PACIFIC BASIN BOOKS

Editor: Kaori O'Connor

Faithfully Yours
Louis Becke

PACIFIC TALES

BY LOUIS BECKE

Introduction by Kaori O'Connor

KPI

LONDON AND NEW YORK

First published in 1897

This edition published in 1987 by KPI Limited
11 New Fetter Lane, London EC4P 4EE

Distributed by
Routledge & Kegan Paul, Associated Book Publishers (UK) Ltd.
11 New Fetter Lane, London EC4P 4EE

Methuen Inc., Routledge & Kegan Paul
29 West 35th Street
New York, NY 10001, USA

Printed in Great Britain by
T. J. Press (Padstow) Ltd., Padstow, Cornwall

ISBN 0 7103 0254 1

INTRODUCTION

Trader, pirate, smuggler, beachcomber, castaway – the Australian adventurer Louis Becke had been all of these before he sat down at a table made of gin cases turned his hand to writing stories. Becke was then thirty-eight, slim and deeply tanned, with a restless gaze and hands that looked, as one observer remarked, 'stong enough to crush a coconut or a skull'.[1] Behind him lay twenty-four turbulent years spent ashore and afloat with some of the roughest, rowdiest, most ruthless men who ever sailed the South Seas. He wrote of what he knew, and it is the honesty and authenticity of his stories that have led James Michener and many others to say that Becke is 'the best writer about the Pacific'[2] in its wild and raffish heyday.

Born on June 18, 1855 in Port Macquarie, New South Wales, where his English-born father Frederick was clerk of petty sessions, Becke was given the names George Lewis, but preferred from boyhood to be known as 'Louis'. Becke ran away from home twice before he was ten, and his formal education was limited to two years at the Fort Street Model School in Sydney, where his family moved in 1867. At fourteen he embarked on his Pacific travels, sailing steerage with his brother Vernon to San Francisco where he worked as a clerk and messenger before returning home by way of Fiji some nineteen months later. Soon he was off again, stowing away on the bark _Rotumah_ bound for Samoa which is those days, as he later recalled, was 'the land of Primeval Wickedness and Original and imported Sin, Strong Drink, and Loose Fish generally'.[3] Becke spent two years working as a clerk in Macfarlane and Williams' store in Apia where he observed the fighting between followers of Talavou and Malietoa Laupepa in the Samoan civil war, mixed with many of the colourful characters who later appeared in his stories, and acquired his abiding dislike of German colonials.

At eighteen Becke became a supercargo – a seagoing business agent, bookeeper and merchant – who handled the commercial aspects of a trading voyage, leaving the captain to attend to maritime matters. Aboard ship the supercargo was in charge of the trade room – a floating general store stocked with Holland gin, fancy hats, fishing hooks, concertinas, soap, Queensland rum, tinned meats, tobacco, cloth, dynamite and many other goods irresistable to the islanders. In practice, the job of a supercargo was a thankless one, for the hapless occupant of the position usually found himself trapped between the conflicting interests of the ship's owners and the captain, the captain and the crew, and the crew and the islanders, but for a poor young man like Becke it offered unrivalled opportunities for adventure at sea. Becke's first voyage as supercargo took him to Mili atoll in the Marshall islands on the rotting ketch _E.A. Williams_, with instructions to deliver the ship to a man who intended to sell her to the natives. Conditions on board were so bad that, on arriving at Mili, Becke left the ship and refused to return, and indeed the ketch was so unseaworthy that she proved unsaleable at any price.

The man to whom Becke had delivered the ketch now abandoned her and signed Becke on as his supercargo, beginning one of the most exciting adventures of the young man's life, for the ship he joined was the sleek brig *Leonora* and his benefactor was none other than the notorious Captain Bully Hayes. By 1874 when he took Becke on at Mili, the American-born Hayes had been twenty years in the Pacific, during which time he had obtained countless ships through fraud, stolen tons of cargo belonging to other traders, held whole villages to ransom, raped scores of native girls and kidnapped thousands of unwilling islanders to work as forced labour on distant plantations, a horrifying practice known as *blackbirding*. Ten weeks off from Mili the *Leonora* was wrecked on the reefs of Kusaie in a gale, and after the survivors swam ashore through shark-infested waters they fell to quarrelling among themselves and terrorizing the natives. Appalled by the behaviour of his shipmates, Becke took his leave of Hayes and withdrew to the village of Leassé where he lived with a native family for what he remembered as the seven happiest months of his life. The idyll came to an end with the arrival of the British warship *Rosario*, which was in search of Hayes with orders to arrest him on ninety-seven charges – 'every count, I believe, except leprosy'[4] as Becke later remarked. But Hayes was an American citizen over whom a British warship had no jurisdiction, and in the end it was Becke who was arrested, put in the brig and taken to Brisbane to stand trial for having stolen the *E.A. Williams*.

On his day in court Becke was acquitted of piracy, having retained through all his adventures the note that instructed him to deliver the ketch to Hayes. Now nineteen, he made the first of several attempts to reconcile himself to life ashore, joining the Palmer River gold rush and working at the Ravenwood station and as a bank clerk in Townville until he was dismissed for 'utter lack of business capacity and distinct disinclination for work'[5] and for keeping kangaroo-dogs at his place of employment. By 1880 Becke was back in the Pacific, working as a trader at Nanumanga in the Ellice islands until the station was destroyed by a hurricane. He opened his own trading store on Nukufetau and married a local girl, Nelea Tikena,[6] but lost most of his possessions when he was shipwrecked on Beru in the Gilbert islands in August 1881. Becke then traded in New Britain, where he witnessed many bloody massacres among the still-cannibal natives and contracted the malaria that would plague him for the rest of his life, finally moving on to Majuro in the Marshall islands. By now he was expert in many island languages, well-versed in island lore and culture, and had developed a deep distaste for many of his fellow traders. As he put it in a letter to his mother written from Nanumanga;

> 'I forgot to say that I had a visitor here in the *Vaitupulemele*, a trader from an adjacent island, Niutao – George Winchcombe. Four years on Niutao and cannot yet talk the language; in fact, I had to interpret for him. Such a man to talk, my ears are tingling now. I don't know how much more I would have suffered if it had not been for a case of gin I produced and by liquoring him up freely I got a little respite. He is a fair sample of too many island traders, fond of liquor and never happy without some grievance to relate against the natives. These are the men that give the missionaries such a pull over *all* traders.'[7]

At thirty, Becke returned to Australia and made another attempt to lead a settled life. He married Elizabeth Mary Stuart, née Maunsell, on February 10, 1886 at Port Macquarie, then worked in Sydney as a contract draftsman for the Lands Department and served as assistant secretary to the New South Wales branch of the Royal Geographical Society of Australia, but city life soon palled. In 1890, Becke took his wife and infant daughter Nora to a trading station in Noumea where Mrs Becke suffered a decline in health. Within two years the family was back in Sydney where Becke, battling with a recurrence of malaria, was unable to find a steady job.

Pressed by creditors, Becke applied for a trading post in the New Hebrides and whiled away the time waiting for a reply by entertaining acquaintances with stories of the islands. One of his listeners, the explorer and writer Ernest Favenc, was so impressed with Becke's tales that he introduced him to J.F. Archibald, editor of the Sydney *Bulletin*, a publication that fostered Australian writers and was the most influential force in the development of a distinctive Australian literature in the years between 1890 and 1918. Recognizing a born story-teller, Archibald asked Becke to contribute something to the *Bulletin*, urging him to write the way he spoke. Becke later credited Archibald with teaching him 'the secrets of condensation and simplicity of language',[8] but from the beginning his style of writing was entirely his own – direct, vital, powerfully realistic and devastatingly honest. Largely autobiographical, his impressionistic stories show island life as it really was in those brutal and lawless times – a paradise where there were no angels, where violent death came as no surprise, and where often the best that could be said of someone was that 'they did no harm to a living soul except themselves when under the influence of liquor, which was not infrequent'.[9] Becke's first published story appeared in the *Bulletin* on May 6, 1893 and his first book, a collection of short stories entitled *By Reef and Palm* was published to popular acclaim in London a year later, where Becke was hailed in literary circles as the 'Rudyard Kipling of the Pacific', a reputation that was considerably enhanced by the publication of *Pacific Tales* in 1897.

Becke had now found fame, but fortune continued to elude him. Constantly in debt, he was forced to sell his books outright to pay off current bills, thereby giving up his right to the substantial royalties that poured in from the sales of his work. Soon after his first book was published his creditors had him declared bankrupt, and in 1896 Becke and his wife separated. Becke then left Sydney with his daughter Nora and his new companion Fanny Sabina Long,[10] travelling to London where he was fêted as a literary celebrity. During the following years Becke lived in England, France and Ireland, writing steadily but failing to achieve lasting content or financial security. In the short story *Leassé* written during his European sojourn, Becke put these revealing thoughts into the mind of Tom Denison, the literary alter-ego who appears in many of his tales;

> 'Still, although three-and-twenty years have passed since then, Denison often wishes he could live those seven months in Leassé over again, and let this, his latter-day respectability, go hang; because to men like him respectability means tradesmen's bills, and a deranged liver, and a feeling that he will die on a bed with his boots off. . .'[11]

In 1908, Becke organized a scientific expedition to the Pacific, with the aim of recording island folklore and collecting marine specimens for museums in London and Berlin, but financial backing for the expedition collapsed before Becke reached his destination and by 1909 Becke, Fanny and their daughters Alrema and Niya were back in Sydney.

Out in the islands, the raffish way of life that Becke had celebrated in his stories was fast passing away, and literary tastes were also changing. The popularity of Becke's work began to wane, and his bills mounted as his earnings declined. Suffering from cancer of the throat, plagued by recurrent bouts of malaria and rheumatism and hounded by creditors, Becke parted from Fanny and sought refuge in drink. His last years were spent in a Sydney hotel room where he was found dead on February 18, 1913, slumped in a chair with the unfinished manuscript of another island tale on the table before him. He was buried in Sydney's Waverley cemetary, his funeral paid for by public subscription, and his tombstone donated by his friends on the *Bulletin*.

Just as Becke never found a niche in society during his lifetime, so his work has never fit easily into the established literary traditions of the time and place in which he wrote. Although he was a native-born Australian and set a number of his stories there – *The Great Crushing at Mount Sugar Bag* in this volume being an example – he has, despite the acclaim he won in his lifetime, never been fully accepted as being in the mainstream of Australian writing. For although many of the major elements and themes in his work – realism, stoicism, rugged individualism, courage in the face of adversity, loyalty between men and the working man as hero– were common to most Australian writers of the period, the Australian literary movement of his time was ultimately a nationalistic one, an affirmation of the Australian dream and way of life. And that is something that Becke was never able to do. He wrote about men like Tom Denison, regarded by relatives at home as 'heartless and dissolute young ruffian(s), who would come to a bad end',[12] who took up life and work in Australia with the sole object of saving up enough to buy a place in Samoa or the Marquesas in which to end their days.

Yet neither do Becke's stories blend comfortably with the popular literature of the Pacific, which is largely in the romantic tradition typified by the work of Robert Louis Stevenson and Pierre Loti. There are plenty of fetching native girls in Becke's stories but no amorous dalliances in the manner of Loti, the relationships being matter-of-fact ones down in the islands where 'it ain't respectable for a man to be livin' by himself.'[13] Becke can describe a pleasing prospect as prettily as Stephenson, but does not draw back from recounting the vile practices that took place beneath the palms – notably in *Collier the Blackbirder*, an indictment of Pacific slaving, and in *Dr. Ludwig Schwalbe, South Sea Savant*, his gothic tale of the secret trade in ethnographic 'curiosities'. Becke is the only writer to show what life in the islands was really like among the nameless, often neer-do-well adventurers, traders and sailors who dominated the island scene in their day, but have found no place in romantic South Sea fictions or standard histories.

Fitting into neither the nationalistic Australian nor romantic Pacific traditions, Becke's work exemplifies the conflict of the men he wrote about – caught between two worlds, never entirely at home in either, happy only when wandering. And it is only through Becke's Pacific tales that one can begin to fully understand the things that drew men to the great ocean, the things that drove them away, and the lure of the drifters life.

Kaori O'Connor

NOTES

[1] in Michener, James and Day, A. Grove; _Rascals in Paradise_. Fawcett Crest, New York, 1983: p 273.

[2] ibid; p 262.

[3] Becke, Louis; _Mrs. Maclaggan's Billy_ (short story). In Day, A. Grove; _South Sea Supercargo_, University of Hawaii Press, Honolulu, 1967: p 26.

[4] Michener and Day, ibid; p 253.

[5] in Day, ibid; p 6.

[6] O'Neill, Sally; _Louis Becke_. Australian Dictionary of Biography, Vol 7: p 238.

[7] in Michener and Day, ibid; p 269.

[8] in O'Neill, ibid; p 238.

[9] Becke, Louis; _A Question of Precedence_ (short story). In Day, ibid; p 114.

[10] Fanny Sabina Long, 1871-1959. Fanny Long and Louis Becke went through a form of marriage at St Pancras Register Office in London on 22 July 1908. O'Neill, ibid; p 239.

[11] Becke, Louis; _Leassé_ (short story). In Day, ibid; p 62.

[12] Becke, Louis; _Denison's Second Berth Ashore_ (short story). In Day, ibid; p 92.

[13] Becke, Louis; _Mrs. Malleson's Rival_ (short story). In Becke, Louis; _Pacific Tales_, KPI, London, 1987: p 56.

To

MY TRUE FRIEND AND GOOD COMRADE,

TOM DE WOLF,

I DEDICATE THESE TALES.

IN MEMORY OF THOSE OLDEN DAYS

WHEN UNDER STRANGE SKIES WE SAILED TOGETHER

IN WEATHER FOUL AND FAIR.

Savage Club,
London, April 15, 1896.

CONTENTS

AN ISLAND MEMORY:
ENGLISH BOB

An Island Memory:
English Bob

THERE was once a South Sea Island supercargo named Denison who had a Kanaka father and mother. This was when Denison was a young man. His father's name was Kusis; his mother's Tulpé. Also, he had several brown-skinned, lithe-limbed, and big-eyed brothers and sisters, who made much of their new white brother, and petted and caressed and wept over him as if he were an ailing child of six instead of a tough young fellow of two-and-twenty who had nothing wrong with him but a stove-in rib and a heart that ached for home, which made him cross and fretful.

But Denison hasn't got much to do with this story, so all I need say of him is that he had been the super-cargo of a brig called the *Leonora*; and the *Leonora* had been wrecked on Strong's Island in the North Pacific; and Denison had quarrelled with the captain, whose name was " Bully " Hayes; and so one day he said goodbye to the roystering Bully and the rest of his shipmates, and travelled across the lagoon till he came to a sweet little village named Leassé, and asked for Kusis, who was the head man thereof.

3

"Give me, O Kusis, to eat and drink, and a mat whereon to sleep; for I have broken apart from the rest of the white men who were cast away with me in the ship, and there is no more friendship between us. And I desire to live here in peace."

Then Kusis, who was but a stalwart savage, nude to his loins, and tattooed from the crown of his head to the sole of his foot, lifted Denison up in his brawny arms, and carried him into his house, and set him down on a fine mat; and Tulpé, his wife, and Kinia, his daughter, put food before him on platters of twisted cane, and bade him eat.

Then, when the white man slept, Kusis called around him the people of Leassé and told them that that very day a messenger had come to him from the King and said that the white man who was coming to Leassé was to be as a son to him, " for," said the King, " my stomach is filled with friendship for this man, because when he was rich and a supercargo he had a generous hand to us of Strong's Island. But now he is poor, and hath been sick for many months, so thou, Kusis, must be father to him and give him all that he may want."

So that is how Denison came to stay at Leassé, and lived on the fat of the land in the quiet little village nestling under the shadows of Mont Buáche, while up at Utwe Harbour on the south side of the island, Bully Hayes and his crew of swarthy ruffians drank and robbed and fought and cut each others' throats, and stole women from the villages round about, and turned an island paradise into a hell of base and wicked passions. But though Leassé was but ten miles from Utwe, none of the shipwrecked sailors ever came there, partly because Captain Hayes had promised Denison that his men should not interfere with Leassé, and partly because the men themselves all liked Denison, and did *not* like the Winchester rifle he owned.

And as he grew stronger and joined the villagers in their huntings and fishings, they made more and more of him, but yet watched his movements with a jealous eye, lest he should grow tired of them and go back to the other white men.

Leassé, as I have said, was but a little village—not quite thirty houses—and stood on gently undulating ground at the foot of a mountain, whose sides were clothed with verdure and whose summit at dawn and eve was always veiled in misty clouds. And so dense was the foliage of the mountain forest of "tamanu" and "masa'oi" that only here and there could the bright sunlight pierce through the leafy canopy and streak with lines of gold the thick brown carpet of leaves covering the warm red soil beneath. Sometimes, when the trade wind had died away and the swish and rustle of the tree-tops overhead had ceased, one might hear the faint murmur of voices in the village far below, or the sharp screaming note of the mountain cock calling to his mate, and now and then the muffled roar of the surf beating upon its coral barrier miles and miles away.

But down from the gloomy silence of the mountain there led a narrow path that followed the winding course of a little stream, which in places leapt from shelves of hard black rock into deep pools perhaps fifty feet below, and then swirled and danced over its pebbly bed till it sprang out joyously from its darkened course above into the bright light and life of the shining beach and the tumbling surf and sunlit, cloudless sky of blue that ever lay before and above the dwellers in Leassé village.

Right in front of the village ran a sweeping curve of yellow beach, with here and there a clump of rocks, whose black, jagged outlines were covered with mantles of creepers and vines green and yellow, in which at night-time the snow-white tropic birds came to roost with clamorous note. Back from the beach stood groves of pandanus and breadfruit and coconuts, whose branches sang merrily all day long to the sweep of the whistling trade wind, but drooped languidly at sunset when it died away.

Straight before the door of Denison's house of thatch there lay a wide expanse of placid, reef-bound sea, pale-greenish in its shallower portions near the shore, but deepening into blue as it increased in depth toward the line of foaming surf that ever roared and thundered upon the jagged coral wall which flung the sweeping billows back in clouds of misty spume. Half a mile away, and shining like emeralds in the bright rays of the tropic sun, lay two tiny islets of palms that seemed to float and quiver on the glassy surface in the glory of their surpassing green.

At dusk, when the shadows of the great mountain fell upon the yellow curve of beach, and the coming night enwrapped the silent aisles of the forest, the men of Leassé would sit outside their houses and smoke and talk, whilst the women and girls would sing the songs of the old bygone days when they were a strong people with spear and club in hand, and the mountain-sides and now deserted bays of Strong's Island were thick with the houses of their forefathers.

.   .   .   .   .

One evening, as Kusis, with Tulpé, his wife, and Kinia, his daughter, sat with Denison on a wide mat outspread before the doorway of their house, listening to the beat of the distant surf upon the reef, and watching the return of a fleet of fishing canoes, they were joined by a half-caste boy and girl who lived in a village some few miles further along the coast. The boy was about twelve years of age, the girl two or three years older. Denison had one day met them, and they had taken him with them to their mother's house. She was a woman of not much past thirty, and the moment the white man entered had greeted him warmly, and pointing to some muskets, cutlasses, and many other articles of European manufacture that hung from the beams overhead, said : "See, those were my husband's guns and swords."

" Ahé, and was he a white man ? "

"Aye," the woman answered proudly, as she brought Denison a mat to sit upon, "a white man, and, like thee, an Englishman. But it is two years now since he died under the spears of the men of Yap, when he led other white men to the attack on the great fort in the bay there. Ah, he was a brave man ! And then I, who saw him die, came back here with my children to Leassé to live, for here in this very house was I born, and this land that encompasseth it is mine by inheritance."

From that day Denison and the two half-caste children became sworn friends, and twice or thrice a week the boy and girl would walk over to see him, and stay the night so as to accompany him fishing or shooting on the following day. The boy was a sturdy, well-built youngster, with a skin that, from constant

exposure to the sun, was almost as dark as that of a
full-blooded native ; but the girl was very light in
complexion, with those strangely deep, lustrous eyes
common to women of the Micronesian and Polynesian
people—eyes in whose liquid depths one may read the
coming fate of all their race, doomed to utter ex-
tinction before the inroads of civilisation with all its
deadly terrors of insidious and unknown disease.
Unlike her brother, who either could not or pretended
he could not, understand English, Tasia both understood and spoke it with some fluency, for, with her
mother and brother, she had always accompanied her
father in his wanderings about the Pacific, and had
mixed much with white men of a certain class—
traders, pearl-shellers, and deserters from whaleships
and men-of-war.

For some minutes Kusis and his white friend
smoked their pipes in silence, whilst Tulpé and the
two girls sat a little apart from them, talking in the
soft, almost whispered tones peculiar to the Malayan-
blooded women of the Caroline Islands, and looking
at some boys who were boxing with the half-caste
lad near by.

"Ha !" said Tasia to the two men, with a laugh,
"see those foolish boys trying to fight like English
people."

"What know you of how English people fight,
Tasia ?" asked Denison.

The girl arched her pretty black brows. "Much.
I have seen my father fight—and he was the greatest
fighter in the world."

"Truly ?"

"Truly. Is it not so, Kusis ?"

" Aye," said Kusis, turning to Denison, " he was a great fighter with his hands as well as with musket and sword. Tell him, Tasia, of how thy father fought at Ebon."

.   .   .   .   .

" When I was but ten years old there came to Lela Harbour on this island a great English fighting ship, and my father, who had run away from just such another ship long years before in a country called Kali-fo-nia, became troubled in his mind, and hid himself in the forest till she had gone. When he returned to his house, he said—pointing to many letters and tattoo marks on his breast and arms— 'Only because of these names written on my skin have I lived like a wild boar in the woods for three days; for see, this name across my breast, were it seen by the people of the man-of-war, would bring me to chains and a prison, and I should see thee no more.' And so, because he feared that another man-of-war might come here, he had the whole of his breast, back, and arms tattooed very deeply, after the fashion of Strong's Island, so that the old marks were quite hidden. Yet even then he was still moody, and at last he took us away with him in a whaleship to an island called Ebon, ten days' sail from here. And here for a year we lived, although the people were strange to us, and their language and customs very different to ours. As time went on, the Ebon people began to think much of my father, because of his great bodily strength and courage in battle, for they were at war among themselves, and he was ever foremost in fighting for Labayan, the chief under whose protection we lived.

"One day a great American warship came into the lagoon of Ebon, and many of the sailors came ashore and got drunk, and as they staggered about the village, frightening the women and children, one of them, hearing that my father was a white man, came to him as he sat quietly in his house, gave him foul words, and then said—

" 'Come out and fight, thou tattooed beast, who calleth thyself a white man.'

"There were many sailors gathered outside the house, and these, because my father took no heed of the drunken man's words, but bade him go away, called out that he was but a beach-combing coward and had no white blood in him, else would he take up the challenge.

"Then Bob—for that was my father's name—put a loaded musket in my mother's hand, and said : ' I must fight this man ; but stand thou at the door, and if any one of the others seeks to enter the house, fear not to shoot him dead.' Then he stepped out to the sailors, and said—

" 'Why must I fight this man ? What quarrel hath he with me, or I with him ? And I shall not fight with a man when he is " tamtrunk " and cannot stand straight on his feet.'

" ' Fight him,' they answered, ' else shall we pull thy house down and beat thee for an English cur.'

"And then I heard the sound of blows, and could see that Bob and the man who challenged him were fighting. Presently I heard the sound of a man falling, and the blue-coated sailors gave a great cry, and I saw my father standing alone in the ring. At a little distance lay the American, whose body was supported by two of his friends. His head had sunk forward on his chest, and those about him said to my father, ' His jaw is broken.'

" My father laughed—' Whose fault is that ? Ye forced me to fight, and I struck him but once. Is there no one man among ye who can do better than he ? 'Tis a poor victory for an Englishman to break the jaw of a man who thought he could fight, but could not.' Then he mocked them, and said they were ' skitas' (boasters) like all the ' Yankeese'; for now he was angry, and his eyes were like glowing coals.

" But they were not all ' skitas,' for two or three stepped out and wanted to fight him, but the others stayed them, and said to my father : ' Nay, no more now ; go back to thy wife ; but to-morrow night we shall bring a man from the other watch on board the ship whom we will match against thee.' Then they lifted up the man with the broken jaw, and carried him away.

" In the morning there came to our house two sailors bearing a letter, which my father read. It said that there would come ashore that night the best fighting man of the ship, who would fight him for one hundred dollars in silver money.

" Now thirteen silver dollars was all the money my father had, so he went to Labayan the chief, who had a strong friendship for him, and read him the letter. ' Lend me,' said he, ' seven-and-thirty dollars, and I will fight this man ; and if I be beaten and the fifty dollars are lost, then shall I give thee a musket and five fat hogs for the money lent me.'

" Now, Labayan could not refuse my father, so without a word he brought him the money and placed it in his hands, and said : 'Take it, O Papu the Strong, and if it be that thou art beaten in the fight, then I forgive thee the debt—it is God's will if this man prove the stronger of the two.'

    .   .   .   .   .

" At sunset two boats filled with men came ashore. Four score and six were they altogether, for my mother and I counted them as they walked up from the beach to the great open square in front of the chief's house. All round the sides of the square were placed mats for them to sit upon, and presently baked fish and fowls to eat and young coconuts to drink were put before them by the people, who were gathered together in great numbers, for the news of the fight had gone to every village on the island, and they all came to see. As darkness came on, hundreds of torches were lit, and held up by the women and boys.

" By and by, when the sailors had finished eating, Labayan and his two wives came out and sat down at one end of the square, and my mother and I sat with them. And then, as fresh torches were lit, so that he great square became as light as day, a man rose up from among the white men and stepped into the centre.

" ' Where is the man ?' he said.

" ' Here,' answered my father, pushing his way through the swarm of people who stood tightly packed together behind the sitting white men, 'and here is my money' ; and he held out a small bag.

" ' And here is ours,' said some of the sailors, coming forward, and the money was placed in Labayan's hands. Then one of them opened a bottle of grog, and my father and the other man each drank

some. Then they stripped to their waists. My
father was thought to be a very big and strong man ;
but when Labayan and his people saw the other man
take off his jumper and shirt, and beheld his great
hairy chest and muscles that stood out like the roots
of a tree when they protrude from the ground, they
murmured. 'He will kill Papu,' they said.

"So Labayan cried, 'Stop!' and standing up and
speaking very quickly, said : ' O Papu, there must be
no fight ! But tell all these white men that the man
they have brought to fight thee shall have the money
that is in my hands. And tell them also—so that
they shall not be vexed—that the women and girls
shall dance for them here in the square till sunrise.'

"My father laughed and shook his head, but told
the white men Labayan's words, and they too
laughed.

"'Nay, Labayan,' said my father, 'fight I must,
or else be shamed. But have no fear ; this will be
a long fight, but I am the better of the two. I know
this man ; he is an Englishman like myself, and a
great fighter. But he does not know me now ; for it
is many years since he saw me last.' And then he
and the sailor shook each other by the hand ; and then
began the fight.

"Ah ! it was terrible to look at, and soon I began
to tremble, and I hid my face on my mother's bosom.
Once I heard a loud cry from the assembled people,
and looking up saw my father stagger backwards and
fall. But only for a moment, and as he rose again the
white men clapped their hands and shouted loudly ;
and again I hid my face as the two met again, and the

sounds of their blows and their fierce breathing seemed like thunder in my ears.

" Presently they rested awhile, and now the torches blazed up again, and, as the women saw that the face of the big man was reddened with blood which ran down his body, their hearts were filled with pity, a great wailing cry broke from them, and they ran up to Labayan and besought him to bid the fight to cease. But the white men said it must go on.

As the two men rested, sitting on the knees of two of the sailors, they each drank a little grog—just a mouthful. Then they stood up again, staggering about like drunken men ; and my mother and I, with many other women, ran into Labayan's house and wept together—for we could no longer look. Suddenly we heard a great cry of triumph from the assembled people, but the white men were silent. Then Labayan called to us to come and see. So we ran out into the square again.

"The big white man lay upon a mat, but he was horrible to look at, and we turned our faces away. My father sat near him, held up by Labayan and one of the white sailors, and lying beside his open hand were the two bags of money. But his eyes were closed, and he breathed heavily.

"As the people—white and brown—thronged around the big man to see if he were dead, we heard the tramp of marching men, and a score of sailors carrying muskets, with swords fastened to their muzzles, came across the square. They were led by two officers, who held drawn swords in their hands.

"'What is this ? ' said he who was leader, sternly, looking first at one and then at another of the white sailors. Then they told him, and said it had been a fair fight.

"'Back to the boats, every man,' he said, 'but first carry this dying man into a house, where he must lie till the doctor comes to him.' And then, when this was done, the armed men drove the others down to the boats, and the square became dark and deserted.

"My father was but little hurt, and all that night he sat beside the man he had fought, who lay sick for many days in Labayan's house. Every morning the doctor from the ship came to see him, and other white men came as well. At last he got better, and then he and my father had a long talk together, and shook each other's hands, and became as brothers. Then the boat came for him, and the beaten man bid us all farewell and went away.

"That night my father told us that this man, who was named Harry, had once been a friend of his, and they had served the Queen of England together in the same man-of-war, and, like him, had run away from the ship. And as soon as my father met him face to face in the square he knew him, 'and,' said he, 'it came hard to me to fight a man who was once my friend, and was still my countryman, but yet it had to be done to shame those boasting "Yankeese," who are but "skitas."'"

.   .   .   .   .

And now, as I think of Tasia's story, there springs upon my memory the tale of the fight told of in "The Man from Snowy River," where an Australian station manager, fresh from England, fought a terrible

fight with an intruding drover. So, only changing
four words of "Saltbush Bill," and with all apologies—

Now the sailor fought for a money prize with a scowl on his bearded
face,
But the trader fought for his honour's sake and the pride of the English
race.

IN THE OLD, BEACH-COMBING DAYS

In the Old, Beach-combing Days

A WHITE, misty rain-squall swept down the mountain pass at the head of Lêla Harbour, plashed noisily across the deep waters of the land-locked bay and whirled away seaward.

Standing upon jutting ledges of the inner or harbour reef, a number of brown-skinned women and children were fishing. The tide was low and the water smooth, and as the fishers shook the raindrops from off their black tresses and shining skins of bronze they laughed and sang and called out to one another across the deep reef-pools.

"*Ai-e-eh!*" cried a tall, slender girl, naked to her hips, around which she wore, like her older and younger companions, a broad, woven sash of gaily-coloured banana fibre—"*ai-e-eh!* 'tis a cold rain, but now will the fish bite fast, and I shall take me home a heavier basket than any of ye here;" and then she deftly swung her long bamboo rod over the pool on whose rugged brink she stood.

"*Tah!* Listen to her!" called out a round-faced, merry-eyed little woman who fished on the other side. "Listen to Niya the Wisehead! She hath

19

not yet caught a fish, and now boasteth of the great basketful she will take home! Get thee home for thy father's seine net, for thou canst not catch anything with thy rod;" and the speaker, with a good-humoured laugh, took a small fish out of the basket that hung at her side and threw it at the girl.

Niya, too, laughed merrily as she ducked her head and twisted her lithe young body sideways, and the fish, flying past her face, struck a boy who stood near to her in the back.

He swung round, and with mock ferocity hurled the fish back at she who threw it.

"That for thee, fat-faced Tulpé; and would that it had gone into thy big mouth and down thy throat and choked thee! Then would thy husband call me friend, and seek out another wife; for, look thou, Tulpé, thou art getting old and ugly now."

A loud shriek of laughter from Niya, a merry, mocking echo from those about her, joined in with Tulpe's own good-natured chuckle, and then, flinging down their rods and baskets, they sprang into the water one after another and played and laughed and gambolled like the children they were all in heart if not in years.

By and by the sun came out, hot and fierce, and the women and children, rods in hand and baskets on backs, made homewards to their village across the broken surface of the reef. Right before them it lay, a cluster of some two or three score of grey-thatched, saddle-backed houses, with slender sharp-pointed gables at either end.

Nearest to the beach and distinguishable from the others by its great size was the dwelling of Togusā, the chief of Lêla Harbour. At a distance of fifty feet or so from its canework sides a low wall of coral slabs surrounded it on four sides, with gateways at back and front. Within, the walled-in space was covered with snow-white pebbles of broken coral, save where a narrow pathway led from the front gateway to the open doorway of the house.

On came the fishers, the older of the women walking first in twos and threes, the young girls and boys following in a noisy, laughing crowd. But as they drew nearer to the low stone wall their babbling laughter died away, and they spoke to each other in lowered tones. For it had ever been the custom of Kusaie [1] to speak in a whisper in the presence of a chief, and Togusā, chief of Lêla, was master of the lives of four thousand of the people. Other chiefs were there on Kusaie who lived at Utwe and Mout and Leassé, and whose people exceeded in numbers those of the chief of Lêla, but none were there whose name was so old and whose fame in battle would compare with his.

So, with softened steps and bodies bent, the women entered through the narrow gateway one by one and knelt down in front of the door in the manner peculiar to the women of the Caroline Islands, bringing their thighs together and turning their feet outward and backward. Apart from them, and clustering together, were the boys, each sitting cross-legged with outspread hands upon the pebbled ground. And then all, women, girls, and boys, bent their eyes to the ground and waited.

Presently there came to the open doorway of the

[1] Strong's Island, the eastern outlier of the Caroline Archipelago.

chief's house an old, white-haired woman, who
supported her feeble steps with a stick of ebony
wood. For a moment or two she looked at the
people assembled before her, and then a girl who
followed her placed upon the canework verandah of
the house a broad, white mat, and spread it out for
her to sit upon. Slowly the old woman stooped her
time-worn frame and sat, and then the slave-girl
crouched behind her, and, with full, luminous eyes,
looked over her mistress's shoulder.

Suddenly the dame raised her stick and tapped it
twice on the cane work floor, and then, with a quick,
soundless motion, the fishers rose, and with bent heads
and stooping bodies crept up near to her and laid their
baskets of fish silently at her feet.

But though they spoke not themselves, each one as
she or he placed a basket down looked at Sipi, the
slave, and made a slight movement of the lips, and
Sipi, in a low voice and looking straight before her,
murmured the giver's name to the old woman.

" 'Tis the gift of Kinio, the wife of Nara, to Seaa,
the mother of Togusā the King."

" 'Tis the gift of Leja, the daughter of Naril, to
Seaa, the mother of the King."

And so, one by one, they laid down their tribute till
the offering was finished and they had crept back
again to the place where they had first awaited old
Seaa's coming, and now they sat and waited for the
King's mother to speak.

"Come hither, Niya."

At the sound of the old woman's voice the girl
Niya came quickly out from amongst her companions
and sat down beside the piled-up baskets of fish.

"Count thee out ten fish for Togusā the King, ten each for his wives, and two for Sipi, the slave."

With deft hands the girl did the old dame's bidding and placed the fish side by side upon narrow leaf platters brought to her by the young slave-girl.

"Good," said old Seaa, smiling at the girl, for Niya was niece to Sikra, and Sikra was one of the King's most trusted warriors and nephew to old Seaa.

"Good child. And now, tell the people that Togusā the King is sick, and so comes not out to-day to see their offerings of goodwill to him and his house. So let them away to their homes, taking with them all the fish they have brought save these fifty and two here before me."

Again the women crept up, and each taking up her basket again walked slowly away through the gateway and disappeared among the various houses. But Niya, at a sign from the King's mother, remained, and sat down beside Sipi, the slave.

By and by, with much stamping of feet and singing a loud chorus, came a party of men, tall, stalwart fellows, stripped to their waists, with their long black hair tied up in a knob at the back of their heads. As they reached the gate their song ceased, and each man placed the basket of taro or yams he carried at the feet of the old dame. From each basket the girl Niya, at old Seaa's command, took one taro and a small yam for the King's household; then the men, picking up the baskets again, followed the women into the village.

So for another hour came parties of men and women and children, brown, healthy, strong and vigorous, carrying their daily offerings to the King of fish and fowl and wild pigeons, and baked pigs and young coconuts, and bananas and other fruits of the rich and fertile Kusaie.

Then, when the last of them had come and gone, the slave-girl Sipi put a small conch shell to her lips and blew a note, and men and women—slaves like herself—appeared from the rear of the house and carried the baskets away to the King's cook-houses.

.   .   .   .   .

This was the daily life of Lêla. At the very break of dawn, when the trees and grass were heavy with the dews of the night, and the flocks of mountain parrots screamed shrilly at the rising sun and the wild boar scurried away to his forest lair, the people were up and at work among their plantations or out upon the blue expanse of Lêla Harbour in their canoes. For though there was no need for them to do but the merest semblance of toil, yet it was and always had been the custom of the land for each family to bring a daily gift of food to the King. Sometimes if a whaleship lay outside the harbour the King would take all they brought, to sell to the ship in exchange for guns and powder, and bright Turkey red cloth ; but beyond this he took but little of all that they gave him day after day. They were a happy, contented race, and their land was a land of wondrous fertility and smiling plenty.

.   .   .   .   .

Sometimes, even in those far-off days, a whale-ship cruising north-westwards to the Moluccas, or the coast of Japan, would sail close in, back her mainyard and send her boats ashore and wait till they returned laden to the gunwales with turtle, yams and fruit. Dearly would the crew—as they gazed upon the bright beaches and the thickly-clustered groves of palms amid which nestled the gray roofs of thatch—have liked the ship to have sailed in, and heard the cable rattle through the hawse-pipes as her anchor plunged through the glassy depths of Lêla Harbour. But Lêla was seldom entered by a ship of any size. Her boats might come in if the captain so choose, and the rough, reckless seamen might wander to and fro among the handsome, brown-skinned people and make sailors' love to the laughing Kusaie maidens till the ship fired a gun for them to return; but the ship herself dared not enter. Not that there was danger of treachery from the people, but because of the narrow, tortuous passage and the fierce, swift current that ever eddied and swirled through its reef-bound sides. Once, indeed, in those olden days the captain of an English whaleship, that lay-to outside, had seen a small schooner lying snugly moored abreast of the King's house, and had boldly sailed his own ship in and anchored beside the little trading vessel. In a week a dozen of his crew had deserted, lured away from the toils of a sailor's life by the smiles of the Kusaie girls. Then he tried to get away before he lost any more men. Three times he tried to tow his ship out with her five boats, and thrice, to the secret joy of the Kusaie people and his crew, had he to return and anchor again; at the fourth attempt the ship struck and went to pieces on the reef.

In those wild days, and for long years afterwards, there were some five or six white men living on Kusaie.

They were of that class of wanderers who are to be met with even now among the little known Caroline and Pelew Groups and on some of the isolated islands of the North Pacific. Of those that lived on Kusaie, however, our story has to do with but one, an old and almost decrepid sailor named Charles Westall, who then lived at Lêla under the protection of Togusā, as he had lived under the protection of that chief's father thirty years before. With those white men who lived in the three other districts of the island he had had no communication for nearly ten years, although he was separated from them but half a day's journey by boat or canoe ; not that he did not desire to see them, but simply because the intense jealousy that prevailed between the various native chiefs who ruled over these districts made visiting a matter of danger and possible bloodshed. Each chief was extremely jealous of his white protégé, who, although he was exceedingly well treated and lived on the fat of the land, was yet kept under a friendly but rigid surveillance lest he should be tempted to leave his own district and settle in another.

Westall, therefore, as his years and infirmities increased, resigned himself to the knowledge that except when a ship might call at Lêla, he would not be likely to ever converse again in his mother tongue with men of his own colour. He was, although an uneducated man, one of singular energy and discernment, and had during his forty years' residence on the island acquired a considerable influence over the chief Togusā and the leading native families. He was by trade a ship's carpenter,

and, attracted by the intelligence of the natives and
the professions of friendship made to him by Togusā's
father, had deserted from his ship to live among
them.   Unlike many of his class, he was neither a
drunkard nor a ruffian ; and eventually marrying a
daughter of one of the minor chiefs of Lêla, he had
settled down on the island for a lifelong residence.
As the years went by and his family increased, so
did his status and influence with the natives, and at
the time of our story he lived in semi-European
style in Lêla village, about a stone's throw from
the house of Togusā.   He had now some twenty
or thirty children by his five wives—for in accordance with native custom he had to increase the
number of his wives as his wealth and influence
grew—and these had mostly intermarried with natives
of pure blood, so that in course of years the old
English sailor's household resembled that of some
Scriptural patriarch who was honoured in the land.

Early in the morning on the day following the
scene described at the King's house, old Westall
was sitting outside his boatshed smoking his pipe
and watching some of his white-brown grand-children
at play, when a young native girl came quickly along
the groves of breadfruit and coconut and called out
that she had news for him—a ship, she said, was in
sight.

"Come thou inside, little one," said the old sailor,
kindly, speaking in the Kusaie tongue. (Indeed he
had but seldom occasion to speak English.)

The girl was Niya, the niece of Sikra, and was betrothed to Ted, one of old Westall's younger sons.
She was about fifteen or so, and was possessed of

that graceful carriage and those faultlessly straight features common to women of the Micronesian Islands.

Seating herself on the ground beside the old man, and, in accordance with native fashion, not deigning to notice her lover, who was that moment at work in his father's boatshed, the girl told Westall that she and some other girls had seen a small white-painted ship about four miles off, making towards Lêla.

The old sailor's face instantly became troubled and he called to his son to come to him.

"Ted," said the old man, speaking in English, "that mission ship has come at last, and now there's goin' to be a bit of trouble. You see if there won't."

Edward Westall, a short, thick-set youth of twenty, with a darker complexion than that of the girl who sat at his father's feet, leant upon the adze he carried and said in his curious broken English: "How you know she's mission'ry? Has you ever seen mission'ry ship?"

"No," replied the old man, shortly; "an' I don't want to see one. But I know it's a mission'ry ship. She's painted white, an' I heard from Captain Deaver of the *Hattie K. Deaver* that there was a mission ship at Honolulu two years ago, an' she was painted white, an' was comin' here right through this group, blarst her!"

"Well, an' what you goin' to do? You think Togusā goin' to let a mission'ry come ashore an' live?"

"That's just what I don't know, boy. Togusā likes the white men, an' maybe he may take to these

Yankee psalm-singers. An' if he does, it just means that you an' me an' all the rest of us will have to clear out of here and seek for a livin' elsewheres. They is hungry beggars, these mission'ries, and drives every other white man away from wherever they settles down. An' I'm gettin' too old now to be badgered about by people like them."

"W'y don' you go and tell Togusā to keep 'em from comin' ashore?"

The old man shook his head. "No good, boy. I managed to block one mission'ry from landing here—that feller that came here in the *Shawnee* whaler when you was a babby—an' I've always been telling Togusā that it will be a bad day for him when he lets one of them come here, but," and he shook his head again, "he's a weak man, and just like a child. His father was another sort, an' had a head chock full o' sense."

For a moment the old seaman seemed sunk in thought, and then suddenly aroused himself.

"Ted," he said, "just you go along with Niya to her uncle Sikra and tell him an' Jorani an' the other big chiefs to come here an' have a talk with me. Togusā is sick, an' so I can't get in to see him."

Throwing down his adze, the young half-caste beckoned to the girl to rise and come with him. With that passive obedience common among women of her race when spoken to by a man, the girl instantly rose and followed her betrothed husband, who, from the broad blue stripes of tattooing that covered his naked arms and thighs, would never have been taken for anything else but a pure-blooded native.

Then old Westall, still wearing a troubled look upon his brown and wrinkled face, walked slowly back

to his thatched dwelling and sat down to wait for the
native chiefs to talk with them over the danger that
—from his point of view—menaced them all.

.   .   .   .   .

Four miles away the mission brig—for such indeed
was the strange ship—was sailing slowly along the pre-
cipitous northern coast of the island.   On the poop
deck were four clerical gentlemen clothed in heavy
black, and each bore in his face an expression of great
interest as the various points of the beautiful island
opened to their view.

Seated a little apart from the others, as befitted his
position and dignity as their leader, was the Reverend
Gilead Bawl.   He was a man of nearly six feet in
height, with shaven upper lip and white beard, and
his eyes, keen, cold and gray, had for the past ten
minutes been bent over a copy of the Scriptures, outspread upon his huge knees.

Of his four colleagues all that need be said is that in
manner of speech, dress, and appearance generally they
were minor editions of the Reverend Bawl.   They
were but strangers in the Islands, having only arrived
at Honolulu from Boston six months previously and
had been selected by their principal—the Reverend
Gilead—to accompany him on his present mission.

Presently Mr. Bawl closed the book and rising from
his seat walked up to the captain, who was anxiously
scrutinising the line of reef along which the mission
brig was sailing.

"Friend," said he, placing his hand with condes-
cending familiarity on the captain's shoulder, and
speaking in soft, gentle tones, "it hath pleased
Gawd to bless us with a prosperous v'yage to this,

the first cawner of the Vineyard, and ere we sail into the haven before us and ventoor our lives among the ragin' heathen, it would be well for us to stay the ship awhile while the brethren and myself, together with the mariners of this chosen bark, render up our offerins' of praise and thanks-givin' for the manifold mercies vouchsafed to us upon the stormy ocean."

A subdued murmur of approval came from one of the younger missionaries, who, clasping his hands together, gazed with a rapt expression at Mr. Bawl.

The captain of the brig looked and felt uncomfortable. "Jest as you please, sir, but I would like to get the ship to an anchor as quickly as possible. I've never been here before and this Strong's Islander we have brought with us seems kinder stupid, and I really believe the creature doesn't know enough for me to take the ship in by his directions. I guess he's a fool——"

The missionary's face assumed a loftily severe expression.

"Captain Branden, you surprise me—nay, more, you pain me. This young man"—and he placed his large, coarse hand on the head of an undersized native, clothed like himself, in a long black coat and wearing a stovepipe hat with a wide, battered rim—"you do, indeed, pain me when you speak of this pious young man—one of Gawd's ministers—as a fool."

The native he indicated, who, twelve months before, had been one of the crew of an American whale-ship, but was now the Reverend Purity Lakolalai, turned a dull, stupid face upon the captain, and, encouraged by the protecting glance of his white leader, muttered something under his breath.

"Well, I meant no offence, Mr. Bawl ; but I feel somewhat anxious about getting to an anchor as soon as possible."

"Captain Branden," said the missionary, pompously, "it is my wish and the wish of the brethren with me that we offer up supplication for the success of our cause. Will you kindly call the mariners to the stern of the ship, so that they may join with us in devotional exercises befittin' the occasion ? "

The master of the brig nodded ; and muttering the words "darned rot " under his breath gave the order for the crew to lay aft.

It is necessary to explain that the presence of the Reverend Mr. Bawl and his brethren was largely due to the fact that twelve months previously the Reverend Purity Lakolalai—then a native sailor—had run away from his ship at Honolulu. He was a low-caste Strong's Islander, and spoke whaleship English fluently. By some means he came under the notice of the Reverend Gilead, who, learning that he was a native of Kusaie, immediately set about his conversion, with the result that Lakolalai, being in a certain sense a man of the world and deeply sensible of the material advantages to be derived from his new friends, expressed the deepest grief at his own and his countrymen's ignorance of the truths of the gospel. In the course of a week or two reports were sent home to Boston that, by a marvellous dispensation of Providence, an intelligent young "chief" had been rescued from the degrading life of a whaler's foc's'cle, and had "greatly moved" the American brethren at

Honolulu by his pictures of the hopeless savagery and sinful customs of his people. Furthermore, he had become "concerned" for his soul's welfare, and was now at that time "eagerly imbibing the Truth with tears of thankfulness." As a natural corollary to this intelligence subscriptions were asked for to send out a band of brethren to plant the Word on the heathen field of Kusaie. In due course the subscriptions and brethren came, and then followed the imposing function of ordaining Lakolalai, formerly a slave and a "burning brand," a minister of the American Board of Missions. Then came the departure of the mission brig from Honolulu with the missionary party just described.

An hour afterward, the devotions concluded, the brig sailed into Lêla Harbour and dropped anchor off the King's house.

.   .   .   .   .

At eight o'clock next morning nearly a thousand natives were assembled on the gravelled space in front of the King's house, all waiting to see the white strangers land. Already a rumour had gone forth that they were the bearers of a message from a great king to their own chief Togusā, but who the white king was and what the message was about none knew.

In a few minutes a boat left the ship and rowed to the beach, and four white men, wearing stovepipe hats and carrying white umbrellas, stepped out and walked up to the King's gateway; at their heels followed Mr. Lakolalai, dressed in exactly the same manner, and carrying, in addition to his umbrella, a large, heavy volume.

At the entrance to the King's grounds the party

halted, and then some discussion took place between them and Brother Lakolalai, who seemed inclined to fall back.

"'Tis but the weakness of the flesh," said Mr. Bawl to his brethren; "our brother is somewhat afraid of venturing into the presence of this pore heathen king."

"Yes," said Brother Lakolalai, with emphasis, and, in his excitement, reverting to his whaleship English. "Me 'fraid. You see, I no belong to Lêla; I belong to Utwe—on other side of this island. By —— I afraid to go inside King's house here. He d—— big king and break my head."

A pained look came into the brethren's eyes, but the Reverend Gilead at any rate was not wanting in courage, and seizing the Reverend Purity Lakolalai by the arm he drew him along ·with him. Followed by the brethren, they ascended the steps that led up to the King's house, and in another moment were inside.

The room was a very large one, capable of holding half the population of the village. At the further end, seated upon mats, were the leading chiefs. Above them, lying upon a slightly raised couch, was Togusā, the sick chief. He was a man of about thirty, with a thick jet-black beard and pale features, and his countenance showed traces of recent illness.

The moment the missionaries entered, the natives, who were gathered outside, followed them in, the men sitting on one side of the room, the women on the other. As soon as Mr. Bawl and his brethren had approached within a few feet of the King, the missionary motioned to his companions to stop, and advanced alone with hand outstretched.

"You are King Togusā; I am the Reverend Gilead Bawl, and I bring you peace beyond price an' a message from the King ev Kings."

The sick chief shook his head feebly in return, and failing to understand Mr. Bawl's remark, inquired in broken English if he had "come to buy pigs and yams."

"Not pigs, my dear brother, nor yet yams; but souls;" and the Reverend Gilead smiled benignantly, and then with the rest of the brethren sat down upon the rude stool to which the King motioned them. The Reverend Purity Lakolalai, however, sat quite apart from them, on the floor, with a very uneasy expression on his face.

For a moment or so Togusā spoke in an undertone to his chiefs. He was anxious to learn the motive of the white men's visit, and felt that his limited knowledge of English was not equal to the task of carrying on a conversation with them. Presently, however, his eye lighted up when he saw, coming through the doorway, the old white man, Westall, who was attended by four or five of his half-caste sons.

"Tell Challi[1] to come and talk to these men in their own tongue," he said to one of those of his chiefs who sat about him.

Dressed in his seamen's suit of blue dungaree, and holding his broad palm-leaf hat in his hand, the old seaman advanced through the crowded room, and first greeting the King and chiefs in the native language, he turned to the missionaries.

"Good-day, gentlemen. My name is Charlie Westall. I live here. The King wishes me to ask

[1] Charlie.

you what is your business and in what way he can
serve you. You see, gentlemen, he doesn't speak but
little English, and so he wishes me to talk for
him."

Then the Reverend Gilead Bawl, rising to his feet,
extended his right hand, and pointing a large forefinger
at the old white man, spoke.

"Old man, I hev' heerd of you. You are one of
those unfor'nit persons who are out of the Lord's fold,
and whose dangerous and pernicious example to these
pore heathens has done sich harm. You may tell the
King from me that I cannot talk to him through such
a wicked man as you air."

Old Westall laughed a soft, sarcastic laugh.
"Thank ye, sir, I'll tell him that," and then,
turning to the King, he said—

"The white men have come here to give thee
and thy people a new religion ; but he will not talk of
it to thee, O Togusā, by my lips."

"Why is that ?" said the King, mildly, his dark
eyes moving alternately from the face of the missionary
to that of the old white man.

"Because, he sayeth, I am a bad and wicked man,
and have taught thee and thy people evil."

The King's eyes flashed angrily, and he made a
movement as if he would spring from his couch, but
in an instant he was calm again.

"That is well, Challi. Let him, then, if he mis-
trusts thee, find some one else to tell me of his
business here in Kusaie."

"The King, sir," said old Westall, again addressing
himself to the missionary, "says that he is willing to
hear what you have to say—if not through me, then

through any one of you or your ship's company who can speak his language."

The calm, quiet tones of the old seaman, covering, as it did the rage and contempt he felt for the person addressed, deceived not only the Reverend Mr. Bawl and his colleagues, but their coloured brother, the Reverend Purity Lakolalai as well. He now stepped forward, Bible in one hand, stovepipe hat in the other. An encouraging smile on Mr. Bawl's face gave him courage to proceed.

Then, in the midst of a dead and ominous silence, the native minister addressed the King. His speech was a curious one, and not at all one that even Mr. Bawl, with all his ministerial pedantry and silly pomposity, would have approved of had he known its gist. First, he warned the King and his people of the wrath to come if they continued in heathenism; secondly, that old Westall and all other white men but missionaries would be taken away by a man-of-war, and cast into a lake of burning fire called Hell; thirdly, that the good and chosen people lived at Honolulu only, and the Reverend Gilead Bawl was a very rich man, and the friend of the President of the United States and God; fourthly, that if Togusā would cast away his idols, and keep but one wife, and take the missionaries to his bosom, that he would not be taken away to the lake of fire with the bad white men, but when he died his soul would be taken in a man-of-war to Honolulu first, and then to Boston, to live with God and President Andrew Jackson; fifthly, that he, Lakolalai, had been a very bad man, but now he had been "washed" and was filled with a powerful "ejon" (witchcraft) which would make him live for ever.

With his chin supported on his right hand the King of Lêla listened with unmoved countenance to the native minister's speech. Then, when he had finished, he turned to Sikra, his favourite chief.

"Who is this man?" he asked, and at the savage energy of his tones the native minister quailed.

"He is Lakolalai, a pig (a slave) from Utwe. He went away from here two years ago."

"Good," and a grim smile stole over the King's features. "Thou hast heard what he has said, and the lies he has told me. Does he and these foolish white men think that I, Togusā, who ever since my birth have known white men, have not heard of these wizards they call missionaries, who would steal the hearts of my people from their gods, and make slaves of them to the god who rules over the lake of fire—bah!" and he spat fiercely on the ground, and then shook his hand threateningly at the missionaries. "Away from here I tell thee. I have heard of thee and know of thy wizardry. Shall I, Togusā, be a like fool to Kamehameha of Hawaii [1] and yield up my country and my wives and my slaves to such dogs as thee? Go, get thee away to some other land while thy lives are yet safe. But yet "—and here he shot a quick glance at old Westall—"shalt thou stay here awhile and see how Togusā shall do justice upon this dog of Utwe, this Lakolalai, who comes into the presence of the King of Lêla and threatens him with the vengeance of the Christ God, and the Lake of Boiling Fire. Take him, men of Lêla, and bind him like as a hog is bound for the slaughter."

But with a wild, despairing cry the native minister

[1] The King of the Hawaiian Islands.

had thrown himself at the King's feet, and was pleading for mercy, while from the assembled crowd of people there came a low, savage murmur—the desire for vengeance upon a slave who had insulted their King.

"Gentlemen"—and old Westall advanced to the now alarmed missionaries—"you had better get aboard again. I bear you no ill-will for the hard words you have spoken, but you have come upon a fool's errand. The King will have no missionaries here."

"Shameless and wicked old man," said one of the younger missionaries, "would you incite these raging heathens to deeds of bloodshed? Think you that we, the ministers of God, are to be lightly turned away by threats? No!" and with a firm hand he grasped Gilead Bawl by the arm. "I for one shall not desert my Master, but cheerfully give up my life for the Cause."

With a contemptuous smile old Westall turned away from him and walked over to and stood beside the King. Then he raised his hand.

"Gentlemen, you have had your say. Now let me have mine. There is no danger to any of you—at least to any of you who are white. But listen; for forty years I have lived here among these people, and as long as I do live here no mission'ry shall ever set foot again on this island. These natives may all go to hell as you say, but that is none of your business—they've been goin' there cheerful enough for the last five hundred years. Now, don't be afraid, no one is going to hurt you, but the King wants to ask you a question or two before you go."

With a pale face, but a certain amount of resolution

in his cold gray eyes, the Reverend Gilead Bawl stepped out from the others and spoke again to the King.

"Beware, O Togusā, of this old man. He is a bad man," and then he suddenly ceased as the King raised himself upon his tattooed and naked arm.

"Christ-man, answer me this. This dog here"— and he pointed scornfully at the grovelling figure of the native minister—"this dog sayeth that he will live for ever by reason of the new faith he hath gotten from thee."

"Man," said the missionary, springing forward, after old Westall had interpreted the King's words, " I implore you, nay, command you, on peril of the loss of your immortal soul, to give this unhappy heathen my true answer. Tell him that Lakolalai, God's minister, will have eternal life hereafter, even if these godless heathens now take his life."

Then Westall turned to the King.

"The Christ-man sayeth, O Togusā, that this man, Lakolalai, will have life for ever."

"Ha," said Togusā, "now shall we see if this be true."

Two men advanced, and seizing the native minister, stood him upon his trembling feet.

"Stand aside, gentlemen, if you please," said old Westall quietly to the missionaries. They moved aside, and then Togusā, calling to Sikra, the chief, pointed to the wretched Lakolalai.

" Take thou thy spear, Sikra, and thrust it through this man's body. And if he live, then shall I believe that he will live for ever."

And Sikra, with a fierce smile, seized his heavy,

ebony wood spear, and as he raised his right hand and poised the weapon, the men who held Lakolalai's arms suddenly stretched them widely apart.

The spear sped from Sikra's hand, and spinning through the convert's body, fell near the feet of the Reverend Gilead Bawl and his brethren at the other end of the room.

.   .   .   .   .

In another hour the mission ship was under weigh again, and old Westall was seated at home smoking his pipe and playing with his grandchildren, and smiling inwardly as he glanced seaward and saw the white sails of the brig far away to the westward.

But, after all, the visit of the mission ship was long remembered by the people of Kusaie, and for their wickedness were they sorely afflicted ; for the garments of the late Reverend Purity Lakolalai were given by Togusā to one of his favourite slaves, who soon afterwards died of measles, and in less than a month seven hundred other godless heathens followed him, and old Charlie Westall, with Ted and Niya his wife, and his maid-servants and man-servants and all that was his cleared away from the disease-stricken island, and sailed in search of a new land called Ponape, which lieth far to the westward.

MRS. MALLESON'S RIVAL

Mrs. Malleson's Rival

JIM MALLESON lived on Tarawa, one of the Gilbert Islands, in Equatorial Polynesia. He was a tall, thin, melancholy looking man, with pale blue eyes and a straggling sandy beard that grew upon his long chin in a half-hearted, indefinite sort of way. His trading station was situated at the most northerly point of the whole atoll—a place where the thin strip of low-lying sandy soil that belted the blue waters of Tarawa Lagoon was narrowed down to a few hundred yards in width—barely sufficient, one would imagine, to prevent the thundering breakers that flung themselves against the weather side of the island from hurtling through the thinly-growing coconut and pandanus groves, and pouring over into the calm waters of the inland sea, carrying everything, including Malleson's ramshackle house, before them. Denison, the super-cargo of the *Indiana*, had, indeed, mentioned the possibility of such an occurrence to Malleson one day, and offered to shift him further down the lagoon, but his offer was declined—he was quite satisfied, he said, to stay where he was and take his chance.

For some unknown reason Malleson, although on perfectly friendly terms with the four or five other white men who lived on Apiang, the nearest island in the Gilbert Group to Tarawa, yet seldom associated with them. He was the only white man on Tarawa, and, although the two islands are not a day's sail apart, he had never raised energy enough to sail his boat over to Apiang and return the many visits he had had from the traders there. But, in spite of his owl-like solemnity, he was not by any means unsociable, and would occasionally unbend to a certain extent. One curious thing about him was that, although he had now been living alone on Tarawa for two years, he had never been married. Now, for a trader to remain single was, in native eyes, extremely undignified, and not calculated to raise him in public estimation ; any white man who could show such a disregard of the conventionalities of native life and custom, necessarily became an object of suspicion to the native mind. However, as he was a quiet, non-interfering man, who quarrelled with no one, conducted himself with the strictest propriety, and refrained from cheating in the pursuit of his business, he gradually begat confidence and respect among the fierce, warlike Tarawans ; so much so that at the end of two years he had become the most prosperous trader in the Gilbert Group, and his huge, ill-built storehouse was generally filled to bursting with copra (dried coconut) and sharks' fins whenever a trading ship entered the lagoon and dropped anchor off his station. So steadily did his business and his reputation for fair dealing increase with the natives, that, after a time, fleets of canoes would visit Tarawa, coming, some from Marakei, fifty miles to the north, and some from the great lagoon island of Apamama, a hundred miles to the south-east, bringing with them their produce of dried coconut to be exchanged with the white man for coloured prints, calicoes, arms, tobacco, and liquor.

The white men living on Apiang and the other atolls in the group could not but experience a feeling of vexation that Malleson, who, as they said, was the laziest man in the South Seas, should divert so much custom and so many dollars from their islands to his. Day after day they would see large sailing canoes filled with dried coconut and other native produce sailing past their very doors bound to Malleson's place ; but being on the whole a decent lot of men, they bore their successful rival no ill-will, accepted matters (after a time) philosophically, and lived in the hopes of Malleson being found cheating by the natives, and either getting himself tabooed from further trading, or being warned off the island by the chiefs.

So one day, after business jealousies had quite subsided, they again manned their boats and visited him, and, knowing that many months had passed since a ship had called at Tarawa, they bore with them the gift of friendship peculiar to the country—some half a dozen or so of Hollands gin—in order to cheer up his lonely existence by endeavouring to make him drunk. But in this they had always failed on previous occasions, for the more liquor he consumed the more melancholy and owl-like of visage he became. They had all also, individually and severally, endeavoured to induce Malleson to give up his single life and permit them or one of the chiefs of Tarawa to find him a suitable wife from among the many hundreds of young marriageable girls on the island. But their kindly intentions proved unavailing, for Malleson distinctly declared his intention of remaining as he was, and put some little warmth into his manner of declaring that rather than have a native wife forced upon him, he would barricade his house.

"I don't want any native wife, boys," he would say, solemnly. "I dessay you chaps mean well, an' wouldn't see me marry a girl as wasn't no good, an' means to try and make me feel more comfortable; but I ain't agoin' to do it."

But a plot against his further celibacy had been formed, not, it must be mentioned, without ulterior views by one of the participants therein, Mr. Andy O'Rourke, a genial, rollicking trader on the island of Apiang. He was agent for a firm trading in opposition to Malleson's employers, had a large half-caste family, and a very extensive native connection generally, both socially and in business, and for a long time past had cogitated upon the possibility of joining his fortunes with those of his successful rival, to his own particular advantage financially, and that of Malleson from a domestic point of view. In short, he intended to get Malleson married, and had already made up his mind that Tera, his wife's sister, was eminently calculated to fill the position of Mrs. Jimmy Malleson. But to avoid any suspicion of underhand work he determined to so arrange matters that no one of his fellow-traders should ever suspect that he had any preconceived idea of making Malleson his brother-in-law, and set about his plans in a thoroughly open, genial Irish manner.

He had, therefore, proposed that on the present trip to Malleson's they should as a matter of conjugal and family duty take their wives, children, and relatives with them.

"We ought to give the women a run over to Malleson's, boys," he said, when the trip was first proposed. "It's the *gogo* (mutton-bird) season over at Tarawa just now, and the women and children would enjoy themselves fine getting the eggs and birds. You'll bring your wife, Davy, won't you? Tom French's missus is coming, and a couple of his daughters; and my wife wants to bring her sister with her. What d'ye say, boys?"

So over they came, each trader sailing his own boat, and carrying with him his native wife and half-caste family, all bent upon having a thoroughly good time at Tarawa, for the people of the two islands were now at peace. Seated aft in Andy's boat, between his wife and himself, was the pretty Tera, who had been well tutored by her sister Lebonnai in the part she was to play in captivating the heart of Malleson. And although Tera had frankly admitted that she had looked to get a handsomer and younger husband than the one her brother-in-law designed for her, she was a dutiful girl, and consented to sacrifice herself upon the altar of family affection with resigned and unobtrusive cheerfulness.

As the boats, with their snow-white sails bellying out to the trade-wind, sped along over the long ocean swell, Davy Walsh, whose boat was nearest, called out to Andy (they were all sailing close together)—

"I wonder how old Malleson's piggy-wiggy is getting on?"

A general laugh followed, for Malleson's affection for his pig was a source of continual amusement to his fellow-traders.

.   .   .   .   .

5

About a year after he had landed on Tarawa, a passing Puget Sound lumber ship, bound to the Australian colonies, had hove-to off Malleson's place for an hour or two. He had boarded her, and in exchange for some young coconuts and bananas, the American skipper had presented him with a pig of the male sex, informing him that the animal was of a high lineage in the porcine line. Malleson had been much struck with the promising proportions and haughty but reserved demeanour of the creature as it poked about the deck, and at once conceived the idea of improving the breed of pigs on the island—not, of course, from disinterested motives, but as a means of adding to his income.

As time went on the pig grew and throve amazingly, and the fame of the beast spread throughout the Gilbert Group ; and Malleson's anticipations with regard to his own profit in possessing such an animal were amply verified. Natives from outlying villages, and finally from islands a hundred miles distant, came to look at his pig, and a deputation of leading old men (*i.e.*, the village councillors) from Apiang visited Malleson with the object of conveying the pig, as a friendly loan, to their august master, the King. But to this he would not consent, pointing out politely, but firmly withal, the risks attendant upon carrying such a valuable animal in an open canoe a distance of forty miles ; besides that, he had become attached to the creature, he said, and would be lonely without him. The deputation thanked the trader, and withdrew.

.   .   .   .   .

As the visitors' boats sailed across the lagoon, and

brought-to in front of Malleson's dilapidated dwelling, the trader came out of his house, and walked down the beach to meet them; and Andy O'Rourke noted with envy that Malleson's storehouses, the doors of which were wide open, were full to bursting of copra.

"Come up to the house," said the melancholy-looking man, shaking hands with them all in a limp sort of manner. "My boys (servants) will bring your traps up out o' the boats; but "—and here he glanced dejectedly at the women—" I'm afraid that my house is too small to hold you all. Perhaps the women and children wouldn't mind sleepin' in my boathouse just for to-night. To-morrow I can get a house run up for 'em."

"That's all right, old chap," said Andy, slapping his solemn-visaged host on the back; "but, if you don't mind, Lebonnai and her sister will stay with me in your house. You see, Tera—that's her coming up now—was a bit seasick coming over, and my wife got a touch of the sun; they are both complaining a bit. However, they won't trouble you much. Just let 'em have a corner to themselves."

"'Tain't much of a place for women," said Malleson, disconsolately, as he looked at his dirty, untidy sitting-room, with its floor covered with ragged, worn-out mats, and then at Lebonnai and Tera, tall, stately, and graceful in their white muslin gowns and broad Panama hats. "You see, I does my own cookin', and on'y straightens up onst a week or so. But I'll get some o' the village women to come in and clean up the place a bit."

"No, you won't, old man," said Andy cheerfully; "my wife has brought plenty of sleeping-mats, and

she and Tera—a smart girl is Tera—will soon fix up
a place." Andy now had an opening to let Malleson
see what a handy girl Tera was, and what an excellent
housewife she would make.

So, while the wily Andy and Tom French, Dave
Walsh, and Pedro Calice sat outside with Malleson,
and smoked and drank lager beer and gin, pretty
Tera, whose mind was full of the possibilities of
becoming Mrs. Malleson and pleasing her sister and
brother-in-law, hustled her sister about, and set to
work. First of all, though, she took off her starched
muslin gown, and hung it up carefully, revealing her
shapely figure (clothed in but a short skirt of pink
print) in the most innocent and natural manner
possible. Then for the next ten minutes she and
Lebonnai were busily engaged in dragging out the
dirty old mats, and replacing them with clean ones
brought from the boats, clearing off the awful
collection of empty salmon and sardine tins from the
soiled table, and touching up the room here and there
and everywhere.

"He's very old-looking, and hath weak, watery
eyes," whispered Tera to her sister, who was carrying
out a basket full of *débris* to throw away on the
beach.

"Speak low, thou little fool ; he may hear thee.
And what if he is old and watery-eyed ? Is he not a
white man and rich, and with a good character ? "

Tera shrugged her smooth, rounded shoulders, and
went on sweeping, glancing now and then at the long,
awkward figure of her prospective husband.

"Well, old man," said Davy, addressing his host,
" how's business, and how's the pig ? "

"Come an' see him," answered Malleson with un-usual promptitude ; " he's lookin' fine."

The traders exchanged sly, amused glances, but at once rose and followed him to a little compactly built pig-pen of thick coconut logs, which was sheltered from sun and rain by a wide roof of pandanus thatch. Inside, on a bed of clean grass, lay an enormous black and white boar pig, asleep.

This was " Brian."

" He don't like bein' disturbed too soon after his breakfast," said Malleson, as the four men bent over the fence and gazed at the recumbent animal ; " he gets mad sometimes, an' don't eat."

" Is that so ? " said French, with an appearance of deep interest.

" Yes. You see he's got very reg'lar habits, an' don't like bein' worried after a meal. But any way, as you chaps don't see him often, I'll wake him."

Hoisting one of his long legs over the low coconut fence, the trader got into the pen, and slapping the huge beast gently on the rump, called, " Brian, Brian, get up, old man ; it's on'y me an' Andy, an' Tom French an' Davy Walsh."

Brian wouldn't move, but his thick, hideous lip gave a slight quiver.

" He wants a lot o' coaxin', don't he ? " said Malleson, with a faint blink of amusement, and then he began to scratch the monster's back with his forefinger. This partially roused the object of his solicitude, who gave vent to a grunt of enjoyment, and lifting one hind leg slightly, pushed it out astern ; then with another and fainter grunt he lay quiet again.

" Won't he stand up ? " queried Andy.

" No, not now. But we'll come back when it gets a bit cooler. He enjoys the wind when it's a bit westerly, like it is now, and generally stands up in the corner there to get a sniff—there, d'ye see that little port-hole I've cut? Well, he likes looking through that sometimes, watching the village pigs cruisin' about on the beach. I've been givin' him cooked fish lately. Don't believe in raw fish for him—heats his blood too much an' gives him a kind o' nightmare."

" Just so," said Davy, sympathetically ; " makes him cry out in his sleep I suppose. Well, he's looking all right, anyway."

.   .   .   .   .

" Come along the beach for a bit of a stroll," said Andy O'Rourke to Malleson that night. The other two men had turned in, and Andy had been waiting for a chance to have a quiet talk to his host. As they went out Andy pointed to the recumbent figures of Mrs. Andy and her sister, who were apparently sound asleep at the end of the sitting-room, and said—

" They look all right and comfy, don't they ? "

They did look all right, and even the owl-like, watery-eyed Malleson smiled approvingly. One of Tera's soft, rounded arms supported her sister's head, and her face rested against her bosom. As the men's footsteps disturbed the coral gravel that was spread over the path outside the house, the younger woman pretended to awake, rose, and followed them.

" Anti," she called in the native language, " tell the white man that if he will give me a piece of soap, Lebonnai and I shall wash his clothes in the morning." (Result of prompting from Lebonnai aforesaid during the night.)

Of course, Malleson understood the native tongue, and as he walked away with Andy he said that Tera "was a good-hearted girl to trouble about his dirty clothes."

"She is that. Look here, old man, she's a regular star of a girl. Now, I ain't going to beat about the bush. I brought her here thinking you might take a likin' to her, and marry her. She'll be a fine wife for you, and make you comfortable. What do you say? She's willin' enough, and there ain't a better-mannered girl anywhere in the Gilbert Group; an' what's more, there isn't any scandal about her."

Malleson made no reply for a minute or two. Then he began filling his pipe. After he had lighted it he spoke.

"Look here, Andy, I'll just tell you the whole thing. I'd be willin' enough, but the fact is I'm a married man. My old woman is livin' in Auckland. She's got a rotten temper, an' to make things worse, she took up with some o' these here wimmen suffrage wimmen, and used to jaw the head off herself tellin' me what a degradin' beast I was to live with. Well, things went on from bad to worse, until one day I seed in the paper as Mrs. James Malleson had said at a meetin' that she too had an unthinkin' husband as hadn't got no intelligence. That just finished me. I cleared out from her, and came down here with Captain Peate to start tradin'. That was two year ago. I send her money every six months by the schooner, but, although I won't ever go back to her again, I ain't a-goin' to marry no native women. It's bigamy."

"No, it ain't. Not down in the islands anyway.

Why, it ain't respectable for a man to be livin' by himself, as you are. You can marry Tera right enough. Who's agoin' to know that you've a wife in New Zealand."

" I would, and Peate would. And besides that I ain't agoin' to do anything like that. My wife's a holy terror, but, at the same time, I know she's an honest woman, and I won't wrong her that way."

Andy gave a long whistle of astonishment. " Well, just as you like, old man ; but you beat anything I ever saw as a trader. You ought to get a billet as a missionary. And do you mean to keep on livin' like this, all alone ? "

" Yes. Why not? I'm all right. I'm doin' pretty well, and Brian takes up a lot of my time when business is dull. How do you think he's lookin' ? "

.   .   .   .   .

A week later pretty, black-browed Tera went away with her sister—still single. As the boats sailed from the white beach Malleson stood in his doorway and waved his hand in farewell.

" She's a pretty little creatur'," he said as he watched the boats heeling over to the breeze, " an' as merry as a lark. I wonder if Brian would ha' took to her ? "

.   .   .   .   .

Sometimes the village children would come near to Brian's sty, and ask Malleson to let them give the creature a young coconut, knowing full well that the pleased trader would reward them individually by a present of a ship biscuit in return. At dusk Malleson, carrying a huge wooden bowl full of tender coconut pulp and milk, would give the pig his last meal for the day, and then stand and lean over the fence and gaze admiringly down, as Brian thrust his round, pink snout into the repast.

Sometimes also Malleson, although naturally a modest man, could not but feel a proud swell of bosom, when, in the bright moonlight nights, he would look and see perhaps thirty or forty natives from the far end of the island, standing around the pig pen, rifles in hand, discussing the magnificent proportions and money value of its slumbering tenant.

.   .   .   .   .

A year went by, and then one day the *Indiana* sailed into the lagoon. The captain and Denison the supercargo soon came ashore and met Malleson standing on the beach.

"How are you, Malleson? Got much for me this trip?"

"About ninety tons of copra, Captain Peate. Did you bring me those two bags of maize for the pig?"

"D—— your old pig, man! But of course I've brought it. And I'm going to take you back with me this trip."

"Why?" asked Malleson, wonderingly.

"Because I've seen Mrs. Malleson, and had a long yarn with her. Here's a letter to you from her. The fact is, Malleson, she's fretting about you, and wants you to come back. She told me it was all her fault, but that if you come back she'll be a different woman, and leave politics and woman suffrage alone."

Malleson opened and read his wife's letter, and then looked with a troubled expression into the captain's face.

"Well," he sighed, "I s'pose I must go. I can't stay away from my lawful wife now she's goin' to

turn over a new leaf, and quit jawin' and naggin'.
Can you put Brian somewhere below? I wouldn't
let him make the voyage on deck! We might get
bad weather on the trip—it's just comin' on for the
hurricane season now."

The skipper gazed at Malleson in wrathful astonishment.

"Curse your infernal beast of a pig! I'm not
going to have the brute aboard my ship. I'll buy him
from you, if you like, and give him to my Kanaka
crew to eat."

Malleson laughed uneasily. "You're fond of your
joke, Captain. However, we can arrange about him
by and by, after the copra is bagged and shipped."

"Arrange be hanged! D'ye think I'm going to
carry a confounded pig as a passenger? Perhaps
you'd like to bring him in the cabin? It might be
'arranged,' though," he continued with bitter sarcasm.
"Denison and the mate and myself could sleep in the
hold—that is, if the pig wouldn't find the cabin too
close for him when we lose the south-east trades."

Malleson turned away indignantly. He did not see
anything to make fun of in his anxiety for Brian.
Yet he went off, feeling that Peate would relent
before the day was out. But his face fell when, later
on in the day, Captain Peate told him plainly that he
could not possibly take the pig, not even on deck.

"Sell him to the natives," suggested Denison, who
was standing near.

Malleson gave an indignant reply. He never used
bad language, but it was very evident that he was
greatly angered at the captain's refusal to even have a
deck house built for the pig's accommodation. How-

ever, in the course of the day he had an interview with the local chief; then he went back to Peate.

"I've arranged with the chief about Brian. He's promised me that when I come back next trip I'll find Brian all right, and well cared for."

"When you come back! What in the name of Heaven are you coming back to this wretched place for? The 'missus' won't hear of it."

"She'll have to hear of it; and what's more, if she doesn't like to come back with me, she can stay behind. I mean to come back, and live here. I'm doin' pretty well, and don't see why I should give up my business to please her. I might have got married native fashion, an' been more comfortable, but wouldn't do it—it was against my conscience. At the same time, if you'll change your mind, an' will take the pig away with me in the *Indiana*, I might settle down again in New Zealand, an' try pig-farmin'."

"Oh, all right; please yourself," said the skipper, shortly. "I'd take the pig, if I could, but I can't. We've none too much room aboard now, and I can't build a deck house for such a hulking beast as your cursed old pig."

Shortly after dawn next morning Malleson was ready. He had spent an hour or so in meditation over the pig pen, fed Brian for the last time, and taken a tender farewell of him. And, as he now stepped out of his house for the last time, he gave the chief a parting injunction.

"See that he eateth nothing but that which is given him by thine own hand, my friend; and that his bed be made with very little, smooth pebbles, covered over with much soft, fine grass; a big stone among them doth both hurt and anger him when he lieth down to sleep."

Then as Malleson and the captain walked down to the beach, the people stood around, and called out in their guttural tongue : *Tiak ápo, Tími* (Good-bye, Jimmy) ; and the trader, with a last look towards the pigsty, stepped into the boat.

Suddenly a hideous sound—a combination of a snort of rage and a squeal of terror—smote upon his ear, and in an instant he had jumped out, and made toward the pig pen. Just as he came in view of the lowly structure he saw a number of native children disappearing round the back of his storehouses, and Teban, the chief, in swift pursuit, shouting out threats of vengeance.

In a few minutes the chief returned and explained matters to the agitated Malleson, who was now in the pen, rubbing the pig's cheeks, and asking him what was the matter. It seemed that the moment Malleson had got into the boat a rude little boy had thrust a sharpened fish-spear into Brian's snout to make Brian squeal.

Teban swore by the shades of his father and two uncles to find the culprit and beat him.

Malleson didn't answer him for awhile. His feelings overpowered him. Presently he got out of the pen and walked down the beach to the boat.

"Come on, man, come on," called the captain, impatiently, "we'll never get away at this rate."

"Look here, captain, I've changed my mind about goin'. Sling my traps out again, will you ? You can tell the old woman that I was glad to hear from her, an' if she likes to come down here to me with you next trip,

I'll try and make her comfortable, an' be a good husban'
to her. . . . But it's no use, I can see, trusting Brian
with these natives. He's trembling now like a asping
leaf. Some d——d boy has just been proddin' the
poor fellow in the nose out o' pure devilment."

And then shaking hands with the disgusted skipper,
the grief-stricken man hurried back to solace and
soothe the angry feelings of his beloved pig.

.   .   .   .   .

Malleson is now living in a swell weather-board
house at Tarawa, with his lawful wife; and Brian
has " took " to Mrs. Malleson.

PRESCOTT OF NAURA

Prescott of Naura

I

ABOUT three or four hundred miles to the westward of the Kingsmill Group, and situated twenty-five miles south of the equator, is an isolated island, with a teeming population of noisy, intractable savages. It is called by the people Naura, and to the white traders and seamen who frequent that little-visited part of the South Pacific, is known as Pleasant Island. At the present time it is under the jurisdiction of the Imperial German Commissioner of the Marshall Islands, having been included in the German-protected area in the Pacific in 1884. Since that time the social conditions and habits of the people have changed but little, save for one important particular—their German masters try to keep a tight rein upon their blood-letting proclivities, and the seven clans with which the island is peopled are no longer allowed to slaughter each other with a free hand; and everything they buy is made in Germany.

But even under the government of a civilised nation, life to-day among the wild denizens of Naura is full of exciting incident, for there is but one German official on the island, and sometimes the old

fighting leaven becomes too strong and the seven clans
shoot merrily away at each other over their stone
boundary walls.   Then a report goes to the Commissioner at Jaluit, and by and by a German man-of-
war comes down and her captain chides the people,
who promise, like the children they are, not to be
wicked any more, but to lay aside their rifles—and
make copra for the German trading firm—else they
won't get any more English tinned beef and American
tobacco made in Germany.

But thirty or forty years ago Pleasant Island was a
wild place indeed.   The ships of the American
whaling fleet that in those days sailed from one end of
the Pacific to the other, called there often enough, but
every man on board, save those working the ship, held
a musket or a cutlass in his hand as long as the vessel
lay off and on at the island.   For bad enough as the
natives were, the white men who lived with them
were worse.   Among them were men who would
have thought no more of cutting off a ship and
murdering all hands than they would of shooting a
native of the island.   And it was on Pleasant Island
that Robert Prescott had cast his lot when he ran
away from the brig *Clarkston*, of Sydney.   This vessel
when cruising through the New Hebrides Group had
found him at Vaté, where he was living with the
natives.

In those times captains of whalers and sandal-wood-
ing ships picked up many such wandering white men
as this man among the islands and asked no questions
from whence they came.   And although the captain
of the *Clarkston* had a good idea that Prescott was
one of a gang of escaped Tasmanian convicts, he cheer-

fully accepted his statement that he had run away from the *Rifleman*, a London whaler, and acceded to his wish to give him a passage to Pleasant Island.

Three months after, Prescott, then an immensely powerful young man, and notorious for his violent temper, landed on the island, and was greeted with much enthusiasm by some eight or ten white beach-combers, most of whom had known him when, as their associate, he was engaged in the laborious occupation of hauling timber at Port Arthur under the supervision of the unappreciative prison officials who " bossed " the chain gang.

Among the hardened criminals who escorted their newly-found comrade to the village in which four or five of them lived in rude, drunken luxury, was an old New South Wales convict named Jasper Dale, whose brute strength and pre-eminence in every imaginable kind of villainy had led to his tacit installation as leader, not only of the majority of the white renegades of Naura, but of one of the most powerful of the natives clans.

With such a man as this for his friend, Prescott— himself a man of the most ferocious courage and cruel nature—soon became a person of influence among the natives, and ere long he and Dale came to open enmity with the other beach-combers, who one by one withdrew themselves to the protection of the chiefs other clans.

. . . . .

A year or two previous to the arrival of Prescott on the island, Dale had taught the natives how to make an ardent spirit from the sap of the inflorescence of the coconut palm; and it was no

unusual sight to see the whole male population of one
village, maddened by drinking this "toddy," as it was
called, sally forth from their houses of thatch, and,
led by their particular white man, engage in bloody
combat with the people of the next village. In these
encounters Dale had always taken the leadership of
the fighting-men of his clan, and his prowess in war
led him to be treated with the greatest consideration
by his native friends. Before Prescott's arrival he had
already given further distinction to his name by shooting
dead a fellow beach-comber named Lawson, and carrying off his wife to his already ample harem. The
savage spirit in which Prescott emulated him in deeds
of bloodshed proved his eminent fitness as a lieutenant,
and it was this partiality that Dale evinced for him
that led to the rupture with the other white
men.

For some time neither Prescott nor Dale came into
actual collision with their former associates till one
day an ex-convict named Cassidy, with three other
whites and two hundred natives at his back, maddened,
like himself, with drinking sour toddy, burst upon the
village in which Dale and Prescott lived and began
firing into and burning the houses right and left.
Seizing his musket at the first alarm Prescott had
taken his stand in front of his house, and the first shot
he fired struck Cassidy, and killed him on the spot.
The loss of their leader made the attacking party
retreat, and the two friends, flushed with their victory,
that night held high revel with their native friends in
the *maniapa*, or council-house, of their village, and
planned the utter destruction of their former colleagues.

Their native allies entered eagerly into the scheme,

and it was finally agreed upon that if they and their two white men succeeded in exterminating the others, that the island should be divided into two districts— one for Dale, the other for Prescott; and after long discussion it was decided to make an attack in two days' time upon a village in which six of the white men lived.

But their plans were thrown suddenly out of gear by an unlooked-for event—next morning at daylight they saw lying-to, close in shore, a large ship, which, by the number of boats and men she carried, it was easy to see was a whaler.

Dale and Prescott, calling loudly to their native friends to come with them in force and board the ship before they were anticipated by the other white men on the island, were just preparing to start, when, to their disgust, they saw that a whaleboat, in which were their former companions, had already reached the ship.

"Curse them!" said Dale, with a fearful oath, to his crime-stained partner, "Klinermann, Ashton, and Cow-faced Bob and the others have got to windward of us this time. They'll buy all the spare arms and ammunition they can get, and then sail in and wipe us two out."

"Never!" said Prescott, passionately, as his hand gripped a pistol savagely. "I tell you, Dale, that if you stand by me we will yet be masters here."

"What is the use of it?" said Dale. "Even if we do wipe 'em out, we can't expect to live here for ever. I tell you, man, that there's bound to be a man-o'-war here before long—and you know what that means"; and with a hideous grimace he pointed to his throat.

" The System[1] ain't agoin' to let us chaps live in clover down here."

Sitting down on an upturned canoe the man Prescott gazed moodily out upon the placid ocean towards the whaleship as she slowly stood out seawards with the shore boat in tow. Suddenly he sprang up, and with clenched hands and working features strode to and fro under the waving plumes of the palm trees.

" Dale," he said, suddenly, and his voice was husky and hoarse with emotion, " you know me. I tell you that if you will stand by me we will see Europe or America in another twelve months. O God, man! O God! I must get somewhere away from these cursed men-o'-war, or I'll go mad."

" Spit it out, then," said Dale, with a savage light in his eye. " I ain't the cove to go back on a man. Wot d'ye want to do ? "

" Come here," said Prescott, clutching his arm and drawing him into the deserted native council-house.

For nearly half an hour the two men talked, and then separated as they saw the whaleship shorten her canvas and heave to, and the boat, crowded with white men, pull for the shore.

.   .   .   .   .

In the boat there were seven white men belonging to the island and four others from the ship. These four useless, dissolute creatures had been told by the captain of the whaleship that as he no longer wanted them on board they might go on shore and stay there. Fired with the desire of leading a lazy, sensuous life among the wild people of Pleasant Island, they had eagerly accepted the invitation of the seven beach-

[1] The Convict System of New South Wales.

combers to " come ashore and live like fighting-cocks."

As the boat drew in to the beach the man who steered, a tall, slender young fellow named Beverley, suddenly uttered an expression of alarm, and pointed to the figures of their two former comrades who were seated on the shore, apparently awaiting their arrival. Behind them were some three or four hundred natives belonging to the village in which the seven beachcombers lived.

" By God, boys," said young Beverley, " there's Prescott and Dale right among our people, sitting down on the beach as if they belonged here—and as if Prescott hadn't shot poor Cassidy less than twelve hours ago."

"What does it matter, Bev.?" hiccupped a crime-hardened ruffian named Greenhaugh ; " they're in our village, and if they meant mischief our natives would have made short work of 'em. Tell you what it is, boys. Dale ain't a bad cove, neither is Prescott—they've come round to make it up with us. An' I votes we makes it up an' has a howlin' drunk all round, and treats each other like gentlemen."

The hospitable sentiments of Mr. Greenhaugh were well received by his companions, and as soon as the boat touched the beach the eleven white men left her to be hauled up by the natives and advanced in drunken, rollicking good-humour to the two men who awaited them.

" Hallo, Beverley," said Prescott, advancing, " you chaps got to windward of me and Dale this time in getting aboard the ship first. Well, never mind, we aren't going to quarrel over it, are we, Dale ? But

what we do want to say is this : we ain't going to
bear no malice for what happened yesterday. Cassidy
got wiped out. We ain't going to deny it. I wiped
him out, an' if you other chaps," pointing to the other
three men who had followed Cassidy in the previous
day's encounter, " hadn't cleared mighty smart, you'd
have all been wiped out too by our crowd. And so
what I say is this, let us make friends again and live
quiet and peaceablelike. You, Beverley, are married
to a sister of my wife ; so here's my hand, and let
bygones be bygones."

"Right you are, Prescott. I don't want no
fighting, and I wouldn't join in the row yesterday. I
have no grudge against you," and so saying young
Beverley held out his hand. In a few moments the
others followed his example.

"Well, look here, boys," said Dale, meditatively,
" our house at the other village is a bigger one than
yours. We've got plenty of grog, and why can't you
chaps all come up to our village, and we'll have a
blazin' spree, and drink repose to poor Cassidy's foolish
soul ? "

" Yes, come on, lads," said Prescott ; " we'll make it
up to-night, and besides that, we can talk business";
and he looked meaningly at Beverley, who, though
so young, he knew possessed great influence over the
other men.

Half an hour's walk brought them to Prescott and
Dale's village, and then, surrounded by a tumultuous
and excited crowd of Prescott's native friends, the
thirteen white men entered his house, and were made
welcome by his and Dale's wives. A case of gin was
passed out to the natives, and, to show that no treachery

was intended towards their guests, Prescott commanded the people to bring all their arms—muskets, clubs and spears—into his house, and lay them down on the matted floor.

Less cruel and treacherous than their white associates, the natives instantly complied, and in a few minutes the floor of the beach-combers' house was covered with weapons. As soon as the natives had withdrawn to their huts, which were within a few hundred yards of Dale and Prescott's house, the latter opened a couple of bottles of liquor, and pouring the fiery contents into coconut shells handed it round to the company.

Throwing off all disguise, Prescott strode into the middle of the room, and drinking off his liquor spoke.

" Boys," he said, and his bright blue eyes glittered and sparkled with cruel lustre, " Dale and I didn't ask you here just to get drunk. Did we, Dale ? "

" No," said Dale, with a fierce laugh as he drained off his liquor and dashed the empty coconut shell to the ground. " We asked you coves here to see if you had any grit in yer, an' was game for a bold stroke."

" What d'ye want us for, then, d——n yer ? " said Greenhaugh, the most reckless of the lot. " D'ye want us to sing a hymn for poor Ted Cassidy ? "

" This is what we want," said Prescott, and advancing to the table he spread out both hands upon it. " Here we are, thirteen men, all got arms, and plenty of niggers to back us up—and there's a ship to be had for very little trouble. Now do you understand ? "

For a moment no one answered him, and then Beverley with his brown arms folded across his brawny chest, advanced to Prescott.

" What do you mean, Prescott—cutting off?"

The ex-convict nodded, and then gazed with keen anxiety into the young man's face. The rest of the men looked from one to the other, but no words escaped their lips.

Dashing his hand upon the table the young beach-comber looked into the dark and lowering face of Prescott.

" Look here, Bob Prescott, if you brought us here to try and work this dodge you've made a mistake. I may be a d——d scoundrel, but I'm not going to murder a ship's crew for the sake of what is aboard the ship," and turning fiercely to the other men who sat silent at the table. " And if any man among you chaps listens to such a thing, by God, I'll go to the ship and tell the skipper !"

Five or six of the men sprang to their feet, and in eager tones assured the speaker that they would not entertain the idea. And then Prescott, with simulated drunken hilarity, clapped Beverley on the back, and swore that his suggestion was only a joke.

" Get another bottle of grog, Terátiko," he said to his native wife, at the same time shooting a glance of terrible meaning towards Dale.

" I'll get it, Bob," said Dale, going to a partitioned-off part of the house, where the liquor was kept. As he stepped past Prescott he muttered—

" Come in with me ;" and then in a loud voice he asked him to come and show him where the grog was.

The moment they entered the partitioned room the man Dale whispered—

" What are you going to do ?"

"Look," said Prescott, with an oath, as he pointed out through the window seaward, " do you see that ship? Well, only for these chicken-hearted dogs that ship would be ours to-night. But they won't do it. And I say that if we can't get away in that ship those eleven chaps in there will wipe us out like we wiped out Cassidy."

"Well," said Dale, in a hoarse whisper, " *I say, what are you a'goin' to do?* "

With a swift glance at his companion, Prescott took a bottle of liquor from a case and handed it to Dale.

" Quick—take this out and open it for them. But mind, don't drink anything yourself from the next bottle when I bring it in."

In a moment or two the white men heard Prescott calling to his wives to bring in some food, and Greenhaugh, with a drunken laugh, staggered to his feet, and said he would assist the ladies to bring in the dinner.

"Sit down, you fool," said Beverley, the youngest and least ruffianly of the seven beach-combers, "haven't you got enough sense to keep quiet in this place?" and he pointed to the muskets, cutlasses, and knives that were lying upon the floor. " Do you think that because we have got all these muskets here that we are safe? Bah, you drunken fool!"

Steadying himself at the doorway, Greenhaugh boastingly asserted that he for one was afraid of neither their hosts nor the natives, and then, meeting an answering look in some of his comrades' faces, he let his caution vanish.

" What's to keep us from shootin' 'em both now?"

he said, lurching up to Beverley again, and speaking in a husky whisper.

At that moment Prescott entered the room, and his quick ear caught Beverley's answer—

"Shoot him yourself if you want to ; but you're not going to do it now. I like fair play. He's acting fair and square now to us, and I ain't going in for any underhand shooting."

"Here, boys," said Prescott, advancing to the table, followed by a number of women carrying leaf platters of baked fish and pork ; "here's some 'chuck.' But let's have another drink first ; " and going to the latticed-in store room he took out a bottle of liquor from the case and set it upon the table.

Little did the unfortunate victims of his dreadful treachery know that the food which this monster had placed before them had been impregnated with a deadly poison. Possibly Prescott might have relented at the last moment but for the conversation he had overheard between Beverley and Greenhaugh, which steeled him in his murderous resolution.

Presently a native woman, instructed by Prescott, came to the door and called to Dale.

"What is it ? " said the ex-convict, going outside to where the woman stood.

"Pápu (Bob) says you are not to eat any food, and to watch him."

Dale nodded and returned inside, and then the coco-nut shells of liquor were passed round again. Without the slightest hesitation Prescott poured some out for himself and drank it off, and then, looking steadily at his colleague, passed the shell to his neighbour. Instantly Dale surmised that he had changed his mind about administering the poison in the liquor, and he too drank some.

Then, waited upon by their two murderers, the wretched men began to eat.

Suddenly, as if inspired with a happy idea, Dale remarked, " Why didn't Davy Terris come with you chaps ? "

Beverley laughed. " He had a hand in that job of Cassidy's."

" Why, that's nothing," said Dale, with rough good-humour ; " d——d if I don't walk down to his place and bring him here."

" By hell, yes," assented Prescott, " and I'll go with you. We'll all be friends now, boys ; " and picking up his hat he strode out with Dale, and took the path that led towards the village in which the man Terris lived. As they went off he called back to his guests not to spare the " chuck," as there were plenty more fish and fowls being cooked, and that Terris, Dale, and himself would eat together.

.   .   .   .   .

The awful scene that followed within a few minutes after these two friends had left the house may be imagined, but not described. On seven of them the poison soon took deadly effect, and within half an hour their writhing figures had stiffened cold in death. Of the four others, Beverley and a seaman from the whaler were least affected, and, although unable to walk, managed to crawl to different portions of the room, where they lay in agony so terrible that the listening and wondering natives, hundreds of yards away, were moved to pity, and besought the two white men to go and put an end to their misery.

With terrible imprecations the beach-combers held the natives back, and waited for another half an hour, till all was silent. Then together they entered the house, and presently the natives, who were still forbidden to enter, heard three shots—the death knell of the poor wretches who were still alive.

.   .   .   .   .

Two or three years passed.

Of the fate of Dale nothing was ever known, but the subsequent career of the wretch Prescott was well known to many an island trader. Filled with horror at the deed the white men had perpetrated, the natives of the island withdrew their countenance entirely from them, and, some months afterwards, Prescott was forced by them to go on board the American whaler *Gideon Hauling*. The captain refused to take him further than Ocean Island, a small spot a few hours' sail from Pleasant Island. Eight months afterwards he again returned to Pleasant Island in the London whaler *Eleanor* (all these latter particulars I take from the log of an old Sydney shipmaster, Captain Beckford Simpson, of the barque *Giraffe*, in a report to the *Nautical Magazine* of 1840), but with cries of horror and disgust the natives repulsed him from landing. Where he went to after this was not known, but in 1843 Captain Stokes, of the whaler *Bermondsey*, reported having seen him in chains at San Juan d'Apra, in Guam; and this was subsequently confirmed by Captain Bunker, of the *Elizabeth*. Whether he had committed some fresh crime, or had merely been given up to the Spanish authorities by some ship as a runaway convict from

New South Wales, does not appear. How he escaped from Guam is not known.

For twenty years this tiger in human form lived a wandering life among the islands of the North-West Pacific, and then disappeared from that part of the South Seas, to re-appear among the French islands of the Society and Paumotu groups. But the tale of his great crime followed him. Only a man of his utterly callous nature could have survived many years of such an existence. There was hardly an island in the Pacific which he had not sought out in the vain hope of finding refuge from the story of his black past.

II

FIVE years ago a trader named Watson was staying at the Waitemata Hotel, in Auckland, slowly recovering from the terrible malarial fever of New Guinea, contracted eighteen months previously in Orangerie Bay. He did not know one single person in the city of Auckland that he could call a friend, and time hung heavily upon him. Only that it was a matter of physical impossibility for him to get about, he would have returned to the islands weeks before. Knowing no one, and taking no interest in local matters, he eagerly read the shipping news in the morning papers, to see if any vessels had arrived from the South Sea Islands; for the best part of his life had been spent in the various groups of the South and North Pacific, and the name of not only every vessel and captain engaged in the island trade from Tonga to New Guinea was familiar to him as his own, but the personality of every trader as well.

One morning he saw notified the arrival of a
schooner from the island of Aitutaki, in the Cook's
Group. The name of her captain at once recalled to
memory his cheery face and rude good-nature when
Watson and he were shipmates in the Queensland
labour trade eight years before.

He wrote a note and sent it on board, and in the
evening the skipper came up to the hotel. They had
much to say to each other, and for nearly an hour
talked of old times and friends in the Solomons and
New Hebrides Group, of which part of the Pacific the
skipper declared he had had enough. " A murderous
low-down crowd of niggers," he said, with a cheerful
smile, drawing up the coat-sleeve of his right arm and
showing Watson a most extraordinary thing in the way
of inartistic butchery of the human form. " Look at
that, my son. Don't it look like as if the flesh had
been parcelled round the bone in strips ? The niggers
did that for me at Bougainville two years ago. I was
rushed on the beach, and my boat backed out before I
could get down to her ; my boat's crew had gone back
on me—planned with the natives that I should be
killed ! Three of them jumped overboard when they
saw that I was wading off, and made for the shore,
leaving only a sooty black devil of a Buka Buka boy
in the boat. He stood his ground, although he was
only a slip of a lad. He was too frightened to try
and shoot me, but the moment I got my hand on the
gunwale of the boat he commenced slicing the flesh
off my arm, from the wrist down, with his sheath-
knife. He didn't want to kill me, only stop me
getting into the boat. Only that my mate saw the
row from the schooner I'd have been killed in the end,

sure enough. She was about a couple of hundred fathoms away, and he and the crew commenced firing over towards the boat, so as to scare the boy away. It did scare him, too, for as the first ball hummed by him he jumped over on the other side and dived ashore, leaving me just able to crawl aboard and fall unconscious in the bottom of the boat. And I don't tackle the Solomon Islands any more, my son."

"Well," said Watson, "you're in a nice quiet trade now, among the Christianised and 'saved' kanakas of the Cook Group, where the once shocking heathen goes about clothed and in his right mind."

"Aye," grinned the old skipper, "they do, the dirty beggars. Once a kanaka gets 'saved,' and wears European clothing, he gets very filthy in his habits, and won't wash himself, and puts on such a look of greasy saintliness that there's no living on the same island with them—unless you chew off the same plug as the white missionary. So it's no wonder that so many of these old white traders among the eastern islands are shoving out to the westward, where they can at least live without interference from the white-chokered gentry. I've got an old fellow aboard now, passenger with me. He's come up here to get away to New Ireland, or the Admiralty Group, *viâ* Samoa."

"What is his name ?"

"Collier—Mike Collier. He's a tough old warrior, nearly seventy, I think. He's been trading for the Tahiti people in the Gambiers, he tells me, but says the French missionaries and he didn't hit it, so he's going west again. He's a nice, pleasant old fellow, doesn't drink, but is a bit queer in his ways."

"Old age," suggested Watson.

7

"Not exactly; but he won't come ashore and live. He says he'll wait till he gets a passage to Samoa. Says he likes the smell of the copra in the hold, and doesn't like mixing with shore people. So I've agreed to let him stay aboard till we're ready for sea again; then he'll have to shift and go to a pub."

The trader saw Captain Ross several times after this, and on each occasion he mentioned that old Mike still remained on board, and had not yet put foot ashore. "However," added Ross, "he'll have to clear out to-morrow, as I'm bound to get away in the forenoon."

"Send him here," said Watson; "he'll be a good mate for me, and the place is quiet enough."

"Right," said Ross, "I'll bring him up to-night."

Sitting in his bedroom after dinner, smoking his pipe, Watson heard Captain Ross's gruff, good-humoured voice on the stairs. He was speaking to some one whom Watson at once surmised was the eccentric old trader from the Gambiers. Presently, in answer to something the skipper had said, he heard the stranger speak.

"Yes, there are a good many stairs, Captain."

The sound of the man's voice—querulous from age—struck the trader like a shot. He remembered when and where he had heard it last. In a few seconds more they entered. Watson had not yet lit the gas, and the room was in comparative darkness.

"Are you in, Watson?" said Captain Ross. "Here's old Mr. Collier come to see you. Can you get him a room?"

"Come in, Captain," replied the trader, striking a match and lighting the gas. "How are you, sir?" and he nodded to the old trader, who had quietly seated himself at the further end of the room.   He had his own reasons for not shaking hands with him. " Oh, yes, you'll get a room here.   Sit down, Ross, and I'll send for something to drink."

But the skipper was in a hurry and would not stay, and shaking hands with the old man and Watson he bade them goodbye, and hurried away downstairs.

Until now the sick trader had not had an opportunity of looking at his visitor.   Turning towards him after bidding the captain goodbye, he caught the stranger's eye fixed upon him.

He was a short but broad-shouldered and muscular man, with a mass of wavy white hair overhanging his temples, which, with the rest of his face and neck, were burnt by long, long years of wandering under the torrid sun of Polynesia to the deepest bronze.   His face was cleanly shaven, and were it not for the whiteness of his hair would have seemed absolutely youthful, so free was it from the lines and indentations of advanced age.   And—a fitting accompaniment to the broad, square jaw and firm, determined mouth—his eyes were of a bright steely blue, and met the trader's in a calm, assured, but yet irritating and aggressive manner.

For a moment or two they looked at each other steadily, and then, leaning back in his chair, the old man placed his dark, sunburnt hands on his knees and laughed.

" Well, young fellow, you'll know me next time, I hope."

The cold, sneering inflexion of his tones irritated the trader.   It was a direct challenge.

"I know you as it is," he answered.   " You are Prescott of Naura."

In an instant the stranger leapt up, stood beside Watson, and seized his hands in a vice-like grip, and the trader heard his teeth grind savagely, and felt his hot, panting breath upon his cheek.

"Yes," he said, in a low, savage voice, "I am Prescott, from Pleasant Island, and I'll strangle you like a dog if you tell it to any one else."

Suddenly he let go Watson's hands.

"Look here, you're a sick man, and I'm not going to take advantage of it. Now listen to me. I am an old man, and life isn't worth much to me. But, look here—what harm have I ever done you?"

"None," said Watson, "nor have I any evil intentions towards you. Whatever you have done does not concern me personally."

The old man sat down again, and bent his fierce blue eyes upon the ground. For a minute or so he remained silent, then he sprang to his feet and paced the room rapidly.

"Where did you see me before?" he asked.

"At Callie Harbour, in the Admiralty Group," replied Watson. "You came on board the *Dancing Wave* to see Captain Leeman about buying some tobacco from him. I was the supercargo."

"Ha! I remember you. And where is Leeman now?"

"Dead," answered Watson. "He died in the Gulf of Carpentaria, and was buried on Adolphus Island."

The old man nodded. Then he stopped short in his walk.

"Are you a poor man?"

"What the devil does that matter to you?" answered Watson, shortly.

He turned away and picked up a small portmanteau that he had brought with him, opened it and took out a small canvas bag and threw it contemptuously on the table.

"Those are sovereigns—good English sovereigns. Will they buy your silence, and let an old and hunted man escape to some unknown spot where he may die in peace ? "

"You may go," said Watson, "and take your sovereigns with you. Murderer and fiend as you are, I cannot give you up to justice. The witnesses of your horrible crime are all dead. But I would like to see you hanged."

He looked at the trader intently for half a minute, and then taking up the bag of sovereigns dropped it back into the portmanteau, closed, locked, and strapped it. Then again he paced to and fro like a tiger in a cage.

"Do you know *all* about me ? " he said, suddenly, in a strangely harsh voice.

"A good deal," replied the younger man.

Again he laughed savagely. "And yet you won't give me away to the white men ! "

"Don't you call yourself a white man ? " said Watson.

"No," he growled back, " I am not a white man. The cat took all of the white man out of me at Port Arthur ; and for fifty years I have lived with kanakas, and I am a kanaka now—backbone and soul."

Without a word of farewell he picked up his portmanteau, passed through the door, and went downstairs.

Watson, looking out through the window into the

street, presently saw his short, square-set figure appear
upon the footpath. For a moment or two he stood
under the glare of a gas-lamp, then, with a quick,
active step, he strode across the street and was lost to
view.

CHESTER'S "CROSS"

Chester's "Cross"

THE *Montiara*, trading schooner, had finished taking in her stores, and hauled out to an anchorage in Honolulu Harbour, ready to start on one of her usual trading cruises to the Caroline Group. The captain, accompanied by his supercargo, had gone ashore again to the British Consulate for his papers, letters, &c., leaving the two mates in charge to amuse themselves till his return by playing cut-throat euchre with some of the brown-skinned kanaka crew—for they were a sociable lot aboard the *Montiara*, and, when he first joined the ship, had given young Denison, the supercargo, much cause for reflection. This, however, was his second voyage ; and he now knew that " Tarawa Bob " and " Rotumah Tom," two huge, soft-hearted, hard-fisted able seamen, whose light brown skins were largely illustrated by fantastic devices in blue and vermilion, were the respective brothers-in-law of the gentlemen who officiated as first and second mates of the schooner —Messrs. Joe Freeman and Pedro do Ray. And if, occasionally, their superior position made these officers in times of emergency address their tattooed brethren-in-law in vigorous and uncomplimentary language, emphasised by a knock-down blow, no ill-will was either felt on one side nor engendered on the other. Therefore, in moments of relaxation, when the ship lay at anchor and there was nothing to do, the two white men seated on one side of the skylight and the two brown on the other, with a large bottle of Hollands gin between them, would endeavour to rook each other at cards. Sometimes, too, Denison had witnessed further proof of the *camararderie* existing between all the hands for'ar'd and the two mates, when the latter, overflowing with generosity and strong drink, would invite their coloured shipmates to come ashore and paint the town red. All these things surprised Denison—for he was very young then, and came from a religious family. But he gained experience later on, when he sailed with Packenham in the brig *Indiana*, as you will see in another story.

So with a parting admonition to his officers to let no one go ashore, and to heave short at four o'clock, as soon as they saw him coming down the wharf, old Hunter, the grizzled skipper and owner of the little schooner, had shoved off and pulled in to the pretty palm-embowered town nestling under the shadows of Diamond Head.

" How are you, Hunter ? " said the Consul, as soon as the captain and Denison entered his office. " I'm glad you've come in just now. I've had a visitor—a lady from San Francisco. She arrived here yesterday by the *Moses Taylor ;* wants to know if I can get her a passage down to the Caroline Group."

" The deuce ! " said Hunter. " *I* can't take her in the *Montiara*. And what on earth does she want to go down there for ? Is she a she-mission'ry ? "

The Consul laughed at the sour expression on the old seaman's face ; then he became grave.

" No, she's not a missionary, Hunter, and I really do wish you could see your way clear to take her—she seems terribly anxious."

" But, man, I can't. My cabin is only a small one, and there's my two mates and Mr. Denison here, besides myself, to occupy all the room, which is very little. But if she's not a she-mission'ry, what in thunder does she want down in the Carolines ? "

The Consul shrugged his shoulders. " I can only tell you that she's a lady—mind, Hunter, a *lady*—a widow, I suppose, as she has a little boy with her—and she is now staying at the hotel. She told me her name—here it is," and he took up a card—" Mrs. Hilda Weston—and that she hurried down here from San Francisco in the mail-boat to catch the *Morning Star*, missionary brig. But, as you know, the *Morning Star* sailed for the Carolines a week ago."

" And I hope she may get piled up there," growled old Hunter, who did not love missionaries, " and the snufflebusting crowd of thieves on board of her go to the bottom with her."

" Well," resumed the Consul, " that seemed to upset her greatly. It seems that she had been promised, and counted upon, a passage in the missionary brig. What was she to do ? she asked, when I told her that the *Morning Star* would not be back here and sail again for the Carolines for another six months. Then I thought of you. It struck me that you might manage to fix her and the little boy a berth somehow. She has plenty of money—that I can vouch for ; said she would pay as much as five hundred dollars for a passage, and not complain of any discomfort."

Hunter looked first at the Consul and then at
Denison doubtfully, and then shook his head. A
hundred pounds was a nice little sum for a passage
that would only take fourteen or fifteen days, and yet
it could not be done. The one small deck-house of
the schooner was occupied by his officers' wives, and
it wouldn't be fair to turn them out of it to sleep on
deck. Joe and Pedro wouldn't mind, provided a
financial reason were adduced for *their* benefit, but the
women would, and so would the ladies' brothers, who
would sulk over the indignity—kanaka sailors have
some blessed privileges over those of the ordinary
British sailor-man.

" Here, take her card," said the Consul, " and go
and see her yourself. You may, perhaps, be able to
make arrangements in some way. Anyway, she seems
very anxious to meet you, and I gave her my promise
that you would call."

" Oh, did you ? " grumbled Hunter. " Well, here
you are, Denison, *you* go and see her—you look so
nice and pretty in that white duck suit of yours, that
I wouldn't think of going myself. And look here,
sonny, tell her that I can't possibly give her a passage
down this trip, but will the next, in about four months
from now. That will be two months sooner than the
Morning Star. But, wait a minute—find out what
island she wants to go to, and if it is anywhere this
side of Ponape I'll land her there for £50—that's
about a fair thing."

.   .   .   .   .

Denison had waited five minutes in a sitting-room
of the hotel when she came in—a pretty, fair-haired
woman, with deep, wistful hazel eyes. Her face was

deathly pale, and Denison's heart somehow went out to her in quick sympathy—there was such an underlying sadness in her looks.

"I am Mrs. Weston," she said in a voice that quivered with trembling excitement, as she motioned the young man to resume his seat, "but surely you are not the captain of the *Montiara?*" as the hazel eyes took in his youthful appearance.

"No, madam. My name is Denison. I am the supercargo." And then he gave her the skipper's message.

A quick mist came into the dark eyes, and she pressed her hand to her throat. Then she found her voice.

"Four months is a long time to wait; but it cannot be helped, I suppose," and she turned her face away from him and seemed to look out over the blue waters of the harbour, but Denison saw heavy tears falling upon a native fan that she held in her hand.

Presently she rose, went to the window and stood there in silence for a few minutes, gazing seaward. Then, with the traces of tears still upon her face, she came back to her seat and said with a brave smile—

"You must think me very childish to show my disappointment so much; but I *am* oh, so very, very disappointed. When I left California I was told that I should be in plenty of time for the *Morning Star;* but unfortunately the *Moses Taylor* broke down when half-way, and we arrived eight days late, to find the missionary ship had gone. But when I heard that there was a trading schooner to sail in a few days I thought—" Again her eyes filled, and Denison bent his head and pretended not to notice. He felt deeply

sorry, but could not venture to tell her so. Then he
rose to go, but she begged him to remain a little while.

"Please don't go for a few minutes," she murmured,
and then smiled. "I am sure you are English, are
you not? Ah, I thought so. I am an English-
woman, but have lived so long in America that I
like to meet an Englishman. Every one in Honolulu
is American, I think, and I have felt very lonely
here." Then her courage seemed to rise, and bending
forward she asked—

"Mr. Denison, is there *any* use at all in my
appealing to your captain to give me a passage in
his vessel. I told Mr. Roche, the Consul, that I
would willingly pay £100; but I shall gladly pay
more. I will give £200—more—if that amount is
not enough."

Denison shook his head. "I am indeed very sorry
to say so, Mrs. Weston, but it is impossible for us to
take you down this trip. In the first place we are
already short of room, and in the second we call at
the Marshall Group for thirty or forty deck passengers
—native divers we are taking down to the Carolines.
No white woman could possibly live on board the
same ship with such a noisy lot."

She sighed deeply. "I *must* be content to wait
then. Now, Mr. Denison, may I ask you if you will
tell me something about the Caroline Islands?"

"With pleasure—that is, all I *can* tell you. I have
only made one voyage there—in fact, the present will
be only my second voyage in this part of the Pacific."

She looked at him for an instant, and then with a
violent rush of colour suffusing her face from temple
to throat asked—

" Do you know Mr. Tom Chester—one of the
traders living down there ? "

" Where does he live—I mean at what particular
island. There are many hundreds of islands in the
Eastern and Western Carolines."

" On Las Matelotas—that is, he did so three or
four years ago. He is very dark—and fond of singing."

Now Denison did know the man she spoke of—
knew him well, and hardly knew what to say. Most
supercargoes do not care about giving information
concerning traders to utter strangers—so many of
them have reasons for burying themselves in the
Pacific Islands. And he knew that old Hunter
thought much of the man, and would not like his
supercargo giving even this beautiful young creature
any information about him, so he hesitated ere he
answered.

" I may know him. I cannot say for certain."

" This is Mr. Chester," she said, quickly, and before
he knew it he was holding a photograph in his hand.
The woman watched him keenly.

Denison recognised it immediately as the man he
knew as Tom Chester—*mata uli*, the dark-faced, as
the Las Matelotas people called him.

He was about to lie, and say, " I don't know him,"
but, looking up, he met her deep, earnest eyes—and
failed.

" Yes, I know him," he said ; " he is one of our
traders. He is well known down there, and liked.
Is he a friend of yours ? "

" Yes " ; and again the red flush leapt to her face,
" a very dear friend," and then with a curious, shaking

intonation, "I am very anxious to see him. He is my cousin. I have not seen him for four or five years. My husband died six months ago in America, and there are family matters which Mr. Chester must be consulted about, and—and a great many things demand his attention. I—that is, my late husband and my relatives have written to him several times during the past three years, but the letters no doubt never reached him. We only knew that he was somewhere in the South Sea Islands, and the letters were directed to the care of the Consuls at the various ports. From one of these we eventually heard that a Mr. Chester had a trading station at Las Matelotas, in the Western Carolines. And so, in despair of communicating with him by letter, I—that is, his and my relatives, consented to my coming out here to him."

Denison bowed, but said nothing, and she went on hurriedly : " I had not the faintest idea of what a task I was undertaking. I really imagined that any part of the South Sea Islands could be reached in a few days from San Francisco."

" It is indeed a difficult undertaking for a lady. I do not want to dishearten you, but could you not send some one else—is there no male relative who——"

" No," she said quickly with a nervous movement of her hands ; " I have no brothers nor any one I would care to ask. I prefer to go myself."

She was silent awhile, and just then a little boy, about five years of age, came into the room and nestled beside her, smiling shyly at Denison. She drew the child to her and then, as she stroked his head, said in a voice that she strove to steady—

"Oh, is—is—he, is Mr. Chester married?"

That question, as Denison told old Hunter later on, took him flat aback. (And yet he might have expected it.) Anyway it was a hard question to answer, especially when the inquirer was a young and pretty woman with perhaps no idea of the unconventionalities obtaining in island life. To say that Chester was married in the orthodox, English sense of the word would not have been correct; to say that he was not was equally misleading, inasmuch as Nirani, the young Bonin Island quadroon girl who controlled his domestic arrangements and looked after his trading business during his absence, was known and spoken of all over the group as "Tom Chester's wife." And so he hesitated before answering. He was young, but yet old enough to know from the look in the woman's eyes that much depended to her upon his answer.

"I don't know," he said, very slowly, lifting his eyes to hers calmly in a manner that said plainly enough, "You should not have asked such a question."

Mrs. Weston rose and extended her hand to him. "You must pardon me, Mr. Denison, if I have seemed unduly inquisitive; but I know perfectly what you mean. I am no silly girl, but a woman of twenty-six . . . and I am told that white people living in the islands think but little of—of—making temporary alliances with the natives. But there, I shall ask you no more. I am much older than you, so you must forgive me if I have annoyed you. Of course you will take a letter for me?"

"With pleasure, I assure you, but you will not

have much time—we shall certainly be under weigh in an hour."

" Thank you.   I shall write it at once, and myself bring it down to your boat.   Good bye, and give my sincere thanks to your captain should I not see him."

Half an hour later as Hunter and his supercargo turned down towards the wharf she met them, gave them the letter, and wished them a prosperous voyage, and, she added with a smile, " a *very* quick return."

     .   .   .   .   .

" I've seen that handwriting before now," said the skipper to Denison as the latter put Mrs. Weston's letter in a rack above his berth ; " seen it a good many times."

" Where ? " said Denison in surprise.

" Here, aboard the *Montiara,* and aboard the old *Talaloo* when I was sailing out o' Samoa to the Gilbert and Marshall Group.   Why, I've carried at least half a dozen letters in that same writing, and all directed to Tom Chester ; but I never knew until now who wrote 'em.   Look here, sonny, Chester has got a cross, like most of us men has, an' that cross is going to follow him up.   You see if she don't."

" She's a cousin of his she tells me."

Hunter grinned.   " O' course, only a cousin or a sister would write to a man so frequent.   I can guess the reason now why Chester is living down in the Carolines.   I suppose this is the woman that threw him over and married another man with money. Well, it isn't any of our business ; but Chester doesn't like getting those letters—in fact, I believe he'd like to tell me to drop 'em overboard."

     .   .   .   .   .

The *Montiara* made a quick run down to the Marshall Islands, ran into Milli Lagoon, took aboard forty wild-eyed, long-haired, half-naked, vociferous native passengers, and then spun away westward before the stiff north-east trades towards the Carolines. Ten days later she worked through the tortuous passage leading into Matelotas Lagoon, and dropped anchor abreast of the native village and half a mile away from the trader's house.

A wild clamour of welcome from some hundreds of handsome light-skinned natives greeted Hunter and Denison, and in a few minutes the decks were thronged with the warm-hearted, simple-minded people—men, women, and children—who all seemed animated by an overpowering desire to embrace and caress the rough, grizzled old skipper of the schooner —a man whom they trusted and idolised. And the girls swarmed into the little cabin without fear.

Presently a whaleboat, manned by five stalwart natives, and steered by a slightly-built but muscular-looking white man, swept alongside, and Chester stepped on the schooner's deck.

"How are you?" he said, shaking hands warmly with Hunter, Denison, and the two mates—the only white men on board. "Ah, I see you've brought down those fellows from Milli. Well, to-morrow we'll pick out the best divers among them and try the deep part of the lagoon, over Ngoli side. I am quite confident, Hunter, that if the water isn't too deep there is a little fortune waiting for us at the bottom."

"Well, I hope so, Chester, but I'm rather doubtful about it—all the pearl-shell I've seen taken out of

these lagoons at any depth was big enough, but badly
worm-eaten. However, I've brought you down
these fellows from Milli, and if the water is too
deep for them, why, we must do the other thing—get
a couple of suits and two good divers down from
Sydney."

A few minutes later, as the three men were sitting
together in the cabin over a glass of grog and talking
about their forthcoming attempt on the deep water
" patches " of pearl-shell in Ngoli lagoon, Denison
said—

" Oh, I've a letter for you, Chester," and stepping
into his cabin he returned with it and handed it to
the trader.

Chester took the letter, looked at the superscription,
and, with an unmoved face, put it in the pocket of
his duck jumper. Then he asked the others if they
were coming ashore with him.

" Not now," answered the captain ; " at least, I'm
not. But Denison can go with you and lend you
a hand with the Gilbert Islanders—a noisy, intractable
lot of devils they are. Have you got a house ready
for 'em ? "

" Oh, yes," answered Chester in his slow, quiet
way ; " I've had a place fixed up for them for a
month past. Nirani will see to them as soon as they
get ashore."

The trader's house stood a little over a quarter of
a mile away from the native village, and was a comfortable one-storied place, built entirely of wood and
cane wickerwork in semi-European fashion. On
the ground floor was Chester's store, the upper
portion of the house being merely a huge combined

sitting, dining, and sleeping-room. As he and Denison entered a pretty, dark-eyed young native woman met them and shook hands with the latter.

"How ar' you, Mr. Denison?" she said, her red lips parting in a smile that showed her pretty teeth. "An' so you an' Cap'en Hunter have brought the divers down this-a-time. W'y, Tom, here, he have been fret like a little child ev'ry day because the *Montiara* so long time comin'. Now, he satisfy, I suppose"; and then with a merry laugh she led the way to the big room upstairs, and a minute later was bustling about scolding and occasionally administering a smart but jocose slap on the shoulders to two half-nude young native girls who were setting the table for Hunter, Denison, and the two mates. Clad in a loose blouse and skirt of thinnest texture, her every movement revealed the outlines of her lithe, graceful form, and Denison watched her as one watches the movements of a beautiful bird fluttering from bough to bough, with a pleased fascination.

A merry time was spent in the trader's house that night, for Chester sang well, and Nirani, who was of Portuguese blood, and Pedro do Ray, the second mate, sang duets and love songs to their own guitar accompaniments, while the forty Gilbert Islanders, overjoyed at getting ashore, gathered beneath, inside Chester's fence, and danced their own wild island dance, and then took to wrestling, till the loud clang of eight bells from the schooner broke up the gathering and sent every one, white and brown, to their couches of soft mats.

Soon after daylight the schooner's two boats, manned by about twenty of the Gilbert Island natives, with

Chester and Hunter in charge, set out to test the deeper water of the lagoon for pearl-shell, while Denison remained on board to see to getting Chester's stores and trade goods ashore.

At noon the boats returned, and Denison at once saw by the captain's face that he was pleasurably excited. His news was soon told—Chester's surmise was correct : there was plenty of splendid pearl-shell in the deep water, but at a depth that it was impossible to work successfully without proper diving gear. Every one of the Gilbert Islanders had gone down ; but only four or five had succeeded in bringing up shell, and were then so exhausted that they could not possibly be sent down again. But, they said, the shell lay very thick amid clusters of young coral.

That afternoon after dinner on board it was decided that the schooner should proceed with all haste to Manila, instead of Sydney, where Hunter was to buy two diving dresses, pumps, and gear, and engage two Manila men as divers. Denison was to remain with Chester and enjoy himself as he best could. And then Chester went ashore to tell Nirani.

As soon as the two mates had left the table Hunter, leaning his grizzled chin on his huge hand, addressed his supercargo.

" Ha' ye told Chester about your meeting wi' the young woman at Honolulu ? "

" No, why should I ? If he mentions her to me I might do so, but although I told him yesterday that the letter was given to me personally, he only nodded and said, ' Yes, I know ; thank you.' "

" Well, I'm thinking that he seems very down in

the mouth, and if she isn't the cause of it, I don't know what is. And, mind ye, had I known who the woman was I would never ha' made her that promise to bring her down here. Ye see, I never thought of it at the time. And then there's Nirani."

Denison nodded. " I see what you mean. It's an unpleasant position. What are you going to do about it ? "

" Just nothing ; but as soon as I leave for Manila you can tell him that I didn't know—and that now as we are on this pearling racket, there's not much chance of the *Montiara* going back to Honolulu this year at all."

"Very well ; but you've forgotten the *Morning Star*. The lady will come down by her if our schooner doesn't turn up."

Hunter gave an angry exclamation. " Devil take the woman ! Here we've dropped on to as fine a patch of shell as lies in the Pacific ; it will take us twelve months to work it out, and if this woman comes down here I can see trouble ahead for us all, and Chester in particular. And Nirani's been a good girl to him, d'ye see. D—— all women as proves crosses to a man, I say ! "

" I don't see what we can do, Hunter. Of course if Chester gives me a chance this evening, I'll tell him of the promise you've made. At the same time I don't think it necessary. No doubt the letter he got told him all this. But you're a mean old dog to put everything on to me."

Early on the following morning Hunter came ashore and wished Denison, Chester, and Nirani goodbye, and an hour later the white sails of the

Montiara swept round the low, palm-clad southern
point of Las Matelotas and were lost to sight from
those who watched on shore.

That night Chester and Denison were walking
slowly to and fro on the white, moonlit path at
the side of the house, smoking and talking. Above
them in the big sitting-room a light shone dimly
through the latticed sides and they could see the
shadow of Nirani sitting at the table with her two
girls, looking at some finery that old Hunter had
brought her from Honolulu.

Chester was speaking. "I am glad you have
mentioned it anyway, Denison. Yes, Mrs. Weston
did tell me that she had seen you and that she
means to come down here. Now, I don't mind
telling you that five years ago she was my promised
wife. I had a civil appointment in South Australia
at that time. From Adelaide I was sent up to
a God-forsaken place called Port Darwin in the
Northern Territory. I was away a year. When
I came back she was gone—had married some
wealthy old American three months before, and left
the colony."

"She wrote to me, blaming her mother, and
said all the usual penny novelette things about
being 'forced' and a 'broken heart' and all that.
Well, God knows if it was true. I know her mother
was a match-making, money-loving old devil, who
looked upon me with aversion—in fact, hated me.
Well, that's the whole yarn. I went back to Port
Darwin, where I knew some pearl-shellers, and
went on a cruise with them to New Guinea,
liked the life, and finally made my way down here

five years ago. And I'd be happy enough if I could only think that I am free of blame. You see I've never answered one of her letters—I swore I would never forgive her. And yet I may have misjudged her cruelly."

For some minutes neither of the two men spoke, and then Denison said—

"It is a hard position to be in, I must admit."

Chester laughed bitterly. "And made worse by my own folly. Of course it's no use my pretending that I have forgotten her. But then Nirani has been with me for three years and loves me in her childish, jealous way. And by G——! I'm not going to desert her now!"

.   .   .   .

Before the month was out the *Montiara* was back in the lagoon and Chester and Denison went aboard.

"Well, boys, I've got everything, two good divers included," said Hunter, gleefully, as he shook hands with them. "Come below an' I'll tell ye all about my doings"; and in a few moments the three men were seated around the little cabin table listening to Hunter's account of his voyage, and discussing their future operations in the lagoon.

"Seen any ships?" asked Denison casually of Hunter.

"Yes, the *Mattie*, of New Bedford; spoke her yesterday just in sight of the land. She's bound up to Honolulu, lost four of her boats, and is leaking like a sieve."

"Where do you think she is now?" asked Chester, slowly.

"Can't be more than ten miles away from the weather side of the lagoon," replied Hunter. "She's beating to windward, or else we could see her from here now. Why, do you want to see Burton?" (the captain of the *Mattie.*)

"No, not particularly, but," and Chester shot a quick glance at Denison, "I would like to send some letters by him. I think I'll go ashore at once and send my boat out to him. If he's anywhere in sight the boat can soon board him—there's no wind to speak of"; and then arranging to meet Denison and Hunter at his house later on, he went ashore.

Late that evening as Chester and Denison walked down to the beach to see Hunter off to the ship, the former's whaleboat came pulling in through the darkness, and cleaving the phosphorescent water like an arrow, dashed up on the sandy shore."

"Find the ship, Baril?" called out Chester.

"Yes, sir," answered the native coxswain, "she no got wind. I give captain letter. He say all right."

"Good boy! Now you and the other men go up to the house and get some supper and a bottle of grog."

As soon as Hunter had left Chester said to Denison, "Thank Heaven that is off my mind. I've written to her and told her exactly how matters are. She'll get that letter within a month . . . I've studied the thing out . . . there's a right and a wrong way in everything. To let her come here if I could stop her would be mean and cruel. Nirani isn't a native girl; she has some white blood in her veins, and I'm not going to let her know that I wished I had never met her."

.   .   .   .   .

For nearly four months the white men worked assiduously at the isolated but rich beds of pearl-shell in the deeper parts of the lagoon, and were well rewarded for their toil. Already over four thousand pounds worth of shell lay in the *Montiara's* hold, and, provided the weather kept fine, they expected to go on working till the rainy season and westerly gales set in.

One evening, however, as the boats were returning to the schooner from the farther end of the lagoon, the breeze, which had been steady all the day, suddenly dropped, the air became close and oppressive, and Hunter and Chester, who were in the same boat, looked at each other in some alarm. At the same time numbers of natives who were either fishing or walking about on the inner beach of the lagoon, uttered loud cries and ran quickly along the shore to the village.

" Down sails ! " roared Hunter to the boats that were following, "and pull hard for the ship ! "

The native crews, knowing well the danger that menaced them, bent to their oars with a will and sent the boats flying through the water. Already they could tell from the changing sound of the surf beating upon the outer reef that there was but little time left ere the hurricane would be sweeping across the now glassy waters of the lagoon and sending roaring billows of foam high up among the dense groves of coco-palms.

In another ten minutes the three boats were

alongside, and Hunter and his crew were striking
the schooner's topmasts and getting awnings down,
while the cutter with the pumping gear was sent
ashore to be hauled up out of danger.

"Go ashore, Chester, and look after your house,
and take all these natives with you," said Hunter.
"I don't want to be cumbered up with a lot of extra
men on deck to-night. I tell you we're going to
get it hot."

"My house is all right, Hunter," replied Chester.
"I can see some of my people on the ridge of it
already, passing rope lashings over it—trust Nirani
for that. She has seen this sort of thing before,
and knows what has to be done. But I'll go presently, as I can't be of any——"

Before he could finish a hot blast of wind struck the
Montiara with mighty force, spun her half round like
a top, and then shot her astern till her cable brought
her up with a jerk ; and then with a savage, droning
sound, the hurricane burst upon her.

"We're all right here !" yelled Hunter a few minutes
later in Chester's ear, trying to make himself heard
through the now appalling clamour of wind and
whistling spray—"unless we get the sweep of the
sea coming in the passage—and which way it'll run
we can't tell yet." And then through the fast-
gathering and premature darkness that was envelop-
ing even the white, seething sea around them he
looked forward to where Freeman, the mate, stood,
holding on to the forestay and standing by the
second anchor.

.   .   .   .   .

At dawn next morning, when those natives who

lived on the western and sheltered side of Las Matelotas looked across the lagoon, they saw that nothing
remained of the eastern chain of islets on which the
principal village had stood but a line of isolated sand-
banks and jagged patches of coral reef—every living
being had perished in the awful night. And whether
the end had come upon them suddenly or they had
been swept away when endeavouring to cross the
narrow channels that separated the palm-clad islets, was
never known.

Six miles away, lying high and dry amid fallen
palms and the wreckage of native houses, lay the
once trim little *Montiara*, broken-backed and dis-
masted, and about her were gathered those of her
crew who were uninjured. She had ridden out the
storm till nearly midnight, when she parted both
cables one after the other. In vain had Hunter
and his crew tried to get enough sail on her to
work up under the western beach of the lagoon
and run her ashore in smoother water—sea after
sea swept her decks and drove her right before them.

" Well, it's a bad job," said Hunter, philosophically to Denison, as he surveyed the wreck ; " and
yet it might ha' been worse. Anyway, we've got
the pearl-shell—and know where we can get more.
How's Chester ? "

" Bad, very bad. I'm afraid he won't pull through,
Hunter. That hole in the back of his head is enough
to settle him, let alone a broken arm and broken ribs.
I've left Pedro with him for a bit. I wish to God we
had a doctor here, Hunter. I say, I wonder why
Nirani hasn't turned up before now. She must have
seen that the schooner was missing at daylight."

"Come with me, my lad, and I'll show you why
Nirani isn't here"; and the old captain, clambering
over the wreckage that lay about them, led the way
down to a point of the beach that commanded a
view of the whole lagoon.

"Look over there!" he said.

"Good God!" said Denison, "the three islands
are gone!"

"Aye, swept away in the night. And not a soul
has escaped, for some of our natives have been
down to see. Chester's house was farthest out too.
Poor little woman! Don't tell him, though—at
least not yet."

.   .   .   .   .

Chester didn't die. He was "too tough to go
under very easy," Hunter said, but for a week he
lay between life and death, nursed with rough ten-
derness by his white and brown comrades, and then
he slowly mended. And until he began to improve
he never knew that Nirani was gone, Hunter and
Denison, in reply to his constant inquiries, telling
him that she was sick and could not come to him,
and instructing the natives who occasionally attended
him to bear out their story. But at last Denison
told him.

"I thought she was dead, Denison," he said, quietly.
"Poor girl, poor girl!"

Then he "worried" and went back again; Denison
said on account of Nirani, Hunter said on account of
his ribs not being yet "setted."

.   .   .   .   .

Another month or six weeks had passed by. Hunter
and his people were busy building a cutter out of

the timbers of the *Montiara*, and the islands of Las Matelotas lay shining white and green in the yellow sunshine, when a lumbering old barque, with many boats hanging from her davits, ran along the weather reef of the lagoon and then hove-to off the passage.

"Hurrah!" cried old Hunter, flinging down his adze; "it's the *Amity Parsons*, an' Turner is sending a boat ashore. We're in luck, Denison. He'll give us a passage to Ponape, and there's a doctor there who'll soon put poor Chester to rights." For Chester had "gone back," as Hunter called his relapse, with a vengeance, and although he heard the loud cries of his excited friends when the ship came in sight, he took no heed of them as he lay in his little thatched house near by.

"Wal, this is er surprise," said Captain Turner as he jumped out of his boat and shook hands with Hunter; "I cert'nly didn't reckon to find the *Montiara* piled up here. Say, whar's Chester?"

Hunter told him as quickly as possible the story of their misfortunes.

"Wal, this *is* real vexin', I thought I done a foolish bit of business in doin' what I hev done—now I'm certain of it. Why, I've got a lady passenger and small child on my hands now. Now what on airth am I to do?"

"*I* know," said Hunter, cheerfully; "just come up to my hut and I'll tell you what you're going to do— and a d—— lucky man you are to come along with your greasy old blubber-hunter. Look here, Turner, you're going to take me and all the *Montiara's* crew to Ponape, and Chester as well. And I'm going to give ye a thousand dollars for it."

"It's a deal," said Turner, laconically, as he followed Hunter up the beach.

At sunset that evening the whaleship's boats took off the *Montiara's* crew and the bags of pearl-shell ; in the last boat were Hunter, Denison, and Chester.

Scarcely able to walk, the sick man was led below and put into Turner's own cabin by the ever-watchful Denison and the whaleship's black steward.

"Thanks, old fellow," muttered Chester, extenuing his hand to his friend ; "you are as good a nurse as a woman."

"Am I?" laughed Denison. "I think you'll change your mind about that when you *do* get a woman nurse ; " and then he slipped out of the cabin.

For some minutes Chester lay listening to the sound of the boats being hauled up to the davits. The cabin was very quiet and he seemed to be all alone.

Then he felt a soft hand upon his arm, and in the dim light saw the face of Alice Weston close to his own.

"Alice!" and he half rose from the bunk. "Didn't you get my letter by the *Mattie?*"

"No, darling. Did you write me one at last?" she said as she kissed him.

.   .   .   .   .

But long after they were married, Burton, the skipper of the *Mattie*, told Denison that "the lady's yarn" was all bunkum—he gave the letter to her himself.

HOLLIS'S DEBT: A TALE OF THE NORTH-WEST PACIFIC

Hollis's Debt: A Tale of the North-West Pacific

ONE day a small Sydney-owned brigantine named the *Maid of Judah*, loaded with coconut oil and sandal-wood and bound for China, appeared off the little island of Pingelap, in the Caroline Group. In those wild days—from 1820 to the end of the " 'fifties "—the sandal-wood trade was carried on by ships whose crews were assemblages of the most utter ruffians in the Pacific Ocean, and the hands that manned this brigantine were no exception. There may have been grades of villainy among them ; perhaps if any one of them was more blood-stained and criminal than the others, it was her captain.

There being no anchorage at Pingelap, the captain sailed in as close as he dared, and then hove-to under the lee of the land, waiting for the natives to come aboard with some turtle. Presently a canoe put off from the long curve of yellow beach. She was manned by some eight or ten natives. As she pulled up along-side, the captain glanced at the white man who was steering and his face paled. He turned quickly away and went below.

.　　.　　.　　.　　.

The mate of the sandal-wooder shook hands with

the white man and looked curiously at him. Only by his speech could he be recognised as an Englishman. His hair, long, rough and dull brown, fell on his naked shoulders like that of a native. A broad-brimmed hat, made from the plaited leaf of the pandanus palm, was his only article of European clothing ; round his loins was a native girdle of beaten coconut leaves. And his skin was as dark as that of his savage native crew ; he looked, and was, a true Micronesian beach-comber.

"You're under mighty short canvas, my friend," said the mate of the vessel by way of pleasantry.

The man with the brown skin turned on him savagely.

"What the hell is that to you ? I don't dress to please a pack of —— convicts and cut-throats ! Do you want to buy any turtle ? that's the question. And where's the captain ? "

"Captain Matson has gone below sick, sir," said the steward, coming up and speaking to the mate. "He says not to wait for the turtle but to fill away again."

"Can't," said the mate, sharply. "Tell him there isn't enough wind. Didn't he see that for himself ten minutes ago ? What's the matter with him ? "

"Don't know, sir. Only said he was took bad sudden."

With an oath expressive of disgust the mate turned to the beachcomber. "You've had your trouble for nothing, you see. The old man don't want any turtle it seems—— Why, what the hell is wrong with *you* ? "

The bearded, savage-looking beachcomber was

leaning against a backstay, his hands tightly clenched, and his eyes fixed in a wild, insane stare.

He straightened himself up and spoke with an effort.

"Nothing. I'm all right now. 'Tis a fearful hot day, and the sun has giddied me a bit. I daresay your skipper has got a touch of the same thing. But gettin' the turtle won't delay you. I want tobacco badly. You can have as many turtle as you want for a couple of pounds o' tobacco."

"Right," said the mate—"that's dirt-cheap. Get 'em aboard as quick as you can. Let's have twenty."

The beachcomber laughed. "You don't know much about Pingelap turtle if you think a canoe would hold more than two together. We've got 'em here five hundredweight. You'll have to send a boat if you want that many. They're too heavy to bring off in canoes. But I'll go on ahead and tell the people to get 'em ready for you."

He got over the side into the canoe, and was paddled quickly ashore.

The mate went below to tell the skipper. He found him sitting at the cabin table with white face and shaking limbs, drinking Sydney rum.

"That beachcombing cove has gone ashore; but he says if you send a boat he'll give us twenty turtle for some tobacco. We want some fresh meat badly. Shall I lower the boat?"

An instantaneous change came over the skipper's features, and he sighed as if a heavy load was off his mind.

"Has he gone, Willis? . . . Oh, yes, we must have the turtle. Put a small twelve-pound case of tobacco in the whaleboat, and send half a dozen

Sandwich Island natives with the second mate. Tell Barton to hurry back. We're in too close, and I must tow out a bit when the boat comes back—and I say, Willis, keep that beachcombing fellow on the main-deck if he comes aboard again. I don't like his looks, and don't want him down in the cabin on any account."

.   .   .   .   .

The second mate and his crew followed the white man and a crowd of natives to the pond where the turtle were kept. It was merely a huge pool in the reef, with a rough wall of coral slabs built round it to prevent the turtle escaping when the tides rose higher than usual.

"A real good idea——" began the second mate, when there was a lightning rush of the brown-skinned men upon him and his crew. At knocking a man down and tying him up securely your Caroline Islander is unmatched, he does it so artistically. I know this from experience.

.   .   .   .   .

"This is rather sudden, isn't it, Barton?" The beachcomber was speaking to him, looking into his eyes as he lay upon the ground. "You don't remember my face, do you? Perhaps my back would improve your memory. Ah, you brute, I can pay both you and that murderous dog of a Matson back now. I knew I should meet you both again some day."

Across the sullen features of the seaman there flashed a quick light—the gleam of a memory. But his time was brief. The beachcomber whispered to a native. A heavy stone was lashed to the second mate's chest.

Then they dropped him over the wall into the pond. The native sailors they left where they lay.

And now ensued a hurried, whispered colloquy. The story of that day's work is not yet forgotten among the old hands of Ponape and Yap. Suffice it to say that by a cunningly contrived device the captain was led to believe that the second mate and his men had deserted, and sent the chief mate and six more of his crew to aid the natives in recapturing them. The presence of numbers of women and children walking unconcernedly about the beach made him assured that no treachery was intended. The mate and his men were captured in one of the houses, where they had been taken by the beach-comber for a drink. They were seized from behind and at once bound, but without any unnecessary rough usage.

"What's all this for?" said the mate unconcernedly to the white man. He was an old hand, and thought it meant a heavy ransom—or death.

The beachcomber was standing outside in the blazing sun, looking at the ship. There were a number of natives on board selling fish and young coconuts. The women and children still sauntered to and fro on the beach. He entered the house and answered the query.

"It means this ; no harm to you and these six men here if you lie quiet and wait till I send for you to come aboard again. The other six Sandwich Islanders are alive but tied up. Barton is dead, I have settled my score with *him.*"

"Ah," said the mate, after a brief outburst of blasphemy, "I see, you mean to cut off the ship."

"No, I don't. But I have an old debt to settle with the skipper. Keep quiet, or you'll follow Mister Barton. And I don't want to kill you. I've got nothing against *you*."

Then the beachcomber, with some twenty natives, went to where the first six men were lying, and carried them down into the mate's boat.

.   .   .   .   .

"Here's the second mate's chaps, sir," said the carpenter to Matson; "the natives has 'em tied hand and foot, like pigs. But I don't see Barton among 'em."

"No," said the captain, "they wouldn't tie up a white man. He'll come off with Willis and the turtle. I never thought Barton would bolt."

The *ruse* succeeded admirably. The boat-load of natives had hardly been ten seconds on deck ere the brigantine was captured. Matson, lashed in a sitting position to the quarter railing, saw the last man of the cutting-out party step on board, and a deadly fear seized him. For that last man was the beachcomber.

He walked aft and stood over him. "Come on board, Captain Thomas Matson," he said, mockingly saluting him. Then he stepped back and surveyed his prisoner.

"You look well, Matson. You know me now, don't you?"

The red, bloated face of the skipper patched and mottled, and his breath came in quick, short gasps of rage and terror.

"Ah, of course you do! It's only three years ago since that Sunday at Vaté in the New Hebrides, when you had me triced up and Barton peeled the

hide off me in strips. You said I'd never forget it
— *and I've come to tell you that you were right.* I
haven't. It's been meat and drink to me to think
that we might meet again."

He stopped. His white teeth glistened beneath the
black-bearded lips in a low laugh—a laugh that chilled
the soul of his listener.

A light air rippled the water and filled the sails, and
the brigantine moved. The man went to the wheel
and gave it a turn to port.

"Yes," he resumed, casting his eye aloft, "I'm
delighted to have a talk with you, Matson. You will
see that your crew are working the ship for me. You
don't mind, do you, eh? And we can talk a bit, can't
we?"

No answer came.

"None of the old hands left, I see, Matson—
except Barton. Do you know where he is now?
No? He's dead. I hadn't any particular grudge
against him. He was only your flogger. But I
killed him, and I'm going to kill you." He crossed
his bare, sinewy arms on the wheel, and smiled again
at the bound and terrified wretch.

"You've had new bulwarks and spars since, I see.
Making money fast now, I suppose. I hope your
mate is a good navigator, Matson. *He's* going to
take this ship to Honolulu.

Then the fear-stricken man found his tongue, and
a wild, gasping appeal for mercy broke from him.

"Don't murder me, Hollis. I've been a bad man
all my life. For God's sake, let me off! I was a
brute to you. I've got a wife and children. For
Christ's sake —— !"

The man sprang from the wheel and kicked him savagely in the mouth with his bare foot.

"Ha! you've done it now. 'For Christ's sake. For Christ's sake!' Don't you remember when *I* used those words: 'For Christ's sake, sir, hear me! I did not run away. I got lost coming from the place where we were cutting the sandal-wood.'" A flicker of foam fell on his tawny hand. "You dog, you bloody-minded fiend! For three years I have waited . . . . and I have you now."

A choking groan of terror came from Matson.

"Hollis! Spare me! . . . . my children."

The man had gone back to the wheel, calm again. A brisk puff was rippling over the water from the westward. His seaman's eye glanced aloft, and the wheel again spun round. "Ready, about!" he called. The brigantine went and stood in again——to meet the mate's boat.

.   .   .   .   .

"Come this way, Mr. Willis. Captain Matson and I have been having a chat about old times. You don't know me, do you? Captain Matson is a little upset just now, so I'll tell you who I am. My name is Hollis. I was one of the hands of this ship. I am owner now. Funny, isn't it? Now, now; don't get excited, Mr. Willis, and look about you in that way. There isn't a ghost of a chance; I can tell you that. If you make one step towards me, you and every man Jack will get his throat cut. And as soon as I have finished my business with our friend here you'll be captain—and owner, too, if you like. By the by, what's the cargo worth?"

The mate told him.

" Ah, quite a nice little sum—two thousand pounds.
Now, Mr. Willis, that will be practically yours. With
only one other white man on board, you can take the
vessel to Honolulu and sell both her and the cargo,
and no questions asked. Hard on our friend here,
though ; isn't it ? "

" Good God, man, what are you going to do to the
captain—murder him ? "

" For God's sake, Willis, help me ! " The mute
agony in the skipper's face, more than the spoken
words, moved even the rough and brutal nature of the
mate, and he opened his lips to speak.

" No ! " said the man at the wheel ; " you shall not
help him. Look at this ! "

He tossed aside the mantle of tangled hair that fell
down his shoulders, and presented his scarred and
hideous back to the mate.

" Now, listen to me, Mr. Willis. Go below and
pass up as much tobacco and trade as will fill the
small boat. *I* don't want plunder. But these natives
of mine do."

In a few minutes the goods were hoisted up and
lowered into the boat. Then the two six-pounders
on the main deck were run overboard, and all the
small arms taken from the cabin by the natives.

" Call your men aft," the white man said to Willis.
They came along the deck and stood behind him.

" Carry that man on to the main hatch."

Two of the strongest of the native sailors picked
up the burly figure of the captain and laid him on the
spot the beachcomber indicated and cut his bonds.

.   .   .   .   .

A dead silence. The tall, sun-baked figure of the

muscular beachcomber, naked save for his grass girdle, seemed, as he stood at the wheel, the only animate thing on board. He raised his finger and beckoned to a sailor to come and steer. Then with quick strides he reached the hatch and stood in front of his prey.

"Captain Tom Matson. Look at me well ; and see what you have made me. Your time . . . and *mine* . . . at last."

He extended his hand. A native placed in it the hilt of a knife, short, broad-bladed, heavy and keen-edged.

"Ha! Can't you speak ? Can't *you* say ' for Christ's sake '? Don't the words stick in your throat ? "

The sinewy left hand darted out and seized the fated man by the hair, and then with a savage backward jerk bent back his head, and drew taut the skin of the coarse, thick throat. Then he raised the knife . . .

.   .   .   .   .

He wiped the knife on his girdle, and looked in silence at the bubbling arterial stream that poured down over the hatch-coamings.

"You won't forget my name, will you ? " he said to the mate. " Hollis ; Hollis, of Sydney ; they know me there ; the man that was flogged at Vaté by him, *there*—and left ashore to die at Santo."

He glanced down at the limp, huddled-up mass at his feet, got into the boat, and with his naked associates, paddled ashore.

The breeze had freshened up, and as the brigantine slowly sailed past the crowded huts of the native village a hundred yards distant, the mate saw the beachcomber standing by his thatched house. He was watching the ship.

A young native girl came up to him with a wooden water-bowl, and stood waiting. With his eyes still fixed on the ship he thrust his reddened hands into the water, moved them slowly to and fro, then dried them on his girdle of grass.

THE ARM OF LUNO CAPAL

The Arm of Luno Capál

WHEN Kermody, the new trainer from the Marshall Group, came to Matupi, in New Britain, and said he was willing to take Colin Murray's trading station at Mutávat, away down the coast, every one said he was mad.

"Don't you do it, young fellow," said Billy Rodman, the greatest fighter and oldest trader from the Solomon's to the Admiralty Group. "Take my advice and don't do it. Look here, there's plenty of places nearer here than Mutávat, where you can do just as well, and get just as much copra as you can in that cut-throat cannibal shop."

"I daresay," said Kermody, a young, fair-featured Irishman of about five-and-twenty, "but the fact is, I want to go there. I mean to have a slap at that patch of black-edged shell about ten miles on the other side of Mutávat. I've got six Yap natives with me—brought them from the Caroline Islands—all good divers, and all d——d good fighting-men as well. And I think I can stick it out there. Levison, of the brig *Adolphe*, told me two years ago, when I met him up in the Pelews, that the shell is there, right enough, and in shallow water, too—whips of it."

"Of course it's there, all of us here knows that," said

Rattray, the trader from Ralune; "but there is no one of us fool enough to go and live there. Why, man, Murray was only there three weeks when they speared him, and his three native boys, and ate them."

"But Murray's station was at Mutávat," said Kermody. "He was killed there, wasn't he? And when I say I'm going to Mutávat — I mean that I only intend using Murray's house as a living station during bad weather. My idea is to sail right down to the place where the shell is, and live on that little island between the reef and the mainland."

"Look here, young fellow. Me and these chaps here"—and old Rodman indicated by a nod of his shaggy gray head the five other white men present— "ain't none too pleased to see you come to New Britain. Not that we doesn't like you—it's not that. But there's quite enough of us trading about here from Blanche Bay to Kabira—the only parts where a man's life is pretty safe. We chaps came here before the missionaries and before the Dutchmen, [1] and used to do pretty well. Then what with the missionaries and the big Dutch firm coming in and sticking traders all over the coast, and underselling all us old hands, with their cheap and rotten German rubbish, times ain't what they used to be; and we don't want to see any more new men coming in and making it harder for us to earn a living. Ain't I right, chaps?"

"In course yer are, Billy," said Cockney Smith, a bleary-eyed, gin-drinking little man, dressed in a suit of dirty duck. "By and by, if many more coves

[1] All Germans, Swedes, Danes, Norwegians, &c., are "Dutchmen," to the English trader.

come here on the trading racket, we'll bloomin' well have to go 'awkin' our stuff round to the natives in baskets like bloomin' pedlars."

"Well, wait a minute," resumed Rodman, continuing his remarks to young Kermody; "as I was saying, we don't want any more traders about here. But at the same time, we don't want to see any white man go down to the place you want to go to, and get his throat cut before he's been there a week. When the German firm opened that station at Mutávat two years ago, they asked me to take charge of it. I wouldn't. I knew what the natives down there are. Two of the firm's own men went down with a lot of New Ireland niggers as a sort of bodyguard. A month afterwards, when the *Iserbrook* brig went down to get their copra, they found that the two Dutchmen and every man Jack of the New Ireland niggers had been killed and eaten, and the station looted. Did the German manager tell you that, when he told you what a fine house and station it was?"

"No," said Kermody; "he didn't."

"And he didn't tell poor Murray, either. We did, but it was too late then. He had signed his agreement, and said he wouldn't back out, but take his chance. Like yourself, he was a new hand here. He'd just come from Fiji way somewheres and thought that as he knew all about psalm-singing Fiji niggers, that he'd get along all right with these New Britain beggars. And in three weeks he and his three native boys went down their d——d gullets."

For a minute Kermody hesitated. He was a courageous man, but not, in his own opinion, a foolhardy

one.   Levison, a wandering trading skipper, had given
him a glowing account of the rich patches of black-
edged pearl-shell he had seen along the coast about
Mutávat.   And these men confirmed it.   And somehow Kermody didn't altogether believe that concern
for him personally was at the bottom of their anxiety
lest he should go.   Perhaps they meant to have a slap
at it themselves.   That's what it was!   So he made
up his mind to go.   He had left the Carolines to come
to New Britain for the purpose of getting that shell
and he meant to have it."

"Well, I'm very much obliged to you all, gentlemen.   But I won't settle down here to buy copra.
I've got a good cutter and six good men, and plenty
of arms.   At the same time, I'll tell the German
manager that he can keep his blasted station.   I won't
go near it—thanks to you—I'll take the cutter in
over the reef and anchor her off the little island.
Levison told me there are no natives living on it,
and that they seldom land on it."

"They'll land on it when you don't expect 'em,"
said Rodman, grimly.   "You don't know these niggers.
They ain't the sort of people you have been used to in
the Marshalls and Carolines.   They are the lowest-
down, most treacherous, bloodthirsty cannibals in the
Pacific, and no one but a madman would go so far
down the coast as you are going, even with six men
well armed.   They are bound to get you in time.   If
they see that you suspect them, they'll get d——d
sociable with you, and cut your throat when you're
asleep.   However, I've had my say, young fellow, and
I'm very sorry you won't take my advice.   When
are you going ? "

"To-morrow."

"Going to take your wife?"

Kermody smiled. "Rather. She's as good as a man. Not a bit scared. Comes from a good fighting stock. She's a Pelew Island girl."

"Well, then, I suppose it's no use talking. But I don't think you should take her. Let her stay here with my old woman; or, better still, with Pedro's wife. She's a young thing, and will be glad of her company. Besides that, Pedro's wife comes from somewhere near the Pelews, don't she, Pedro?"

"Yes," answered the man addressed, a small, slender-built Portuguese. "She coma from Las Matelotas; speaka sama languaga as Pelew."

"No, thanks. You're very kind, but she wouldn't stay behind," said Kermody (and, indeed, what Pelew girl would leave her white husband through fear or death or danger?), and with a kindly nod to the five traders he went out, walked down to the beach, got into his boat, and went off to the cutter, which lay at anchor just off old Billy Rodman's station.

.   .   .   .   .

At daylight next morning Pedro Unzaga and his Matelotas wife, standing at the door of their house, saw the cutter get under way, and with the first breath or the trade wind bellying out her mainsail, sail slowly past the curving palm-lined beach that fringed the shore for a long ten miles.

"Pedro," said his wife, laying her hand on her husband's arm, and looking wistfully at the little vessel as she passed, "she speaketh my tongue. . . . And it is long since I last heard it. . . . And it may be that she will never come back. . . . And she is but a child."

. . . . .

For two days the cutter sailed westward, and Kermody—as he steered her past the long, long stretches of white, sandy beach, and saw the groves of stately palms and rich verdure of the hills in the background, and the flash and gleam of many a mountain torrent far inland—called to his young wife to come and sit beside him.

" 'Tis a fair green land," said he, as she came to his call, and sitting beside him leant her cheek upon his shoulder, and looked dreamily across to the shore.

"Aye, Kermotee," she answered, in her native tongue. "A fair green land ; but yet not so green to my eyes as Uruloong, the land of my father. And Seta, the wife of Pedro, sayeth that the men who dwell here are eaters of men's flesh. And they are black and ugly to look upon. Kermotee," and she lifted her eyes, soft, black, and lustrous, to his face, "let us not live here in this evil land always."

"But for six months, my bird," said Kermody, stroking her glossy hair—"only for six months, till we have filled the cutter with this pearl-shell, and I have a string of pearls for that white throat of thine. Then will we be rich, and sail to Singapore. There will I sell the pearl-shell, and then shall we return to Uruloong and live."

A soft, tender smile flitted across her pale face, and Kermody, taking her hand in his, pulled up the loose sleeve of her blouse to the shoulders and looked at the thin spiral lines of blue tattoo that ran in graceful curves from her shoulder down to her slender wrist.

" Thou art for ever looking at my arm," she laughed, in her sweet, low voice ; " is not the marking to thy liking, my husband ? "

" Nay, not that, Luno-Capál. But I wonder that thou, child of a white father, should so follow the fashion of thy country."

" I was but a little child when my white father died. And my mother's people desired me to be as any other girl of Uruloong. So I was tattooed as thou seest, but only on mine arms."

Kermody smiled. She was but a child even now ; and as he looked at her fair young face and graceful, delicate figure, and thought of the rough life he was bringing her to on this shelling trip, his conscience smote him for not having left her with the wife of Pedro the Portuguese till he returned.

" Kermotee," she said, presently, toying with his hand, " would it please thee better if my arms were as the arms of a woman of thy own land ? "

" No," he answered, pinching her chin playfully. " Thy arms are to my liking. Yet us white men like not the fashion of tattooing. Still to me it matters nothing."

" And thou would'st know my arm from that of any other, even were the tattoo marks like these ? " she said, with childish vanity—" even if my face were hidden from thee ? "

" Even as I would know thy eyes among the eyes of ten thousand, though the rest of thy face were hidden from me," he answered, drawing her to him.

.   .   .   .   .

A month had passed, and then one day, when the trade wind blew strong, and the lines of palms along

the beaches swayed and bent their plumèd crowns,
and the sea was white-horsed away to the horizon, the
cutter came in sight again, and dropped her anchor
within a mile of Pedro's house.

"How are you?" said Kermody, as, half an hour
later, he jumped out of his boat, and met the Portuguese
on the beach. "I've had grand luck; got two tons
of shell in the first week, and am getting more every
day. But Luno Capál is a bit sick."

"Gotta th' fev'?" suggested Pedro.

"No, I don't think it's fever, Pedro. I think she's
fretting a bit ever since she saw your wife. You see
I'm away in the boat all day, and she's left on the
little island by herself. And I've come up to ask you
to let your wife come with me, and keep her company
for a week or two. Will you?"

"Yes," said Pedro, who was a good-natured fellow,
and who felt reassured now that Kermody had returned
safely, "I'll let her go wis you. She what you call
'fretta' too for your wife. All daya long she talk
about her, and aska question about when she come
back."

Then Kermody asked Pedro to come as well, and
after some little hesitation he consented. He did not
like leaving his station without any one to take care of
it, but at the same time was anxious to see Kermody's
pearling ground. In a few minutes they were at his
house, and his pretty little Matelotas wife clapped her
hands with joy when she heard the reason of Kermody's
visit. In two hours they were all on board, and the
cutter was lying over to the breeze, with the water
swirling and slopping over her lee rail. Only two of
Kermody's crew were on board, the other four having

been left with his wife on the island, with strict instructions to keep a good watch for any native canoes.

"But I don't think there's the slightest danger," said Kermody to Pedro, as they sat smoking in the cabin, and listening to the rush and seeth of the water as the little cutter swept through the night. "We haven't seen a native yet, although we've seen any amount of fires on the mainland ; and Levison told me there was a big town of two thousand natives about ten miles away from the little island."

Yes ; Pedro knew that the town was inhabited by a branch of the Mutávat tribe—the Narra. When the Mutávat people killed the two Dutchmen and Murray, they had sent portions of their bodies over to the big town mentioned by Levison. And when the Narra people had a cannibal feast they "always sent a limb over to the Mutávat crowd."

"What infernal brutes!" said Kermody. "I wouldn't live in such a cursed country for a fortune. However, I'm pretty safe where I am now, and mean to stay on the island till I fill the cutter with pearl shell. I may come back again, Pedro, with a bigger crowd of men next year—that is if my little woman doesn't buck. I promised her a month ago that I would not stay here over six months. But, by Jove, Pedro, there's a dozen fortunes lying around here. And . . . well, to tell you the truth, I'm only telling her a lie. I do mean to come back here, and I know she won't let me come alone."

Pedro nodded, and wishing Kermody good-night, he turned in.

.   .   .   .   .

The breeze fell during the night, and at daylight the cutter was slipping along over a smooth sea, with a clear blue sky overhead. The little island was still ten miles away, and just as the sun rose, Kermody could see the faint, dim outlines of its palm-covered shore pencilled against the horizon.

"Hallo," said Pedro, "I see a canoe right ahead."

"I see that canoe just a couple of minutes ago," said Harry, a native of Yap, who acted as Kermody's mate. "She was coming this way, then she slewed round and made back."

"We'll soon overhaul them, anyway," said Kermody to Pedro. "But, by the Lord, they *are* paddling!"

Pedro had his dark, deep-set eyes fixed steadily on the canoe, which contained four men. Then he turned to Kennedy with an uneasy look upon his face.

"What's the matter?" asked Kermody.

Pedro shook his head solemnly, and said he thought it was very curious that they should meet this canoe. She seemed to have been coming from the island towards Mutávat, which was now astern of them. But now she had turned back, and was making for the mainland.

"We'll soon see what the devil they're in such a hurry about," said Kermody, and he altered the cutter's course a point or two, so as to intercept the canoe. At the same moment Pedro came up from below with his rifle, which he laid down on the deck.

In twenty minutes more the cutter was within three hundred yards of the canoe, and Pedro taking up his rifle, sent a shot through her. The four natives, who had been paddling as if for their lives, at once jumped overboard and dived towards the shore.

"What did you do that for?" said Kermody, angrily, to Pedro.

"Look at that," answered the Portuguese, pointing to the canoe.

Kermody could see nothing but the empty canoe floating about. Amidships, and suspended between two slender upright sticks, was a basket of coconut leaf, which swayed to and fro with the motion of the sea.

"What is it?" asked Kermody, impatiently. He was angry at Pedro's wanton shot.

The Portuguese took the tiller from him, and let the cutter run up alongside the rocking canoe. As she swept by he let go the tiller, and reaching out his hand caught the basket from between the sticks and dropped it down upon the deck.

Kermody picked it up, and cutting the lashing of cinnet that secured the sides, turned it upside down upon the skylight.

"It's not very heavy, Pedro, anyway. . . . Oh, my God! . . ."

It was the arm of Luno Capál.

IN A SAMOAN VILLAGE

In a Samoan Village

SIXTY years ago, when not a score of white men lived in Samoa, and when, as now, the greatest chief in the country bore the name of Malietoa, there ruled over the district of Lefanga, in the western end of Upolu, a chief of singular courage and most undaunted resolution. His name was Tuisila; and although scarcely past his youth, he had already distinguished himself in battle on many occasions. Like the valorous but ferocious Finau of Tonga, with whom he was contemporary, and whose name first became known to English people by his cutting off of the London privateer, *Port-au-Prince*, in 1805, the young Samoan chief had associated with him in his warlike enterprises some few white men, whom misfortune or their own crimes had led to their abandonment of all civilised ties and associations. In the case of Finau, a young English seaman named William Mariner, who was one of the survivors of the *Port-au-Prince* massacre, preserved in his journal of his four years' residence in Tonga, a record of the names of many of the white mercenaries who aided Finau to subjugate his enemies. Most of these men, like Mariner himself, had been spared from the general slaughter of the privateer's crew by the astute Finau in order that they might instruct his people how to use the cannon which belonged to the armament of the captured ship. And so readily did the adventurous privateersmen enter into his wishes that in a very short time Finau was able to subdue all those who contested his authority, for his white artillerymen soon destroyed forts hitherto considered impregnable to attacks conducted in the ordinary Tongan method. While, however, there were in the service of the chief Finau about sixteen Englishmen, the Samoan chief Tuisila had but three, and at the time of this story he was lamenting the death of one of these, who, a few days before, had been mortally wounded in an encounter with a foray party from another district, and whose body had just been buried by his two comrades, assisted by the natives.

. . . . .

One evening, a few days after this man's death, Tuisila, to show the respect in which he held his white friends, assembled the people in front of his house and ordered a "lagisolo," or funeral dirge, to be sung in honour of the memory of the dead white man, and sent a message to his surviving comrades to honour the ceremony by their presence.

Living somewhat apart from the other houses of the village, some little time passed ere they presented themselves to Tuisila, who, receiving them with that dignified courtesy which is innate in all Samoans of whatever rank, bade them be seated beside him in the place of honour. Then, at a signal from the chief, the opening solo was begun by an aged woman, and the two white men, rough and stern as were their natures, could not be but affected somewhat as the plaintive, wailing notes that recounted their comrade's achievements resounded through the quiet evening air. The scene of the ceremony was a small fortified village situated at the foot of Mount Tofua, and looking seaward over the wide, blue expanse of Falelatai Bay.

The trade wind was slowly fading away, and the dense fringe of cocos that studded the beach of the verdant littoral between the mountain village and the shores of the bay scarce moved their drooping leaves to its dying breaths.   Far up, towards the summit of Tofua, the purpling shades of the setting sun were giving way to the night mantle of soft, white cloud that crept up and around its deeply-verdured sides and bold, outspreading spurs.

For some minutes the men sat smoking in silence and gazing at the foaming curves of the barrier reef encompassing the bay of Falelatai, and apparently taking but little heed of what was going on around them.   Presently, however, at the conclusion of the dirge, they heard the full, manly tones of the young chief directing some young women to prepare a bowl of kava.   The sound of his voice aroused them from their thoughts, and brought them back to their wild surroundings.

" Bill," said the elder, a grey-bearded, muscular man of fifty, " I wonder if you an' me is going to get finished off like poor Tommy Lane?   Or is you an' me goin' to spend all our lives here among a race o' savages, livin' like 'em, thinkin' like 'em, and dyin' like 'em ? "

The younger man, who was known to the natives as Tuifau ("the blacksmith," or "ironworker") for some minutes made no answer. Unlike his companion—who was evidently but a rude, uncultured seaman—his countenance, tanned and roughened as it was by his wild and adventurous life, showed not only intelligence but a degree of refinement that would not be looked for in one whose conditions of existence were so degrading. Both men were dressed like natives, naked to the waist, and save where their girdles of *ti* leaves protected their skins, their tattooed bodies and limbs were darkened as deeply by the rays of a tropic sun as were those of their native associates. At last " Bill " spoke, but with such a strange bitterness in his voice that his comrade stared at him in wonder.

" Aye, Dick, as you say ; are we indeed to end our days here among these people, or meet the fate of poor Tom ? Think of it, man. Let us look things in the face. What are we in our own minds ? What would any of your or my countrymen think of us but that we are a pair of shameless, degraded beings, unfit to associate with ; sunk too low to even think of returning to civilisation again ? "

The elder man moved uneasily, and then glanced somewhat curiously at the other.

" That's comin' it rather strong, Bill. We ain't no worse than any other *papalagi tafea*[1] in Samoa. I don't mean to say as I'd like to go aboard ship like this "—and he touched his naked body and pointed to his tattooed legs—" but, at the same time, it ain't my fault, and it ain't yourn. I runned away from my ship twenty years ago, because she was a floatin' hell. Perhaps, if I could ha' got away again from here in a

[1] Beachcombers.

year or so, I would ha' gone. But I took to the native live, and the life took to me. An' I says I've had a better time among these here people than I would ha' had at sea. What's the use o' gettin' hell knocked out o' you all your life at sea and dyin' in the poor-house in the end? O' course, wi' you it's different. You is on'y a young man, an' has a eddication. I'm on'y a old shell-back as doesn't care a dam' 'bout anything. But now as you've started talkin' 'bout these things, I does own I've sometimes had a kind of a wision like of bein' in London again, and sittin' down in front o' a frothin' mug o' stout. God alive, just think of it!"

A slight smile flickered across the younger man's lips. Then he asked, "Isn't there anybody you'd like to see again in the old country, Dick?"

The grizzled old beachcomber shook his head. "No—leastways, not as I knows of. I s'pose every one thinks I'm dead. I say, Bill, what made you take to this kind of life?"

"Bill," otherwise William Trenchard, once a petty officer on the American frigate *Huron*, clenched his browned hands and stared moodily before him. Then he said slowly, "Because, like yourself, I was tired of a life at sea. And because one day three years ago I was taken by the pretty face of a native girl—I deserted from the *Huron* at the Sandwich Islands, and came here in an American whaler."

"Well, ain't you satisfied? Doesn't you and me live like fightin'-cocks? Tell yer what it is, Bill— this here cove, Tuisila, thinks a hell of a lot o' us. An' jest you remember this—he's going to be king o' Samoa before long. You see, you've on'y been here two years. I've been here twenty, an' I knows what's goin' on. Malietoa would like to see Tuisila dead—he's afeerd he's gettin' too powerful."

"Well, even so, what good will that do us?"

"Lots! Why, you an' me will be two of the biggest men in the country. Your wife is a sort o' adopted sister to Tuisila, an' if he wipes out Malietoa, you'll be the second man in the country."

Trenchard rose to his feet and laughed bitterly. 'Yes, and even then only a disgrace to my own."

He was about to walk away when he remembered that he would be expected to remain and drink a bowl of kava with his native master, and so resumed his seat upon his mat again in sullen silence.

.   .   .   .   .

Among the many hundreds of women and girls who were seated around were his wife Malama and her infant child. Scarcely out of her girlhood, she possessed to a very great degree all that beauty of face and figure and vivacity of expression that are met with in the Malayo-Polynesian races of the Pacific Islands, and a smile lit up her features as she heard her husband's name called out next to that of her adopted brother, the chief, as the bowl of kava was presented to him to drink.

Hitherto the name of the older of the two men had, by reason of his long services and valorous conduct, been held in such esteem by Tuisila—and his father before him—that at all ceremonious kava-drinkings it had always been called out immediately after that of the chief himself.

So as the stalwart young native who officiated as cup-bearer presented the bowl to Trenchard with a respectful obeisance, the younger white man waived it aside, and nodded his head towards old Richard Mayne.

" That's all right, Bill," said the old beachcomber, without the slightest trace of bitterness in his voice, and, of course, speaking in English, " I ain't put out a bit. You're goin' to be the big man here now, an' I ain't fool enough to get mad over what's werry natural. You has a eddication, an' these natives knows it. Drink it, man, an' good luck to us both."

Trenchard, however, turning to the chief, who sat looking at him with a smile on his face, still declined the honour, and it was not until the chief's orator, or " talking man," who sat behind him, rose, and leaning on his staff, said that it was not only the wish of Tuisila, but of the older white man himself, that Trenchard yielded and drank.

For some minutes or so the ceremony continued, the kava bowl being passed round to the various sub-chiefs in order of rank, and then Tuisila whispered to his orator, who, again rising, addressed the assemblage. His speech was brief, but the excited looks and expressions of pleasure that immediately followed showed its importance—a messenger had that morning arrived from Apia with the news that an American man-of-war had dropped anchor in the harbour, and that her captain, desiring to meet Tuisila and the chiefs of his district, wished them to visit his ship. His reason for making the request was that, learning of the disturbed state of the island, and the bloody encounters that had occurred between Malietoa and his tributary chiefs, he wished to effect a reconciliation.

For a moment or two no one spoke, and then Tuisila

asked the white men to tell the assembled people their opinion of the naval officer's request ; would it be safe for him to accede, or did they think that the captain was acting in collusion with Malietoa and intended to make him (Tuisila) a prisoner?

Trenchard at once expressed the opinion that the man-of-war captain's request concealed no evil intention, and urged the chief to comply. He pointed out to him the probability of Malietoa having already seen the captain, and, through his white interpreters, sought to gain his armed aid in bringing his rebellious chiefs to submission ; and that the naval officer no doubt wished to hear both sides, and then endeavour to reconcile them to one another.

Placing as he did the greatest faith in his two white men, the chief at once announced his intention of setting out on the following day, and preparations were at once begun to make the journey in three or four large *taumualua*, or native boats.

.   .   .   .   .

It now became necessary for Trenchard to tell the chief that he could not accompany him. He gave his excuse that he had no desire to ever again come in contact with white men while in his present condition. The mere absence of clothing, he said, would subject him to insult and place him in an ignominious position. The only garments he had were in such a ragged state that he could not possibly venture to clothe himself in them ; therefore he begged the chief to permit him and his comrade, who was in precisely the same situation, to remain behind, or at least to only accompany the expedition to within a certain distance of Apia

Harbour. To this suggestion Tuisila reluctantly assented.

Unaware of the real reason of Trenchard's objections to visit the man-of-war (for the chief did not know that he was a deserter), Tuisila expressed the most lively sympathy, and stated that he would endeavour to get them some clothing from the two or three white men who lived under the protection of Malietoa, so that the next time that a ship touched at the island they should not be debarred from visiting her and hearing the sound of their country's tongue again.

At dawn the boats left the village, and Mayne and Trenchard, who were in the same boat as the valorous young chief, could not but see that he was visibly depressed at their not being able to accompany him on board the man-of-war and assist in any negotiations that might take place. Trenchard was accompanied by his wife, and his comrade Mayne by one daughter. Malama, as was natural enough, looked forward with pleasure to the prospect of visiting a man-of-war, for in those days whole years passed without a ship touching at the group, which was but little known to navigators, and the sight of white strangers was a rare event.

Early in the afternoon the chief's flotilla ran into Vaitele Bay, on the western side of the point of Mulinu'u, some three miles from Apia Harbour, and Trenchard could see through the serried lines of cocos the lofty spars of a large frigate that lay at anchor off Matautu Point. At the place where they landed Tuisila was met by messengers from King Malietoa. They brought him the customary presents from their master, and expressed the king's hope that their meeting would result in bringing their disastrous quarrel to an end. A bowl of kava was at once prepared in one of the houses and partaken of by Tuisila's party and the messengers from Malietoa, and then the two white men saw him, accompanied by Malama and Mayne's daughter, step into the boats again and paddle away towards the ship.

For nearly two hours Trenchard and his companion lay in the house awaiting Tuisila's return, and then, becoming wearied, they set out for a walk towards a village a mile or so away, where lived people who were related to Mayne's wife. Both men were possessed of muskets, but, feeling perfectly sure of the good intentions of Malietoa's people, they had had no hesitation in leaving their arms in the care of the people of the house they had just left.

.   .   .   .   .

As soon as Tuisila reached the ship he at once, without the slightest hesitation, ascended to the deck, where he was met by the captain and his officers, who received him most hospitably, for they were struck with his dignified and imposing bearing. On the other side of the deck were a group of natives, and among them the young chief recognised the stately figure of his foe, the King Malietoa, who quickly advanced towards him and greeted him in a friendly manner.

With the king was a white man named Collis, who acted as interpreter, and who was now desired by the American captain to ask the two chiefs to come below into his cabin and have a friendly conference. To this both Malietoa and Tuisila immediately consented, and they were about to follow the interpreter when the latter caught sight of the figure of the graceful Malama, who was standing on the main deck with old Mayne's half-caste daughter. Both the young women seemed lost in timid wonder at the strangeness of their surroundings, and Collis, knowing them both by repute, called to them to go on to the quarter-deck, where they would feel more private.

Holding each other by the hand like two children, they walked shyly along the deck, till Tuisila, just as he was about to descend to the cabin, addressing Malama and her friend, told them not to be frightened—there was no one on the ship who would seek to do them harm.

"Nay," answered Malama, with a smile, "we are not now afraid; but yet did I desire to stay a little while on the lower deck among the *auva'a* (the common sailors), and then would I have liked thee, Kolli (Collis), to ask some of them to sell me some clothes for my husband. See," and she pointed to a bundle that lay upon the deck, "behold this roll of fine mats and new *tappa* cloth. These have I brought to exchange with the sailors for some of their clothing, so that my husband, who hath none, can sometimes dress himself as becomes a white man."

The eager, earnest manner in which the young woman spoke and her engaging and modest appearance at once attracted Captain Wilkes, who, with some of the officers of the *Vincennes*, was standing near, and he asked Collis pleasantly what it was that she wanted.

Collis, a good-natured but careless and thoughtless man, laughed as he answered—

"She wants to barter some native mats, sir, for clothes for her husband, who is a white man."

"Indeed ; where is he ; is he on board ? "

" No, sir. He's like a good many of us here—he's got no clothes. He lives with this chief Tuisila, and this girl, who is Tuisila's half-sister, tells me that her husband and another white man are ashore here at a village quite close to. They are waiting there till these young women come back and bring them some clothes, I expect."

" Ha," said Captain Wilkes, quickly, "are these two of the men that Malietoa tells me are allies of his enemies ? "

" Yes, sir ; old Mayne and Trenchard are both fighting for the Lafanga people."

" I understand. Now, Collis, I would like to see these men, and mean to see them. Tell the young woman that I will give her some clothing to take ashore to her husband. Mr. Wallis, pass the word for my steward to come to me, and then will you please get ready to go ashore with these young women. They will take you to a village where two white men are staying. Give these men the clothes that my steward will give you, and then bring them back with you to the ship. They may not want to come ; but if they object, bring them by force. One, I am told, is an Englishman, the other an American. I wish to see them both, and especially the latter, as I have no doubt he is a man of whom I have a written description. But, any way, they are a pair of scoundrels, so don't be too delicate with them. I shall endeavour to keep the chief here till you return."

. . . . .

Trenchard and Mayne, after walking about a mile, reached the village where the friends of the latter's wife lived. They had been made very welcome in true Samoan fashion, and, after spending an hour or two with the natives, set out on their return, for they were feeling somewhat anxious at the length of time that Tuisila had been absent. Malietoa was recognised by naval officers as king, and it was not very unlikely that Tuisila had been delayed by some action of the commander of the war-ship who was anxious to restore peace between the king and the chiefs who contested his sway.

Night had fallen by the time they returned, and as they drew near the little village they heard the sound of Malama's voice calling for her husband. She was about two hundred yards away from the house, standing in the path, and the moment she heard her husband's voice she gave a glad cry and came towards him.

"Billee," she said, "the white chief of the ship hath sent thee some clothes. Come, see, they are here in the house. And there have come with us an *alii* (officer) and six men to bring thee and Dikki to the captain of the fighting ship; he desireth to talk with thee both."

"Good God, Dick!" and the young man clutched his comrade by the shoulder, "they know who I am."

For a moment or two he spoke hurriedly to the wondering Malama, who saw that his whole form was quivering with excitement, and then he turned to Mayne.

"You go on, Dick. You have nothing to fear. You are an Englishman; they cannot harm you. I will get back into the mountains, and return home through the bush," and then, grasping his comrade's hand, he turned to go.

"Bill," said Mayne, earnestly, "you're making a mistake. They doesn't know who you are—that I'm sure of. They're all sitting down there in front of the house talkin' and smokin'. Come along and face 'em."

"Yes, you might as well," exclaimed a strange voice, and an officer, closely followed by two seamen, sprang upon and seized him.

Then began a deadly struggle between the two half-naked beachcombers and the officer and his men. Old as he was, Mayne possessed such strength and suppleness of body that he not only succeeded in freeing himself, but soon stretched the officer out senseless by a terrific blow. Trenchard, too, fought with savage desperation, and, although the men-of-warsmen had now drawn their cutlasses, they could not use them on account of the darkness and for fear of injuring each other. Mayne, after knocking the officer down, seized his pistol, and, springing to Trenchard's aid, whispered, "Make for the beach."

Then, before the excited seamen could realise what had happened, the naked figures of the two beachcombers vanished into the night, but not so quickly but that Malama and Mayne's young daughter fled with them.

The darkness rendered pursuit hopeless, and the officer, as soon as he came to, ordered his crew into the boat and returned to the ship.

An hour or so afterward Tuisila and his party, who had been delayed, returned, and search was made for his white friends. Half a mile away they discovered a place on the beach from where a canoe had been run down into the water.

"Ha!" said the chief, "it is well. See, they have

gotten away safely, and are now returning home before us."

.   .   .   .   .

But Trenchard and Mayne were never seen in the village that nestled under the shadow of Mount Tofua. But long, long years afterwards, when the chief Tuisila had become a middle-aged man and the infant half-caste child of Malama had grown to be a woman, a ship one day touched at a lonely little island called Motu-iti, a thousand miles or more to the westward of Samoa. As the captain of the ship landed he was met on the beach by an old, grey-headed white man, whose bronze-hued skin told of a lifetime spent in the South Seas. With feeble steps he conducted the captain to his house, and offered him such hospitality as lay within his means, but his tongue could scarcely frame the forgotten English words that came to his lips.

The seaman looked at him curiously, and then in an off-hand manner asked him if he was the only white man on the island.

"Yes," he answered, "I am the only white man on the island. . . . Twenty-one years ago I came here. I drifted here. . . . I had a companion with me, but he died . . . seven years ago."

He bent his head upon his chest awhile. "And Malama died long before that. The hardships, sir, oh, God! the awful hardships of that long, long time upon the sea—poor girl, poor girl——" and then he ceased to speak.

For some little time he remained silent, and then, rising from his seat, extended his hand to his visitor, and in tremulous tones bade him farewell.

COLLIER :
THE " BLACKBIRDER "

Collier : " *The Blackbirder* "

THE trading brig *Airola*, belonging to Sydney, dropped her anchor at noon in Papiete Harbour, at Tahiti, after a smart run up from Fakarava, in the Paumotu Group. The skipper had then immediately gone ashore to report, and owing to various causes—the principal of which was his careless and indiscriminate manner of mixing his drinks—had not yet returned, although the lights had begun to glimmer from the shore. The second mate and Allan, the half-caste boatswain, professing an ardent anxiety for their superior officer's welfare, had been allowed to go in search of him, with a parting warning from the mate that if they were found drunk in the streets after gunfire, the "Johnny darms" would run them in till the British Consul took them out again. And so, just before eight bells struck, Jack Collier, the first mate, and Denison, the supercargo, found themselves the only persons in the after part of the ship, the mulatto steward having gone for'ard to pursue his nightly pastime of swindling the copper-coloured Polynesian crew out of sundry pounds of tobacco by means of the cheerful game of poker. Then Collier, speaking in his usual quiet

tones, said to Denison, as they sat down on the skylight to smoke—

"I am rather glad the captain isn't likely to turn up
a while, as I'm expecting a visitor, and I want you to
see him—he's likely to be my father-in-law. If all
goes well, and the brig isn't collared by the French-
men for trading in the Paumotus without a license,
or some other such charge, I mean to leave next
voyage, and settle down in Vavitao, in the Austral
Group. For'ard there! strike eight bells!"

.   .   .   .   .

The sound of the bell had scarce died away when
the *tweep, tweep!* of a canoe paddle was heard, and
then the little craft ran alongside, and an old man and
two girls stepped quietly on deck.

Collier, from the gangway, greeted them in Tahitian,
and then the three figures followed him below. As
they came in under the full light of the cabin lamp,
Denison saw that the man was a native, old, but erect
and muscular, and with the keen, hawk-like features
peculiar to many of the people of Eastern Polynesia.
The girls were both young, with pure, olive-tinted
skins, and big, dreamy eyes. The old man, straw
hat in hand, motioned them to a lounge that ran along
the transoms, where they seated themselves demurely,
and then turning silently to Collier, almost sprang at
him, and with a soft, pleased laugh, embraced him
again and again. Then the girls greeted him in low,
almost whispered tones.

.   .   .   .   .

But after their first shyness had worn off at the
presence of a stranger, they too, came to the cabin
table, and the five people all sat and laughed and made

merry over the few bottles of wine that were the last
shots in the brig's lockers, the girls sweetening theirs
with sugar, and smiling at Denison's laboured
attempts to follow them in their soft Tahitian
tongue.

Melanie—so was Collier's flame called—was the
older; and as Denison looked into her dark, melting
eyes, glowing with excitement at her lover's return,
he inwardly called his shipmate a lucky fellow, and
thought this dark-faced daughter of the blue Pacific to
be the most witching little creature he had ever seen
in all his ocean wanderings.

   ·   ·   ·   ·   ·

They are all gone now, all but Denison. Gone is
the tall, erect figure of old Marama, with the sinewy,
muscular frame, and keen, eager face. Gone the
honest smile and deep tones of Collier ; and gone,
too, the soft voice and dreamy, love-lit eyes of Melanie
and her sister. And to all of them the end came
suddenly, when—a year after that night they spent in
the cabin of the old brig—Collier's schooner, the
Leonie, turned turtle in a squall off Vavitao, and went
to the bottom with every soul on board.

   ·   ·   ·   ·   ·

After the old man and girls had gone ashore again,
Collier told his story to Denison, who then wondered
no longer at the strong affection existing between the
wandering, taciturn seaman and the old Aitutaki
native, and why Collier had given his rough affection
to his daughter, and intended to marry her, "straight,
fair, and square in ship-shape fashion." And this was
the story he told.

   ·   ·   ·   ·

"Seven years ago I was dead broke in Sydney. I had come out second mate in one of Green's ships. We were over three months in port waiting to fill up with wool, and one day I got too much liquor aboard, and the skipper, a drunken, hasty-tempered bully, used words to me that sobered me in two minutes. The skippers of the *Ascalon* and *Woolloomooloo*, two ships lying near ours, were looking on, and I turned away to go below, when my captain called me a 'soldier.'

"Then, before I knew what I had done, I knocked out two of his teeth and stove in a rib—and got put in gaol for three months. When I came out I had nine shillings in my pocket and a heart bursting with shame. I knew that as far as my prospects in the old company went I was a ruined man. But I was only twenty-two, and knew I could always get a berth on the coast; so I turned to and spent my nine shillings —mostly in whisky.

.   .   .   .   .

"Three months afterwards I landed in Tahiti from the barque *Ethan Allen*, from Sydney to 'Frisco. We put in for repairs, and I took the liberty of remaining on shore until the barque had left. Most of her fore-mast hands were dead-beat Sydney men, and as the skipper knew I was about the only seaman on board except himself and his officers, I was afraid he would have search made for me, but he didn't. He was too anxious to beat the barque *James Hannell*, also from Sydney, that had sailed the same day.

"There was plenty doing in the blackbirding trade then (God's curse rest on those who first started it in Polynesia, I say), and I soon got a berth in a barque bound to the Gilbert Islands as first mate. The skipper was a Frenchman. Most of the others aft were of mixed nationalities, and a ruffianly crowd they were, too ; and the barque was armed like a privateer of fifty years ago. We were to bring back labourers for Stewart's swell plantation at Atimaono, in Tahiti.

. . . . .

" We sailed first for Aitutaki, in Cook's Group, to get some natives for boats' crews ; and when in about latitude 17 deg. 50 min. S. and longitude 158 deg. W., we sighted a disabled vessel. I boarded her, and found her to be a native-owned schooner from Mangaia (one of Cook's Group) to Aitutaki. She had lost seven of her people overboard by a heavy sea, which made a wreck of her, and the rest—ten men and two female children—were almost dead from starvation.

" The two children were old Marama's daughters. Marama himself we had found lying on the deck with a broken arm. The little girls soon picked up, and their father and the rest of his people—Aitutaki and Mauke natives—agreed to do the cruise in the barque and work the boats—white sailors are no good for working boats where there is much surf—and our captain was very pleased to get them. So we headed N.W. for the Gilberts, and in another two weeks we had made Arorai Island and begun our work of getting in a cargo of copper-coloured Line Islanders.

. . . . .

" Villacroix, our French skipper, was new to the trade, and had not had time to become brutalised. He gave Melanie and her little sister a cabin to themselves,

and told me to see to their welfare. After Marama's
arm had got all right again he was put into my watch,
and from that time began our friendship. He was a
good sailorman, always had a willing heart for his
work, and, if for nothing else, thought much of me
because I was an Englishman.

"Things went very well at first. So far we had
got thirty or forty natives without using violent
means to bring them on board ; then one day we made
Peru, or Francis Island, one of the Gilbert Group.
Villacroix and the second mate went ashore and did
the 'recruiting,' and in two days we had nearly
two hundred fierce, wild-eyed, black-haired natives
on board.

"Marama—who was in charge of one of the boats
—told me on the second evening that many of these
people had been driven down to the beach by the
chiefs and forced into the three boats. Those of them
that didn't hustle and get in quick were cut at and
slashed about with sharks' teeth swords and spears.
And when the boats came alongside the barque I saw
that they were splashed with blood from stem to
stem.

.   .   .   .   .

"At nightfall we had them all under hatches, and
made sail on our long beat back to Tahiti ; and when
I turned in that night I swore to God that once I got
out of that barque I would never ship in such a bloody
trade again. All that night we made no headway, as
the wind had fallen light. At eight bells in the
morning the skipper let a batch of fifty natives come
up on deck to get something to eat and wash their
bruised and blood-stained bodies. They seemed quiet

and docile enough now, but none were hungry, and all turned away from the food offered them. Most of them crowded together on the deck, talked in low tones, or looked blankly at one another. And the skipper—who, to do him justice, showed compassion for their condition—let the whole lot up from below during the day in batches of fifty.

" Night came, and again the breeze died away. From aloft I could see the glimmer of the natives' fires on the island beach, by which I knew that the strong westerly current had set the ship very fast towards the land. The night was close and muggy, and on account of this the captain did not send all the natives below as he would otherwise have done, but allowed about a hundred of them to bring up their sleeping-mats and lie on deck.

" When my watch below came, after seeing that the guard were all posted with loaded rifles, some for'ard, some at the break of the poop, and some on top of the deck house, I laid down in one of the quarter boats and soon fell asleep, for I was tired out for want of rest. I had slept about an hour when I was awakened by loud cries and groans and rifle shots, and looking over the side of the boat I saw that the whole of the main deck was in possession of the natives, and that the crew were being savagely slaughtered.

. . . . .

" As I jumped out of the boat, Marama and two of the native crew rushed on deck from the cabin, all carrying Vetterli rifles, and, standing at the break of the poop, they began firing into the blood-maddened crowd on the main deck. But it was too late to save any of the watch on deck or those of the crew who had turned in. The captain, second mate, and third mate and carpenter were already killed, as well as thirteen of the crew ; and then the natives attempted to carry the poop and finish those of us who were left. Marama handed me a seaman's cutlass, and for a space of five minutes or so we tried to beat them back, shooting, slashing, and thrusting at them as they tried to ascend the poop ladders. Presently the two native sailors ran out of cartridges, and made a bolt down into the cabin. Marama and I followed ; but the boys had shut the doors in their flight, and shot the bolts inside. We just had time to fling ourselves bodily through the open skylight into the cabin and make it fast from below, when the blood-stained mob got entire possession of the poop.

"We lay there awhile, utterly done up, beside the two native sailors, one of whom had a great, gaping wound in his chest, from which the blood poured and ran along the cabin floor. His mate seemed to be all right, and getting his courage up again, he went to the captain's cabin and brought out more rifles and commenced to load them. Melanie and her sister then crept out of their cabin, and at a few quick words from their father brought us water to drink and then fled again to their retreat to be away from the sound of the firing, the thick smoke, and the yells and groans of the bloody pandemonium that followed.

.   .   .   .   .

"That was the first time in my life I had ever shed blood. But we were all mad by this time—mad with the scent of blood and the hot lust of slaying; The natives had taken about twenty cutlasses from the sailmaker's room, and others, with axes, were hacking and hewing at the skylight and companion doors to get at us. And we loaded and fired as quick as we could through the glass sides of the skylight, until both sides of it were smashed, and all the brass bars cut away with bullets. And scarcely a bullet went astray.

" At last they drew off and left us, and we got together in the steward's pantry. Marama pulled a wicker bottle of brandy out of a locker and served us out a drink each ; all except the boy with the wound in his chest, who didn't want any kind of drink—his wound had stopped bleeding and his heart beating.

" If I live to be a hundred, the horrors of that night will never fade from my memory—only when I get drunk and try to drown them—as I did do pretty often for a long time afterwards.

. . . . .

" They were now again all crowded together on the main deck. Marama had crawled up and opened the companion-door, listened, and then looked out. The land was not more than six miles distant, and some of the natives had tried to alter the ship's course by hauling the yards about, but had only succeeded in putting the ship in irons.

" Then Marama, drawing me aside, whispered something to me, and I, God forgive me, consented to do what he proposed.

" In the lazarette were ten kegs of powder, belonging to the four six-pounders the barque carried. We lifted off the hatch under the cabin-table, got up one of the kegs, and then hurriedly bored a hole through the head and put in a very short fuse.

" Then, covered by the Aitutaki boy, who carried three loaded rifles in readiness, in case we were blocked at the companion, we quietly crept up and unshipped the door bolt. In my hand I carried a lighted piece of twisted rag ; Marama had the keg.

" For a minute or so we listened anxiously, and then, throwing open the door, we sprang out and gained the break of the poop on the port side. The moment we were seen there was a wild yell of rage, and half a dozen shots were fired at us—they had evidently got some cartridges from the pouches of the murdered crew, and knew how to use them. Then they made a rush, but quick as lightning the Aitutaki sailor unshipped the heavy poop ladder and turned it over on top of them ; we had, during the first attack, hauled up and hove the ladder on the starboard side overboard. Before they could get together for another rush I lit the fuse, and Marama, with blazing eyes and a fierce oath, hurled the keg right among them, and we rushed back towards the companion.

" But as we gained the door the shock came, and the crazy old bark trembled from truck to keelson. I did expect to see a bit of a burst-up, but I never, as Heaven is my witness, thought that the thing would cause such awful slaughter among the poor wretches, who were so closely packed together that the explosion took full effect on them. There was a great hole torn in the deck ; from the after-coamings of the main hatch right up to the poop deck there was nothing left but a wreck of timbers.

" And then, after that bursting roar had pealed over the quiet, starlit ocean, there came silence, and then the moans of poor, mutilated humanity. All those who were not much injured sprang overboard and made for the shore—six miles off ; and I was told by

Frank Voliero, the trader who lived on Peru Island afterwards that thirty-seven of them did get ashore safely, but twice as many perished in the long swim from exhaustion—and the sharks."

. . . . .

Collier paced the deck awhile in silence, and then knocked the ashes of his pipe out against the rail.

" Well, that's all, Denison. As for us three men and the two girls, we managed somehow to get the ship before the wind at daylight, and then I let her run steadily to the westward for a couple of days. . . . I daresay you've heard of how we did eventually get her back to Tahiti again. I left her there, sick at heart, and as long as I can go aloft with a slush-pot in an honest trading ship, I'll never ship in another blackbirder.

" Two days after we had hauled up to try and make a south-east course, I looked down through the shattered skylight and saw the two girls kneeling on the cabin floor, clasping each other's hands. They were crying. I went below quietly to ask what was the matter. The younger one raised her face and said—

" Nay, we are well. But Melanie and I have been praying to God to forgive my father and thee for the shedding of blood."

IN THE EVENING

In the Evening

THE brave south-east trades had carried our schooner
well down into the straits dividing Upolu from misty,
cloud-capped Savaii, and then left us at sunset to drift
about, hoping for the land breeze to set in. Two
miles off, on our port hand, lay the little verdant island
of Manono, the gem of all Samoa, and the stronghold
of Mataafa. From the schooner's deck we could see
the evening fires in the village of Saleaula sending out
streaks and patches of intermittent light through the
palm-trunks upon the white sandy beach, and revealing at intervals the huge, ill-built native church of
white coral in all its ghastliness.

I think the captain of our schooner was the prince
of all island-trading shippers. No one had ever known
him to be angry for more than ten minutes, even
under the most aggravating circumstances ; and on
this particular evening, the fact that the wind dying
away probably meant the loss of a day to us, seemed
to him the veriest trifle. Other captains would have
sworn at the wind, at the calm, at the crew, and,
lastly, at the supercargo.

I was leaning over the rail looking shorewards,
when the skipper lounged up on deck, cigar in

mouth, and joined me. These were the days of the troubles between Mataafa—the loyal lieutenant of his exiled king — and the Germans. Thrice had the valiant old warrior, with his naked fighting-men, faced the deadly Mausers of the Teuton, and thrice had they proved victorious. Then came the great gale of March, 1889, when, in one wild smother of surf and foam, the six foreign warships in Apia harbour went down at their anchors, and the *Calliope* alone escaped.

We were speaking of that awful day, and of the gallant manner in which Mataafa and his warriors, dashing into the boiling surf, and fierce, sweeping back-wash, had rescued many of the foes they so bitterly hated—the German bluejackets of the *Adler*, the *Olga*, and the *Eber*.

Presently Packenham said, in his slow, lazy way—-

" Say, sonny, what do you say if we lower the boat and take a run ashore, have a drink of kava and come off again ? "

" And find the schooner drifted clean out of the straits and out of sight."

" That's all right, my lad, don't you worry. Here, one of you fellows, pass that lead line aft."

Packenham sounded and got eighteen fathoms, and then, to the mate's disgust, we dropped our anchor. In a few minutes, with a crew of four Savage Island boys, we had left the schooner for the white beach of Saleaula, the principal village of Manono. As we pulled in the sound of the rowlocks brought a crowd of people to the beach. Among them we saw the gleam of many a rifle barrel, and our crew began to get funky. Now, although there were no Germans in the boat, we took good care to keep bawling out in Samoan, " Don't fire, good friends, we are English ! "

Suddenly a huge blaze burst out. A great pile of _au lama_ (coconut torches) had been lit, and by its light every one in the boat became clearly visible.

A deep voice challenged us from the sea face of the _olo_ (fort), "_O ai ea outou ?_ " (" Who are you ? ") and then added, " Answer quickly."

We did answer quickly, and then came a loud chorus of welcome. As we pulled in the boat bumped heavily on a knob of coral. Both Packenham and myself were standing at the time. I tried to save myself by making a grab at the skipper's sleeve, missed, and went overboard.

Yells and shrieks of laughter followed. The _manaia_—the flash young warriors — leaping down from the _olo_ and from out their various places of ambush, rifle and knife in hand, danced with delight, and the soft, merry tones of the women's and girls' laughter mingled with theirs as they looked at me wading ashore.

Now, I happened to know Manono and the Manono people pretty well, although ten years had passed since I was last there. Saying nothing, and taking no notice of the continuous merriment, I went in for a little by-play.

Said I, in as solemn and dignified tone as I could command, " Ye be ill-mannered people here."

" _Aue !_ " they cried. " Who is this ? He speaketh our tongue."

" I am not a German," I said.

" Sorry am I, then," said a fat-faced, clean-shaved, young fellow stepping up to me, and balancing in his hand a huge *nifa oti* (the "death knife") used for decapitation. "The soul of my knife hungereth for the head of a German."

A young chief, whose name I had for the moment forgotten, but whose face was familiar, gave the saucy fellow a cuff, and said, "Shame, shame, fool!"

Here Packenham joined me. "*Talofa* all you good people," said he in very good Samoan; "and so you were going to fire into the boat? And I am an American and my friend an Englishman. Oh, shame!"

"Bah!" said a fat old woman, "Americans are good. Steinberger, the friend of Grant, was one, and he was a good man, and taught us how to fight; but English—pah! they fear the Germans, and won't help us to fight the pigs."

Applause and dissent. Packingham looked meaningly at me. I could see that we were not likely to have an extra cordial welcome on the strength of my being an Englishman, so I changed my tactics.

"Listen," I said; "I am a *perofeta ma tagata poto* (a wise man and one who prophesies). I can tell you of some things that you have forgotten. If I lie, then give us no kava to-night."

They all crowded round us; the men with wild, bushy heads, grasping their rifles in their hands; the women, long-haired and bare-bosomed, some with smiling faces, others dark and lowering.

Said I: "There lived here in Manono once—this Manono, which all the world knows is the place where the people get as fat as pigs by eating *foli*" (shell-fish)—they laughed—"a missionary, not a white missionary, but one of yourselves. His name was

Leutelu, that of his wife Salomê, that of his daughter
Elinê, that of his son Taisami, that of the Englishman that dwelt with him ——" I paused a minute ;
the fat old woman put her face close and peered into
mine, then dropped the torch she was carrying and
swooped down upon and hugged me, and then they
all recognised me, and I shook hands with the men
and rubbed noses with the women until I was fairly
exhausted. Packenham came in for his share too.
He kissed all the young girls—much to their anger—
a Samoan girl looks upon kissing with disgust.

However, we were all right now. They carried
us off to the village, and brought us to the chief's
house. Mataafa was then away at Apia, deep in
politics, and we were not sorry ; for the girls promised
us a dance after our kava. Mataafa is a Catholic, and
somewhat rigid in his ideas, and did not permit the
poula, or native dance, in his lines. We had no
sooner seated ourselves in the big house than a whole
bundle of garments was placed before me—shirts,
coats, pyjamas, trousers, &c. Among them were
German and American sailors' uniforms—sad me-
mentoes of the *Trenton, Vandalia,* and *Nipsic,* and the
three German ships.

Taking a suit of pyjamas, I retired outside and
changed my wet clothing. When I entered again
the preparations for kava-making had commenced.
Meantime Packenham had sent to the boat, and our
crew brought up half a dozen of beer and a bottle of
brandy. The women made short work of the beer,
and the chiefs each pledged us in a stiff tot of brandy.

Beside Packenham there sat a very pretty girl
called Maema. She flirted with him most out-

rageously. The young lady who sat by my side had
the appropriate name of Manuia (Happiness), for she
was as bright as a fairy. Ten years before she was a
little thing of eight, and used to bring me every Sunday
morning in that very village a roasted fowl and a
basket of cooked taro from her father, who was a
particular crony of mine. She was now a splendidly
formed young woman, with perfectly oval features
and a wealth of long silken hair. Her father, she
told me, was fighting then on the side of Tamasese,
the German puppet king and the usurper of Malietoa's kingdom. Yet her brother and her husband
(she was now a widow, at eighteen) were both killed
fighting against the Germans in their attack on
Saluafata a month previously. Such instances as this
were common enough in distracted Samoa, and
showed the fratricidal nature of the struggle.

Said I, in a whisper, "Manuia, would you marry
again, a white man, for instance, an American say,"
and then I added, "my friend in particular?"

She nodded nonchalantly. "*Faatalia ia* (if it please
him), and my people consent. I would rather
have an American—*they are not afraid of the Germans.*"

Then at the chief's command Manuia, Maema,
and five or six other young girls, rose up and sat
themselves down again beside the kava bowl, and the
utmost decorum and silence prevailed during the
important ceremony. After the kava drinking was
over the *poula* commenced, and we were treated
to some high-kicking, beside which the *fin-de-siècle*
ballet is but a hollow mockery.

We remained in the village till dawn, and the

genial and hospitable people treated us like long-lost brothers. Our boat was loaded to the gunwales with fruit and vegetables, and Packenham was the recipient of innumerable fans, tortoise-shell rings, and native combs. My quondam acquaintance, the sweet-faced young widow with the star-like eyes, embraced both Packenham and myself tenderly, and candidly confessed her inability to decide whom she liked best. She was a merry-hearted creature, and I honestly believe that handsome Packenham had inspired her with false hopes.

As the boat pushed off the whole village gathered on the beach and called out their farewells—" *To fa oulua, to fa ! Manuia oulua i le alofa lo tatou Atua !* (Farewell you two—farewell ! May you both be happy in the love of God !)"

THE GREAT CRUSHING AT
MOUNT SUGAR-BAG

The Great Crushing at Mount Sugar-Bag

A QUEENSLAND MINING TALE

" LET's sling it, boys. There's no fun in our bullocking here day after day and not making tucker ! I'm
sick to death of the infernal hole, and mean to get out
of it."

"So am I, Ned. I was sick of it a month ago,"
said Harry Durham, filling his pipe and flinging himself down at full length upon his luxurious couch—a
corn-sack suspended between four posts driven into
the earthen floor of the hut. "I'm ready to chuck it
up to-morrow and drive a mob of nanny-goats to the
Palmer, like young Preston did the other day." [1]

" How much do we owe that old divil Ikey
now ? " said Rody Minogue, the third man of the
party, who sat at the open doorway looking out upon
the disreputable collection of bark humpies that con-
stituted the played-out mining township of Mount
Sugar-bag.

" About £70 now," said Durham ; "but against
that he's got our five horses. The old beast means
to shut down on us, I can see that plainly enough.

---

[1] In the early days of the rush to the Palmer River Goldfield
nanny-goats brought £2 10s. each.

When I went to him on Saturday for the tucker he had a face on him as long as a child's coffin."

"Look here, boys," said Buller, the pessimist, "let the infernal old vampire keep our three saddle-horses —they are worth more than seventy quid—and be hanged to him. We'll have the two pack-horses left. Let us sell one, and with the other to carry our swags, we'll foot it to Cleveland Bay, or Bowen, I don't care which."

"An' what are we goin' to do whin we get there?" asked Rody.

Buller shrugged his shoulders. "Dashed if I know, Rody; walk up and down Bowen jetty and watch the steamers come in."

"And live on pack-horse meat," said Durham.

"Now, look here," and Rody got up from the doorway and sat upon the rough table in the middle of the room, "I want you fellows to listen to me. First of all, tell me this : Isn't it through me entirely that we've managed to get tick from old Ikey Cohen at all ?"

"Right," said Durham ; "no one but you, Rody, would have had courage enough to make love to greasy-faced Mrs. Ikey."

"Don't be ungrateful. Every time I've been to the place I've sympathised with her hard lot in being tied to an uncongenial mate like Ikey Cohen, and for every half a dozen times I've squeezed her hand you fellows have to thank me for a sixpenny plug of sheep-wash tobacco."

"By Heavens! how you must have suffered for that tin of baking-powder that we got last week, and which didn't go down in the bill ! "

Rody laughed good-naturedly.

"Well, perhaps I did. But never mind poking fun at me, I'm talking seriously now. Here we are, stone-broke, and divil a chance can I see of our getting on to anything good at Sugar-bag. We've got about forty tons of stone at grass, haven't we? What do you think it'll go?"

"About fifteen pennyweights," said Durham.

"I say ten," said Buller.

"And I say it's going to be the biggest crushing on Sugar-bag since the old days," said Rody.

"Rot!" said Durham.

"Now just you wait and listen to what I've got to say. We've got forty tons at grass now. Now, we won't get a show to crush for some weeks, because there's Tom Doyle's lot and then Patterson's to go through first. It's no use asking old Fryer to put our stuff through before theirs. Besides, we don't want him to."

"Don't we? I think we want to get out of this God-forsaken hole as quick as we can."

"So we do. But getting our stuff through first won't help us away. Reckon it up, my boys! Forty tons, even if it goes an ounce, means only about £140. Out of that old Cohen gets £70—just half, that would leave us £70; out of this we shall have to give Fryer £40 for crushing. That leaves us £30."

"That'll take us to Townsville or Cooktown, anyway," said Durham.

"Yes," said Rody, "if we get it. But we won't. That stone isn't going to crush for more than ten pennyweights to the ton."

A dead silence followed. Rody was the oldest and most experienced miner of them all, and knew what he was talking about. Then Buller groaned.

"That means, then, that after we've paid Fryer £40 for his crushing we'll have £30 for old Cohen and nothing for ourselves."

"That's it, Ned."

No one spoke for a moment, until Durham, who had good Scriptural knowledge, began cursing King Pharaoh for not crossing the Red Sea first in boats and blocking Moses and his crowd from landing on the other side.

"Well, wait a minute," resumed Rody, "I haven't finished yet. We gave our mokes to old Cohen, didn't we, as a guarantee? He said he'd send them to Dotswood Station, because there was no feed here. What do you think the old beast did?"

"Sold 'em," said Buller.

"No, he'd hardly be game to do that. But instead of sending them to Dotswood, he's got the two pack-horses running the mail coach between the Broughton and Charters Towers, and the three saddle-horses are getting their hides ridden off them carrying the mail between Cleveland Bay (Townsville) and Bowen."

"The infernal old sweep!" said Durham, springing up from his bunk. "Who told you this, Rody? Greasy-face?"

"My informant, Mr. Durham, was Mrs. Isaac Cohen, or, as you so vulgarly but truly call her, 'Greasy-face.'"

Presently, after taking due notice of his mates' wrathful visages, Rody began again—

"So this is how the matter stands. We three

fellows, who are working like thundering idiots to pay off old Ikey's store account, are actually running a coach for him, and conveying her Majesty's mails for him, and he gets the money! Now, I don't want to do anything wrong, but I'm hanged if I'm going to let him bilk us, and if you two will do what I want we will get even with him. But you'll have to promise me to do just exactly what I tell you. Are you willing?"

"Right you are, Rody. Go ahead."

"I'm not going into details just at present, but I can promise you that we'll leave Sugar-bag in a month, or less, from to-night, with £50 each. And old Ikey is going to give it to us; and what is more, he won't dare to ask us to give it back again."

"How are you going to do it?"

"You'll know when the proper time comes. But from to-morrow fortnight we don't raise a bit more stone from our duffing old claim. We're going to start on those big mullocky leaders in Mason's and Crow's old shafts, and raise about ten tons before we crush the stone. We must have it ready at the battery as soon as the stone is through. Now, there you are again, making objections. I know that it didn't go six pennyweights, but it's going to be powerful rich this time."

. . . . .

Mr. Isaac Cohen was the sole business man at Mount Sugar-bag, and although the majority of the miners working the claims on the field were not doing well, Mr. Cohen was. In addition to being the only storekeeper and publican within a radius of fifty miles, he was also the butcher, baker, and saddler, this

last vocation having been his original means of liveli-
hood for many years in Sydney. A small investment,
however, in some Northern Queensland mining shares
led him on the road to fortune, and although never
entirely forsaking his old trade, by steady industry
and a rigid avoidance of such luxuries as soap and a
change of clothing, he gradually accumulated enough
money to add several other businesses to that of
saddlery. He had arrived at Sugar-bag when that
ephemeral township was in the zenith of its glory,
and now, although it was on the eve of the days
that lead to abandoned shafts and grass-grown, silent
crushing mills, wherein wandering goats camp on the
water tables, and death adders and carpet snakes crawl
up the nozzle of the bellows in the blacksmith's forge
to hibernate, he still remained. No doubt he would
have left long before had it not been for the fact that
the remaining ninety or a hundred miners in the place
were all in his debt. Then, besides this, he had
bought a mob of travelling cattle and stocked a block
of country with them. The drover in charge, a
fatuous young Scotchman, with large, watery-blue
eyes and red hair, had succumbed to Ikey's alleged
whisky and the news that there was no water ahead
of him for another sixty miles. Ikey buried him
decently (sending the bill home to the young man's
relations, including the cost of the liquor so freely
consumed on the mournful occasion) and took charge
of the cattle, at the same time writing to the owners
and informing them that their cattle were dying by
hundreds, and advising them to place them in the
hands of an agent for sale. And to show Mr. Cohen's
integrity, it may be mentioned that he named Mr.

Andrew M'Tavish, the local auctioneer, as a suitable person, but neglected to state that Mr. M'Tavish had died in Bowen hospital a month previously, and that Ikey Cohen had bought his business. Consequently the cattle went cheap, and Ikey bought them himself. Thus by honest industry he prospered, while every one else in Sugar-bag went to the wall—*i.e.*, the bar of Ikey Cohen's Royal Hotel. And at the bar they were always welcome, for even if—as sometimes did occur—a disheartened, stone-broke customer drank too much of Mr. Cohen's irregular whisky and died in his back yard, leaving a few shillings recorded against his name on the bar-room slate, Ikey forgave the corpse the debt and buried him (he was the Mount Sugar-bag undertaker) for the trifling sum of £10— paid by sending round the hat on the day of the funeral. In due course Ikey was made a J.P., and then began to think of Parliament.

About two years after his arrival at Sugar-bag, Ikey had occasion to visit Townsville on business, and on his return was accompanied by his newly-wedded wife, a Brisbane-dressed lady of thirty or so. Somewhat to his surprise, a number of the miners at Sugar-bag who had, during their travels, visited the southern capitals, greeted her as an old friend, and congratulated him on securing such an excellent life-partner; and, as he had married the lady after only a few days' acquaintance, he naturally enough accepted her explanation of having presided over various bars in Melbourne and Sydney, where she had met a great number of Queenslanders. Of course there were not wanting, even at Sugar-bag, evil-minded beings to openly assert that Mr. Cohen's expression of surprise at the wide circle of his wife's friends was all bunkum, and that "Greasy-face," as the lady was nicknamed, was only another of his cute financial investments.

If this was correct it certainly showed his sound judgment, for her presence in the bar of the Royal proved highly lucrative to him ; and showed as well that he was above any feelings of unworthy jealousy. For although the title of " Greasy-face " was not altogether an inappropriate one, the bride was by no means bad-looking, and possessed to a very great degree that peculiar charm of manner and freedom from stiff conventionality so noticeable among the fair sex on new rushes to goldfields. Perhaps, however, Mr. Cohen did think that her preference for Rody Minogue was a little too openly shown to the neglect of his other customers and her admirers ; but, being a business man, and devoid of sentiment, he said nothing, but charged Rody and his mates stiffer prices for the rations he sold them, and was quite satisfied.

.   .   .   .   .

On the morning after the three mates had discussed their precarious condition, Rody, instead of going up to the claim with Durham and Buller, remained in camp to write a letter. It was addressed to " Mr. James Kettle, c/o Postmaster, Adelong, N.S. Wales," and contained an earnest request, for old friendship's sake, to send Mr. Harry Durham a telegram, as per copy enclosed, as quickly as possible.

Then, lighting his pipe, Rody left the hut, and walked up towards the Royal. When about half-way he sat down on a log and waited for the mailman, who he knew would be passing along presently on his way down to Cleveland Bay. He had intended to go up to Cohen's the previous evening and write and post his letters there, but Ikey being the postmaster, and Rody a particularly cute individual, the latter changed his mind. The mailman usually slept at Cohen's on his way down to the Bay, and being a good-natured and convivial soul, and a fellow-countryman of Rody, the two were on very good terms.

Presently Rody saw him ride out of Cohen's yards, leading a pack-horse, and turn down the track which led past the place where he was waiting.

"How are you, Dick?" said Rody; "pull up a minute, will you? I've got a letter here I want you to post for me in Townville. It's not good enough leaving a letter in old Ikey's over night."

"Right," said the mailman, taking the letter; "want anything else done, Rody?"

"Yes; would you mind bringing me out as much lead as you can carry when you come back, 40 or 50 lb. Don't bring it to the humpy; just dump it down here behind this log, where I can get it. I'll pay you for it in a week or two; and buy me a horse-shoer's rasp as well."

"O.K., old man. I can get it easily enough, and drop it here for you when I come back on Thursday. So long;" and Dick the mailman jogged off.

.   .   .   .   .

Ten minutes later Rody sauntered up to Mr. Ikey Cohen's store. Mrs. Isaac was there, opening a box of mixed groceries.

"Hallo, Rody! how are you? Here, quick; stick this in your shirt before the little beast comes in;" and "Greasy-face" pushed a bottle of pickles into his

14

hand, just as Ikey entered—in time to see the pickles.

" Not at work this morning, Mr. Minogue ? "

" No ; I've come up to have a bit of a chat with you.   How much are the pickles, Mrs. Cohen ? "

" Two shillings, Mr. Minogue," she answered, with a world of sorrow expressed in the quick glance she gave him, knowing that Ikey had detected her.

" How vas the claim shaping ? " asked Ikey, presently.

Rody shook his head.   " Just the same.   We don't like the look of the stone at all.   Of course the gold is as fine as flour, and you can't tell what it's going to turn out till you get it under the stampers.   We are thinking of raising some of that mullocky stuff out of Mason's and Crow's old claims.   We got some good prospects lately."

" Vell, you'd better do somedings pretty qvick.   I can't go on subblying you and your mates vid rations for noding," said Mr. Cohen, with an unpleasant look on his face.   He was not in a pleasant temper, for he disliked Rody and his mates—the former in particular —and would have shut down on them long before only for the fact that all three men were such favourites on the field that an action like this would have meant a big hole in his bar profits.

" That's true enough," said Rody, with apparent humility, but with a look in his eye that had Ikey noticed it would have made him step back out of his reach, " and I've come to have a talk with you on the matter.   Will you mind just showing us how we stand ? "

"Here you are ; here's your ackound up to the tay

pefore yestertay—the last of the month," and the storekeeper handed him the bill.

Rody looked at it—£70 10s. 6d.

"You charge us pretty stiff, Mr. Cohen, for some
of the tucker and powder and fuse."

"Vell, ven you can't bay gash!" and the little man
humped his shoulders and spread his ten dirty fingers
wide out.

Rody continued to scrutinise the items on the bill.
"We're paying pretty stiff for keeping those mokes at
Dotswood—eight quid is a lot of money when we get
no use out of 'em."

"Vy, you vas full of grumbles. Vat haf you to
comblain of? Thirty-two veeks' grass and vater for
five horses at a shilling a veek each. My friend, if
dose horses had not gone to Dotswood dey would haf
died here."

"All right," said Rody, putting the bill in his
pocket and turning to go, "as soon as Doyle and
Patterson's stuff goes through, our crushing follows.
They start to-day."

"Vell, I hopes ve do some good," snorted Cohen,
as he sat down to his accounts.

.   .   .   .   .

"What the blazes is that for?" said Buller, as late
on Thursday night Rody came into the hut and
dumped a small but extremely heavy parcel, tied up in
a piece of bagging, down on the table.

Rody cut the string that tied it, and the mates saw
that it contained a compact roll of sheet lead and a
farrier's rasp.

"Never you mind; I know what I'm doing.
Now, boys, we're got to slog into that mullocky stuff

at Mason's all next week, and look jolly mysterious if any of the chaps tell us we're only bullocking for nothing."

A light began to dawn on Durham as he looked at the rasp and lead ; a few days before he had seen Rody bringing home an old worn-out blacksmith's vice that he had picked up somewhere, and stow it under his bunk.

Taking up the articles again, Rody stowed them away, and then drew a letter out of his pocket.

" Read that," he said.

Durham took it up and read aloud—

> " DOTSWOOD STATION, BURDEKIN RIVER,
> " *June* 7, 188—.
>
> " DEAR SIR—In reply to your note, I beg to state that no horses with the brands described by you have ever been received on this station from Mr. Isaac Cohen, nor any other person.
>
> " Yours, &c.,
> "WALTER D. JOYCE,
> "MR. RODY MINOGUE,   " *Manager.*
> " *Sugar-bag.*"

" The thundering old sweep ! Why, we could jail him for this," said Durham. " Are you quite sure about his using them ever since he took delivery of them ? "

" Quite ; I can bring a dozen people to prove that the two pack-horses have been running in the Charters Towers coach for the past six months, and the three saddle-horses have been carrying the Bowen mail from Townsville for five months."

Durham thumped his fist on the table. "I wish we could get him to tell us before a witness that the horses were at Dotswood."

"We needn't bother ; this is better," and Rody, taking out Cohen's account, read—

"To 32 weeks' agistment for 5 horses at Dotswood Station, at 1s. per week—£8."

"That's lovely, Rody. We've got him now."

.   .   .   .   .

For the next week or so the three mates worked hard at Mason's and Crow's old shafts, to the wonder of the rest of the diggers at Sugar-bag. And they would have been still more surprised had they gone one Sunday into a thick scrub about a mile from the camp, and seen Rody Minogue fix an old vice on a stump, and spreading a bag beneath it, produce a rasp, and begin to vigorously file a thick roll of lead into fine shavings, that fell like a shower of silver spray upon the bag beneath.

Rody spent the best part of the day in the scrub. He had brought his dinner, and enjoyed his laborious task. As soon as it was finished he carefully poured the bright filings into a canvas bag, and threw the vice and rasp far into the scrub. Then, just at dusk, he carried the heavy bag home unobserved.

That night, as they turned in, he said to his mates—

"We must all be up at old Ikey's to-morrow night, boys, to see the mailman come in. I think we are pretty sure to get Jim Kettle's wire to-night. I asked him to send it at once."

It may be mentioned here that although there was no telegraph station at Sugar-bag, there was at Big

Boulder, a small but thriving mining township five miles away, and telegrams sent to any one at Sugar-bag were sent on by the postmaster at Big Boulder by Dick the mailman.

. . . . .

"Here's Dick the mailman coming!" and the crowd of diggers that sat in Ikey Cohen's bar lounged outside to see him dismount.

In a few minutes he came inside, and first handing the small bag that contained the Sugar-bag mail to Mr. Cohen, who at once, by virtue of his office, proceeded to open it and sort out the few letters, he went to the bar at Buller's invitation for a drink.

"How are you, boys? How goes it, Rody? I'll take a rum, please Missis. How's the claim shapin', Durham?"

"Here's a delegram for you," said Ikey, handing the missive to Durham, and wishing that he could have kept it back till the morning, so as to have made himself acquainted with its contents.

"Thank you," said Durham. "I wonder who it's from?"

"No bad news, Harry, is there?" said Mrs. Ikey, sympathetically; "you look very serious."

"Oh, no; it's from Jimmy Kettle; he and I and Tom Gurner—who went to South Africa—used to be mates on the Etheridge;" and without further explanation he walked away, accompanied by Rody and Buller.

. . . . .

Early next morning, as Mr. Cohen opened his store and pub., Durham walked in.

"Look here, Cohen, I want to sell out and get

away. Will you give me something for my horse, and ten pounds for my share in the crushing ? Rody can't do it, of course ; neither can Buller."

" No, I von't," said Mr. Cohen; " I ain't going to throw away any more money. Vere do you want to go to ? "

Durham, with a gloomy face, handed him the telegram he had received. It ran as follows :—

" *From* JAMES KETTLE, *Adelong.*
" *To* HENRY DURHAM, *Sugar-bag,* N.Q.
" Tom Gurner returned. Has done well. Wants you and me to go back South Africa with him. Will stand the racket for passage money. Steamer leaves Sydney in four weeks. Hurry up and join us."

" Can't you give me a lift at all ? " said Durham, after Cohen had read the telegram.

" No, I can't."

" Then blarst you, don't ! I'll foot it to Townsville, you infernal old skunk."

Sure enough that day he did leave, but not on foot, for some one lent him a horse, to be returned by the mailman. Rody accompanied him part of the way and gave him some final instructions.

.   .   .   .   .

On the day that Durham reached Townsville Rody and Buller began crushing their stone at the mill. The forty tons of stone were to go through first, and were to be followed by the stuff from Mason's and Crow's old claims, which had been carted down to the mill. As Rody surmised, the stone showed tor about ten pennyweights, and the second day, about

dusk, they "cleaned up," squeezed the amalgam into
balls, and placed it in an enamelled dish, ready for
retorting.

"Four of these will do us," said Rody, taking out
that number of balls of amalgam, pressing them into
a flat shape, and thrusting them into his trousers
pockets ; "here's that old swine Ikey coming now to
see if we are robbing him."

"Vell, how does she look ? " inquired Cohen.

Rody, with a face of gloom, pointed to the amalgam
in the dish. "It'll go about ten pennyweights," he
said, "but we're going to start on that other stuff
to-morrow. It's patchy, but I believe there's more in
it than there was in the quartz."

"Vell, vat are you going to do with this amalgam ?
Von't you redord (retort) it now ? "

"No," answered Rody, "it's not worth while
having two retortings. Take it away with you—
you have the best right to it—and lock it up. Then,
as soon as we have put this mullocky stuff through, we
will retort the lot together. It won't take long
running that stuff through the battery—it's soft as
butter."

Then, after carefully weighing the amalgam, Rody
handed it over to Mr. Cohen for safe keeping, and he
and Buller went up to their humpy for the night.
But before they bade Mr. Cohen good-night, Rody
wrote out a few words on a slip of paper, and handed
it to Ikey, with a two-shilling piece.

"Send that along to Big Boulder by any one passing,
will you ? I told Durham I'd send him a wire. He
won't leave Townsville until to-morrow. The
steamer goes at four in the afternoon to-morrow."

When Mr. Cohen got home he read Rody's message, which was brief, but explicit—

"Crushing going badly ; not ten weights. Mullock may go as much or more."

.   .   .   .   .

At eight o'clock next morning Rody and Buller were ready to feed their second lot of stone into the boxes. At Rody's suggestion the mill manager, who was also the engine driver (and who employed but two Chinamen to feed and empty the sludge pits in connection with the wretched old machine), put on very old coarse screens ; and whilst he was engaged in doing this, Rody stowed a certain small but heavy canvas bag in a conveniently accessible spot near the battery boxes.

As soon as the screens were fixed, old Joe Fryer came round and started the engine, whilst Rody "fed" and Buller attended to the tables and blankets.

"We'll feed her, Fryer," said Rody. "These Chinkies are right enough with hard stone, but they're no good with mucky stuff like this. They'd have the boxes choked in no time."

Fryer was quite agreeable, and as soon as he turned away to attend to the furnace Rody seized the canvas bag and poured about a quart of the lead filings into the box. At the same time, Buller came round from the tables with a cupful of quicksilver, and poured that in. This was done at frequent intervals.

In a quarter of an hour Buller came round to Rody and said, in Fryer's hearing, that the amalgam was showing pretty thick on the plates.

Fryer went to look at it, naturally feeling pleased at

such good news. In a minute he was back again, and
seizing Rody by the hand, his dirty old face beaming
with excitement.

"By Jingo! You fellows have struck it this time.
I haven't seen anything like it since the time Billy
Mason and George Boys put ten loads of stuff like this
through and got four hundred ounces. And look here,
this stuff of yours is going to be as good."

"Well, look here, Fryer," said Rody, modestly, " I
may as well tell you that I somehow thought it was
pretty right. And I believe we've just dropped on
such another patch as Mason and Boys did in '72."

Buller by this time was apparently as much excited
as old Fryer, and was now sweeping the amalgam off
the plates with a rubber, like a street scraper sweeps
up mud—in great stiff ridges—and dropping it into an
enamelled bucket. And every time that Fryer was
out of sight shoving a log of wood into the furnace,
Rody would pour another quart of lead filings in the
feed-box, and Buller would follow with a pint of
quicksilver.

"Lucky we got him to put on those old worn
screens," muttered Rody to Buller, "the cursed stuff
is beginning to clog the boxes as it is."

At last, there being no more lead left and but little
quicksilver, the stampers worked with more freedom,
and in another hour Rody flung down his shovel—the
final shovelful of mullock had gone into the box.

"I'll help you clean up as soon as I draw my fire,"
said old Fryer. "By thunder, boys, what'll the chaps
say when they see this? What about old Sugar-bag
being played out, eh?"

Fortunately for Rody and his partner the mill was

a good two miles away from the main camp, there being no nearer water available, and no one had troubled to come down to see how the crushing was going, except one Micky Foran, who had carted their stone down from the claim. But when Micky saw Fryer and Rody go round to the back of the boxes, lift the apron, and take off the screens, he gave a yell that could have been heard a mile :

"Holy Saints, it looks like a grotto filled wid silver!"

And so it did, for the whole of the sides of the box, the stampers, and dies were covered with a coating of amalgam some inches thick and as hard as cement.

In five minutes Micky was galloping up to the camp with the glorious news of Sugar-bag's resurrection, leaving Fryer, Buller and Rody hard at work digging out the amalgam with cold chisels and butcher knives.

By the time the boxes had been cleaned, and the quicksilver—or rather amalgam—scooped up from the wells, and the whole lot placed in various dishes and buckets, the excited population of Sugar-bag began to appear upon the scene. Among them was Mr. Cohen, who advanced to Rody with a smile.

"Vell, my boy, you've struck id and no misdake. I knew you vas a good——"

"Oh, to blazes out o' this!" said Mr. Minogue, roughly. "I don't want any of your dashed blarney. Ten days ago you wouldn't give poor Harry Durham a fiver to take him to the bay, and here you come crawling round me, now that our luck has changed. Go to the devil with you! I can pay you your dirty seventy quid now and be hanged to you!"

And with this he pushed his way over to where

Fryer and Buller were, keeping guard over the white gleaming masses of precious amalgam.

"Going to retort it now, Rody?" said a digger.

"No; we can't. There isn't a retort big enough to hold a quarter of the hard stuff, let alone the quicksilver, which is as lumpy as porridge, as you can see," and he lifted some in the palm of his hand out of a bucket. We'll have to send over to Big Boulder for Jones' two big retorts."

"Boys," said a digger, solemnly, "so help me, I believe there's a thousand ounces of gold going to come out of that there amalgam. What do you think, Rody?"

"About eight hundred," he answered, modestly; and Ikey Cohen metaphorically smote his breast and wished he had lent Durham all he asked for.

Placing the amalgam in the big box Fryer kept for the purpose, Rody was about to lock it, when some one made a remark—just the very remark he wanted to hear and be heard by Isaac Cohen, who was still hanging about him.

"Sometimes there's a lot of silver in these mullocky leaders. I heard that at the Canton Reef, near Ravenswood, there was a terrible lot of it."

"Oh, shut up! What y'r gassin' about? There ain't no silver about this field, I bet," called out two or three miners in a chorus.

Rody's face fell. "By jingo, boys, I don't know. Perhaps Joe is right. I've seen Canton Reef gold, it's only worth about twenty-five bob an ounce owing to the silver in it."

"Try a bit of amalgam on a shovel," suggested some one.

Rody lifted the cover of the box and took out a small enamelled cup half full of hard amalgam—the contents of his trousers pockets surreptitiously placed with the rest while cleaning up.

In a few minutes a fire was lit and a shovel with an ounce of amalgam on it was held over the flame. As the shovel grew red hot and the quicksilver passed away in vapour there lay on the heated iron about eight pennyweights of bright yellow, frosted gold.

" Right as rain ! " was the unanimous opinion, and then every one went away to get drunk at Cohen's pub. in honour of the occasion.

. . . . .

" Vere are you going to, Mr. Minogue ? " said Cohen, oilily, to Rody.

" To Big Boulder, to send another wire to Durham and tell him to come back."

" My friend, you will be foolish. Now you and me vill talk pizness. I vant to buy Mr. Durham out. If you vill help me to ged his inderest in the crushing sheap I will call my ackound square and give you — vell, I will give you £200 for yourself."

Rody appeared to hesitate. At last he said, " Well, I'll do it. I'll wire him that the stuff is going about two ounces, and that you want to buy him out. I'll tell him to take what you offer. But at the same time I won't see him done too bad. Give him £200 as well."

" No, I vill give him £150."

" All right. I'll wire to him at once. The steamer goes to-morrow."

" And I rides in with you to Big Boulder and sends him a delegram, too," said Ikey joyfully.

. . . .

In another hour the two messages were in Harry Durham's hand.   He read them and smiled.

" Rody's managed it all right."

At five in the afternoon Mr. Cohen received an answer—

" Will sell you my interest in the Claribel crushing, now going through, for £150 if money is wired to Bank New South Wales before noon to-morrow."

Mr. Cohen wired it, grinning to himself the while as he thought of the rich mass of amalgam lying in Fryer's box.   Nothing much under £350 would be his share, even after paying Rody £200, in addition to Durham's £150.

    .   .   .   .   .

There was a great attendance to see the retorts opened two days afterwards, and Mr. Cohen went into a series of fits when the opening of the largest cylinder revealed nothing but a black mass of charred nastiness (the result of the lead filings), and the other (which contained the amalgam from the first crushing) showed only a little gold—less than twenty ounces.

Of course he wanted to do something desperate, but Rody took him aside, and showing him certain documents concerning horses, said—

" Now, look here ; you had better let things alone. It's better for you to lose £350 than go to gaol. This crushing is a great disappointment to me as well as you.   We've both been had badly over it."

    .   .   .   .   .

It was not many weeks before the three mates met again in Sydney, Durham having wired them half of the £150 sent him by Ikey Cohen before he left Townsville, not knowing that they had got £200 out of Ikey themselves. And about a year later Rody sent Mrs. Cohen a letter enclosing the amount of old Fryer's bill for crushing, and £80 from himself and mates for Ikey. "Tell him, Polly, that he can keep the horses for the £70 against us. The money he sent to Harry Durham—to swindle him out of that rich crushing, and what he gave Buller and me—set us on our legs. We have been doing very well at the Thames here, in New Zealand, since we left Sugar-bag. Of course you can please yourself as to whether you give him the £80 or keep it yourself. And if you send us a receipt signed by yourself, it will do us just as well as his, and please in particular your old friend, RODY MINOGUE."

THE SHADOWS OF THE DEAD

The Shadows of the Dead

I

"IT is bad to speak of the ghosts of the dead when their shadows may be near," said Tulpé, the professed Christian, but pure, unsophisticated heathen at heart; "no one but a fool—or a careless white man such as thee, Tenisoni—would do that."

Denison laughed, but Kusis, the stalwart husband of black-browed Tulpé, looked at him with grave reproval, and said in English, as he struck his paddle into the water—

"Tulpé speak true, Mr. Denison. This place is a bad place at night-time, suppose you no make fire before you sleep. Plenty men—white men—been die here, and now us native people only come here when plenty of us come together. Then we not feel much afraid. Oh, yes, these two little island very bad places; long time ago many white men die here in the night. And sometimes, if any man come here and sleep by himself, he hear the dead white men walk about and cry out."

. . . . .

They—Denison, the supercargo of the *Leonora*, Kusis, the head man of the village near by and Tulpé, his wife, and little Kinia, their daughter—had been out fishing on the reef, but had met with but scant success ; for in the deep coral pools that lay between the inner and outer reefs of the main island were hundreds of huge blue and gold striped leather-jackets, which broke their hooks and bit their lines. So they had ceased awhile, that they might rest till nightfall upon one of two little islets of palms, that like floating gardens raised their verdured heights from the deep waters of the slumbering lagoon.

Slowly they paddled over the glassy surface, and as the little craft cut her way noiselessly through the water, the dying sun turned the slopes of vivid green on Mont Buache to changing shades on gold and purple light, and the dark blue of the water of the reef-bound lagoon paled and shallowed and turned to bright transparent green with a bottom of shining snow-white sand—over which swift black shadows swept as startled fish fled seaward in affright beneath the slender hull of the light canoe. Then as the last booming notes of the great grey-plumaged mountain-pigeons echoed through the forest aisles, the sun touched the western sea-rim in a flood of misty golden haze, and plunging their paddles together in a last stroke they grounded upon the beach of a lovely little bay, scarce a hundred feet in curve from point to point ; and whilst Kusis and Tulpé lit a fire to cook some fish for the white man, Denison clambered to the summit of the island and looked shoreward upon the purpling outline of the mainland a league away.

Half a mile distant he could see the sharp peaks of the grey-thatched houses in Leassé village still standing out plainly in the clear atmosphere, and from every house a slender streak of pale blue smoke rose straight up skywards, for the land-breeze had not yet risen, and the smoky haze of the rollers thundering westward hung like a filmy mantle of white over long, long lines of curving reef. Far inland, the great southern spur of the mountain that the Frenchman Duperrey had named Buache, had cloaked its sides in the shadows of the night, though its summit yet blazed with the last red shafts of gold from the sunken sun. And over the tops of the drooping palms of the little isle, Denison heard the low cries and homeward flight of ocean-roving birds as they sped shoreward to their rookeries among the dense mangrove shrubs behind Leassé. Some pure white, red-footed boatswain birds, whose home was among the foliage of the two islets, fluttered softly about as they sank like flakes of falling snow among the branches of the palms and breadfruit trees around him. All day long had they hovered high in air above the sweeping roll of the wide Pacific, and one by one they were coming back to rest, and Denison could see their white forms settling down on the drooping palm-branches, to rise with flapping wing and sharp, fretful croak as some belated wanderer fluttered noiselessly down and pushed his way to a perch amidst his companions, to nestle together till the bright rays of sunlight lit up the ocean blue once more.

At a little distance from the beach stood a tiny thatched roofed house with sides open to welcome the cooling breath of the land-breeze that, as the myriad stars came out, stole down from the mountains to the islet trees and then rippled the waters of the shining lagoon.

The house had been built by the people of Leassé, who used it as a rest-house when engaged in fishing in the vicinity of the village. Rolled up and placed over the cross-beams were a number of soft mats, and as Denison returned Kusis took these down and placed them upon the ground, which was covered with a thick layer of pebbles. Throwing himself down on the mats, Denison filled his pipe and smoked, while Tulpé and the child made an oven of heated stones to cook the fish they had caught. Kusis had already plucked some young drinking coconuts, and Denison heard their heavy fall as he threw them to the ground. And only that Kusis had brave blood in his veins, they had had nothing to drink that night, for no Strong's Islander would ascend a coconut tree there after dark, for devils, fiends, goblins, the ghosts of men long dead, and evil spirits flitted to and fro amid the boscage of the islet once night had fallen. And even Kusis, despite the long years he had spent among white men in his cruises in American whaleships in his younger days, chid his wife and child sharply for not hastening to him and carrying the nuts away as they fell.

Then, as Denison and Kusis waited for the oven to be opened, Tulpé and Kinia came inside the hut and sat down beside them, and listened to Kusis telling the white man of a deep, sandy-bottomed pool, near to the islets, which, when the tide came in over the reef at night-time, became filled with big fish, which preyed upon the swarms of minnows that made the pool their home.

"'Tis there, Tenisoni, that we shall go when we have eaten," he said, and he dropped his voice to a whisper, "and there shall we tell thee the story of the dead white men."

So, when the fish was cooked, Tulpé and Kinia hurriedly took it from the oven and carried it to the canoe, in which they all sat and ate, and then pushing out into the lagoon again they paddled slowly along in shallow water till Denison saw the white sandy sides of a deep, dark pool glimmering under the star-light of the island night. Softly the girl Kinia lowered the stone anchor down till it touched bottom two fathoms below, on the very edge ; and then payed out the kellick line whilst her father backed the canoe out from the quickly shelving sides into the centre, where she lay head-on to the gentle current.

For many hours they fished, and soon the canoe was half-filled with great pink and pearly-hued groper and blue-backed, silver-sided sea salmon, and then Denison, wearying of the sport, stretched himself upon the outrigger and smoked whilst Tulpé told him of the tale of the white men who had once lived and died on the little islets.

"'Twas long before the time that the two French fighting-ships came here and anchored in this harbour of Leassé. Other ships had come to Kusaie,[1] and white men had come ashore at Lêla and spoken with the king and chiefs, and made presents of friendship to them, and been given turtle and hogs in return. This was long before my mother was married, and then this place of Leassé, which is now so poor, and hath but so few people in it, was a great town, the houses of which covered all the flat land between the two points of the bay. She, too, was named as I am

[1] Strong's Island.

—Tulpé—and came from a family that lived under the strong arm of the king at Lêla, where they had houses and many plantations. In those days there were three great chiefs on Kusaie, one at Lêla, from where my mother came, one at Utwe, and one here at Leassé. Peace had been between them all for nearly two years, so, when the news came here that there were two ships at anchor in the king's harbour, many of the people of Leassé went thither in their canoes to see the strangers, for these ships were the first the people had seen for, it may have been, twenty years. Among those that went from Leassé was a young man named Kasi-lak—Kasi the big or strong, for he was the tallest and strongest man on this side of the island, and a great wrestler. There were in all nearly two hundred men and women went from Leassé, and when they reached the narrow passage to Lêla, they saw that the harbour was covered with canoes full of the people from the great town there. These clustered about the ships so thickly that those that came from Leassé could not draw near enough to them to look at the white men, so they rested on their paddles and waited awhile. Presently there came out upon a high part of the ship a chief whose name was Malik. He was the king's foster-brother, and a great fighting-man, and was hated by the people of Leassé for having ravaged all the low-lying country from the mountains to the shore ten years before, slaying women and children as well as men, and casting their bodies into the flames of their burning houses.

" But now, because of the peace that was between Leassé and Lêla, he showed his white teeth in a smile of welcome, and, standing upon the high stern part of the ship, he called out, 'Welcome, O friends!' and bade them paddle their canoes to the shore, to the great houses of the king, his brother, where they would be made welcome, and where food would be prepared for them to eat.

"So, much as they desired to go on board the ships, they durst not offend such a man as Malik, and paddled to the shore, where they were met by the king's slaves, who drew their canoes high up on the beach, and covered them with mats to protect them from the sun, and then the king himself came to meet them with fair words and smiles of friendship.

"'Welcome, O men of Leassé,' he said. 'See, my people have covered thy canoes with mats from the sun, for now that there is no hate between us, ye shall remain here at Lêla with me for many days. And so that there shall be no more blood-letting between my people and thine, shall I give every young man among ye that is yet unmarried a wife from these people of mine. Come, now, and eat and drink.'

"So all the two hundred sat down in one of the king's houses, and while they ate and drank there came boats from the ships, and the white men, whom Malik led ashore, came into the house where they sat, and spoke to them. In those days there were but three or four of the Kusaie men who understood English, and these Malik kept by him, so that he could put words into their mouths when he desired to speak to the white strangers. These white men, so my mother said, wore short, broad-bladed swords in sheaths made of thick black skins, and pistols were thrust through belts of skin around their waists. Their hair, too, was dressed like that of the men of

Kusaie—it hung down in a short, thick roll, and was
tied at the end.[1]

"Kasi, who was the father of this my husband,
Kusis, sat a little apart from the rest of the Leassé
people. Beside him was a young girl named Nehi,
his cousin. She had never before left her home, and
the strange faces of the men of Lêla made her so
frightened that she clung to Kasi's arm in fear,
and when the white men came into the house she
flung her arms around her cousin's neck and laid her
face against his naked chest. Presently, as the white
men walked to and fro among the people, they
stopped in front of Kasi and Nehi, and one of them,
who was the captain of the largest of the two ships,
desired Kasi to stand up so that he might see his great
stature the better. So he stood up, and Nehi the girl,
still clinging to his arm, stood up with him.

"'He is a brave-looking man,' said the white officer
to Malik. 'Such men as he are few and far between.
Only this man here,' and he touched a young white
man who stood beside him on the arm, 'is his equal
in strength and fine looks.' And with that the young
white man, who was an officer of the smaller of the
two ships, laughed, and held out his hand to Kasi, and
then his eyes, blue, like the deep sea, fell upon the
face of Nehi, whose dark ones looked wonderingly
into his.

"'Who is this girl? Is she the big man's sister?'
he asked of Malik. Then Malik told him, through
the mouth of one of the three Kusaie men, who spoke

[1] Several English and French privateers cruised through the Caroline
Islands between 1804 and 1819. Fifteen men belonging to one of them
were cut off by the Strong's Islanders.

English, that the girl's name was Nehi, and that with many of her people she had come from Leassé to see the fighting-ships.

"By and by the white men with Malik went away to talk and eat, and drank kava in the house of the king, his brother; but presently the younger white man came back with Rijon, a native who spoke English, and sat down beside Kasi and his cousin Nehi, and talked with them for a long time. And this he told them of himself. That he was the second chief of the little ship, that with but two masts; and because of the long months they had spent upon the sea, and of the bad blood between the common sailor men and the captain, he was wearied of the ship, and desired to leave it. Ten others were there on his own ship of a like mind, and more than a score on the larger ship, which had twenty-and-two great cannons on her deck. And then he and Rijon and Kasi talked earnestly together, and Kasi promised to aid him; and so that Rijon should not betray them to Malik or the two captains, the young white man promised to give him that night a musket and a pistol as an earnest of greater gifts, when he and others with him had escaped from the ships, and were under the roofs of the men of Leassé. So then he pressed the hand of Kasi, and again his eyes sought those of Nehi, the girl, as he turned away.

"Then Rijon, who stayed, drew near to Kasi, and said—

"'What shall be mine if I tell thee of a plan that is in the mind of a great man here to put thee and all those of Leassé with thee to death?'

"'Who is the man? Is it Malik?'"

" ' It is Malik.'

" ' Then,' said Kasi, ' help me to escape from this trap, and thou shalt be to me as mine own brother; of all that I possess half shall be thine.'

" And then Rijon, who was a man who hated bloodshed, and thought it hard and cruel that Malik should slay so many unarmed people who came to him in peace-time, swore to help Kasi in his need. And the girl Nehi took his hand and kissed it, and wept.

" By and by, when Rijon had gone, there came into the big house where the people of Leassé were assembled a young girl named Tulpé — she who afterwards became my mother. And coming over to where Kasi and his cousin sat, she told them she brought a message from the king. That night, she said, there was to be a great feast, so that the white men from the ships might see the dancing and wrestling that were to follow; and the king had sent her to say that he much desired the people from Leassé to join in the feasting and dancing; and with the message he sent further gifts of baked fish and turtle meat and many baskets of fruit.

" Kasi, though he knew well that the king and Malik, his brother, meant to murder him and all his people, smiled at the girl, and said, ' It is good; we shall come, and I shall wrestle with the best man ye have here.'

" Then he struck the palm of his hand on the mat upon which he sat, and said to the girl Tulpé, ' Sit thou here, and eat with us,' for he was taken with her looks, and wanted speech with her.

" ' Nay,' she said, with a smile, though her voice trembled strangely, and her eyes filled with tears as she spoke. 'Why ask me to sit with thee when thou hast so handsome a wife?' And she pointed to Nehi, whose hand lay upon her cousin's arm.

"''Tis but my sister Nehi, my father's brother's child,' he answered. 'No wife have I, and none do I want but thee. What is thy name?'

"'I am Tulpé, the daughter of Malik.'

"Then Kasi was troubled in his mind; for now he hated Malik, but yet was he determined to make Tulpé his wife, first because he desired her for her soft voice and gentle ways, and then because she might be a shield for the people of Leassé against her father's vengeance. So drawing her down beside him, he and Nehi made much of her; and Tulpé's heart went out to him; for he was a man whose deeds as a wrestler were known in every village on the island. But still as she tried to eat and drink and to smile at his words of love, the tears fell one by one, and she became very silent and sad; and presently, putting aside her food, she leant her face on Nehi's shoulder and sobbed.

"'Why dost thou weep, little one?' said Kasi, tenderly.

"She made no answer awhile, but then turned her face to him.

"'Because, O Kasi the Wrestler, of an evil dream which came to me in the night as I lay in my father's house.'

"'Tell me thy dream,' said Kasi.

"First looking around her to see that none but themselves could hear her, she took his hand in hers, and whispered—

"'Aye, Kasi, I will tell thee. This, then, was

my dream : I saw the bodies of men and women and children, whose waists were girt about with red and yellow girdles of *oap*, floating upon a pool of blood. Strange faces were they all to me in my dream, but now two of them are not. And it is for this I weep; for those two faces were thine own and that of this girl by my side.'

"Then Kasi knew that she meant to warn him of her father's cruel plot, for only the people of Leassé wore girdles of the bark of the plant called *oap*. So then he told her of that which Rijon had spoken, and Tulpé wept again.

"'It is true,' she said, 'and I did but seek to warn thee, for no dream came to me in the night; yet do I know that even now my father is planning with his brother the king how that they may slaughter thee all to-night when ye sleep after the dance. What can I do to help thee?'

"They talked together again, and planned what should be done; and then Tulpé went quietly away lest Malik should grow suspicious of her. And Kasi went quickly about among his people telling them of the treachery of Malik, and bade them do what he should bid them when the time came. And then Rijon went to and fro between Kasi and the big white man, carrying messages and settling what was to be done.

"When darkness came great fires were lit in the dance-house and the town square, and the great feast began. And the king and Malik made much of Kasi and his people, and placed more food before them than even was given to their own people. Then when the feast was finished the two ship captains came on shore, and sat on a mat beside the king, and the women danced and the men wrestled. And Kasi, whose heart was bursting with rage though his lips smiled, was praised by Malik and the king for his great strength and skill, for he overcame all who stood up to wrestle with him.

"When the night was far gone, Kasi told Malik that he and his people were weary, and asked that they might sleep. And Malik, who only waited till they slept, said, 'Go, and sleep in peace.'

"But as soon as Kasi and those with him were away out of sight from the great swarm of people who still danced and wrestled in the open square, they ran quickly to the beach where their canoes were lying, and Kasi lit a torch and waved it thrice in the air towards the black shadows of the two ships. Then he waited.

"Suddenly on the ships there arose a great commotion and loud cries, and in a little time there came the sound of boats rowing quickly to the shore. And then came a great flash of light from the side of one of the ships and the thunder of a cannon's voice.

"'Quick,' cried Kasi; 'launch the canoes, lest we be slain here on the beach!' And ere the echoes of the cannon-shot had died away in the mountain caves of Lêla, the men of Leassé had launched their canoes and paddled swiftly out to meet the boats.

"As the boats and canoes drew near, Rijon stood up in the bows of the foremost boat, and the white sailors ceased rowing so that he and Kasi might talk. But there was but little time, for already the sound of the cannon and the cries and struggling on board the ships had brought a great many of the Lêla people to the beach ; fires were lit, and conch shells were blown, and Malik and his men began to fire their muskets at the escaping canoes. Presently, too, the white men in the boats began to handle their muskets and fire back in return, when their leader bade them cease, telling them that it was but Malik's men firing at Kasi's people.

" ' Now,' said he to Rijon, ' tell this man Kasi to lead the way with his canoes to the passage, and we in the boats shall follow closely, so that if Malik's canoes pursue and overtake us, we white men shall beat them back with our musket-fire.'

" So then Kasi turned his canoes seaward, and the boats followed ; and as they rowed and paddled, all keeping closely together, the great cannons of the two ships flashed and thundered and the shot roared above them in the darkness. But yet was no one hurt, for the night was very dark ; and soon they reached the deep waters of the passage, and rose and fell to the ocean swell, and still the iron cannon-shot hummed about them, and now and again struck the water near ; and on the left-hand shore ran Malik's men with cries of rage, and firing as they ran, till at last they came to the point and could pursue no farther, and soon their cries grew fainter and fainter as the canoes and boats reached the open ocean. Then it happened that one of the white sailors, vexed that a last bullet had whistled near his head, raised his musket and fired into the dark shore whence it came.

" ' Thou fool ! ' cried his leader, and he struck the man senseless with the boat's tiller, and then told Rijon to call out to Kasi and his people to pull to the left for their lives, for the flash of the musket would be seen from the ships. Ah, he was a clever white man, for scarce had the canoes and boats turned to the left more than fifty fathoms, when there came a burst of flame from all the cannons on the ships, and a great storm of great iron shot and small leaden bullets lashed the black water into white foam just behind them. After that the firing ceased, and Rijon called out that there was no more danger ; for the cunning white man had told him that they could not be pursued—he had broken holes in all the boats that remained on the ships.

" When daylight came, the boats and canoes were far down the coast towards Leassé. Then, as the sun rose from the sea, the men in the boats ceased rowing, and the big white man stood up and beckoned to Kasi to bring his canoe alongside. And when the canoe lay beside the boat, the white man laughed and held out his hand to Kasi and asked for Nehi ; and as Nehi rose from the bottom of Kasi's canoe, where she had been sleeping, and stood up beside her cousin, so did Tulpé, the daughter of Malik, stand up beside the white man in his boat, and the two girls threw their arms around each other's necks and wept glad tears. Then as the canoes and boats hoisted their sails to the wind of sunrise, the people saw that Tulpé sat beside Kasi in his canoe, and Nehi, his cousin, sat beside the white man in his boat, with her face covered with her hands so that no one should see her eyes.

" As they sailed along the coast Tulpe told Kasi how she and Rijon had gone on board the smaller of the two ships, and seen the tall young white man

16

whispering to some of the sailors. Then, when they saw the flash of Kasi's torch, how these sailors sprang upon the others and bound them hand and foot while a boat was lowered, and muskets and food and water put in. Then she and Rijon and the young white leader and some of the sailors got in, and Rijon stood in the bows and guided them to the shore to where Kasi and his people awaited them on the beach.

II

" For nearly three months these white men lived at Leassé, and the father of Kasi, who was chief of the town, made much of them, because they had muskets, and bullets, and powder in plenty, and this made him strong against Malik and the people of Lêla. The ships had sailed away soon after the night of the dance, but the two captains had given the king and Malik many muskets and much powder, and a small cannon, and urged him to pursue and kill all the white men who had deserted the ships.

" ' By and by, I will kill them,' said Malik.

" The young white man took Nehi to wife, and was given a tract of land near Leassé, and Kasi became husband to Tulpé, and there grew a great friendship between the two men. Then came warfare with Lêla again, and of the twenty and two white men ten were killed in a great fight at Utwé with Malik's people, who surprised them as they were building a vessel, for some of them were already weary of Kusaie, and wished to sail away to other lands.

" Soon those that were left began to quarrel among themselves and kill each other, till only seven, beside the husband of Nehi, were left. These, who lived in a village at the south point, seldom came to Leassé, for the big white man would have none of them, and naught but bitter words had passed between them for many months, for he hated their wild, dissolute ways, and their foul manners. Then, too, they had learnt to make grog from coconut toddy, and sometimes, when they were drunken with it, would stagger about from house to house, musket or sword in hand, and frighten the women and children.

"One day it came about that a girl named Luan, who was a blood relation of Nehi, and wife to one of these white men, was walking along a mountain-path, carrying her infant child, when her foot slipped, and she and the infant fell a great distance. When she came to she found that the child had a great wound in its forehead, and was cold and stiff in death. She lifted it up, and when she came to her husband's house she found him lying asleep, drunken with toddy, and when she roused him with her grief he did but curse her.

"Then Luan, with bitter scorn, pointed to the body of the babe and said, 'Oh, thou wicked and drunken father, dost thou not see that thy child is dead?'

"Then in his passion he seized his pistol and struck her on the head, so that she was stunned and fell as if dead.

"That night the people of Leassé saw the seven white men, with their wives and children, paddling over towards the two little islands, carrying all their goods with them, for the people had risen against them by reason of the cruelty of the husband of Luan, and driven them away.

"So there they lived for many weeks, making grog from the coconut trees, and drinking and fighting among themselves all day, and sleeping the sleep of the drunken at night. Their wives toiled for them all day, fishing on the reef, and bringing them taro, yams, and fruit from the mainland. But Luan alone could not work, for she grew weaker and weaker, and one day she died. Then her white husband went to the village from whence they were driven, and seizing the wife of a young man, bore her away to the two islets.

" The next day he whose wife had been stolen came to the husband of Nehi, and said, 'O white man, help me to get back my wife ; help me for the sake of Luan, whom this dog slew, and whose blood cries out to thee for vengeance, for was she not a blood relation to Nehi, thy wife ? '

" But though the husband of Nehi shook his head and denied the man the musket he asked for, he said naught when at night-time a hundred men, carrying knives and clubs in their hands, gathered together in the council-house, and talked of the evil lives of the seven white men, and agreed that the time had come for them to die.

" So in silence they rose up from the mats in the council-house and walked down to the beach, and launching their canoes, paddled across to the islands under cover of the darkness. It so happened that one woman was awake, but all the rest with the white men and their children slept. This woman belonged to Leassé, and had come to the beach to bathe, for the night was hot and windless. Suddenly the canoes surrounded her, and, fearing danger to her white husband, she sought to escape, but a strong hand caught her by the hair, and a voice bade her be silent.

" Now, the man who held her by the hair was her own sister's husband, and he desired to save her life, so he and two others seized and bound her, and quickly tied a waist-girdle over her mouth so that she could not cry out. But she was strong, and struggled so that the girdle slipped off, and she gave a loud cry. And then her sister's husband, lest his chief might say he had failed in his duty, and the white men escape, seized her throat in his hands and pressed it so that she all but died.

" Then the avengers of the blood of Luan sprang out upon the beach, and ran through the palm grove to where the white men's house stood. It was a big house, for they all lived together, and in the middle of the floor a lamp of coconut oil burned, and showed where the seven white men lay.

" And there as they slept were they speared and stabbed to death, although their wives threw their arms around the slayers and besought them to spare their husbands' lives. And long before dawn the canoes returned to Leassé with the wives and children of the slain men, and only the big white man, the husband of Nehi, was left alive out of the twenty and two who came from the ships at Lela. So that is the story of the two islets, and of the evil men who dwelt there."

. . . . .

Denison rose and stretched himself. " And what of the big white man—the husband of Nehi ? " he asked ; " doth his spirit, too, wander about at night ? "

" Nay," said Tulpé, " why should it ? There was no

innocent blood upon his hand. Both he and Nehi lived and died among us ; and to-morrow it may be that Kinia shalt show thee the place whereon their house stood in the far-back years. And true are the words in the Book of Life—' He that sheddeth blood, by man shall his blood be shed.' "

*" FOR WE WERE FRIENDS
ALWAYS "*

" *For we were Friends Always* "

LANGLEY, the white trader of Uhomotu,[1] came to his door and looked seawards at the smoky haze which almost hid the ocean swell sweeping westward from Beveridge Reef, three hundred miles away, to crash against the grey coral cliffs that lined the weather side of the island from Uhomotu to Liku. In the village street, sweltering even under the rows of coconut and breadfruit trees, not a sign of life was visible. For your true Polynesian dreads heat as much as cold.

  .   .   .   .   .

 " What an infernal day, and what a horrible-looking coast ! " muttered the trader, as he looked at the line of dark grey rocks rising a sheer hundred feet from the boiling surf at their base. Now and then a heavy roller would hurl itself against the wall of rock and leap high in the air, drenching with spray the stunted, tangled scrub that covered the jagged summits of the cliffs to their very edge, and pouring down the face in a seething white avalanche of humming foam.

 The tide was falling, and here and there at the foot of the wall of rock, the trader could see the protruding mounds and knobs of the black reef of coral which, at

---

[1] A village on the northern shore of Savage Island, in the South Pacific.

low tide, formed a border of relief to the lighter hue of the cliffs above it. For twenty feet or so the reef stood out, presenting a perpendicular weed-clad face to the rolling Pacific.

.　　　.　　　.　　　.　　　.

The hot, depressing calm irritated the trader. He was not a drinking man, or he might have drunk till the land-breeze set in and cooled the air.

"I'll shut up the store and camp under the teacher's orange-trees ; it's cool there. Hallo ! what do *you* want ? "

A native boy was standing in the room, holding out a piece of paper. Langley took it from him. It was written upon in the usual sprawling manner of natives, and was a request to hand the bearer the articles mentioned.

"In the name of the evil spirits, who be these that write—Mahekê, Kitia, and Minea ? " he asked, crossly.

"*Mahekê, Kitia, ma Minea.*"

"O wood-head ! am I any wiser now ? "

The boy stared solemnly, and then by a˙sudden inspiration showed him a roll of money tied up in the dangling end of his dirty waist-cloth.

"Ha ! " said the trader, "now do I see. Stolen money, eh ? And these women have sent thee to spend it. Now will I call for the *fakafili* (judge) and have thee beaten with twenty stripes."

"Nay, nay," whined the boy, "I be honest."

"Then why come to this door, which is *tabu ;*— for in here do I eat and sleep. Do I buy or sell in this room ? Have I not a store ? "

" True, O white man, but I was forbidden to go there, lest I be seen."

" Ha, 'tis stolen money then, else why fear to be seen ? "

" Mahekê forbade me."

" And who is Mahekê ? '

" The friend of Kitia ? "

" And who is Kitia ? "

" The friend of Minea."

" O dolt ! O half-awakened hog ! How do I know these names ? Who, in God's name, then, is Minea ? "

" She be friend to Kitia and Mahekê—they be friends to one another."

" So. I see. These three, then, have stolen the money between them—the *fakafili*——"

The boy began to blubber.

" Nay, it is not so, my master. I do not lie to thee. It be honest money. And these three gave it me with the *tuhi* (letter) for thee, and bade me tell no one. And when I come safely to them with those things for which they ask, I am to have one piece of silver money for myself—and that Mahekê hath now in her hand to give me when I return."

.   .   .   .   .

Langley was puzzled. It was so unusual for native women to send any one to buy goods for them. The rule with the natives of Savage Island was to make their purchases ostentatiously, and show every one that they *had* money. He read the note again.

" Send us, O good white man, three white handkerchiefs, three white poll combs, a bottle of musk, three *pili àlo* (chemises), one fathom of blue gossamer to shade our faces from the sun, and a little tobacco and one box of matches."

.   .   .   .   .

"What the deuce can it be?" he thought, as he went into the adjoining store. He got the articles named, and tied them into a parcel. Then he looked again at the rude, scrawling signatures—

"*For us, Mahekê, Minea, ma Kitia.*"

"Here, boy, take these. Stay, what is thy name?"

"Vetsi, the son of Soseni."

"So. And who are these women that send thee to buy? Hast thou three wives? Who is Mahekê?"

The boy laughed at the white man's pleasantry, and began—

"Mahekê is the friend——"

The trader darted out his hand, caught him by the shoulder, and shook him.

"Now, tell me where does Mahekê live?"

"In Uhomotu, with her mother. She it is whose lover died in the Pokulā (Guano Islands) last year."

"Good. And Minea?"

The parrot-like repetition of "She is——" was again issuing from his lips, when another shake brought the boy to his senses.

"Minea is the thin girl with the foot that wasteth away."

"Ha!" said the trader, and he asked no further questions; while the boy, glad to be released, went cautiously away with the parcel, looking fearfully about him lest he should be seen by any of the villagers.

.   .   .   .   .

Although not yet six months on Savage Island, and unfamiliar with the names of many of the natives in

his own locality, the trader now remembered these
three girls.   Sometimes they would bring fruit or a
little cotton for sale, and, unlike the generality of the
people, who would hang about and bandy words with
him, they would take payment in cash and go quietly
away.   One of them, Minea, walked with a stick.
She was the youngest of the three, and her two
companions seemed tenderly anxious for her.   Some
terrible bone-disease had crippled her foot, which was
slowly wasting away.   Mahekê, a sombre-faced, black-
browed creature, had one day been pointed out to him
as the girl who refused to marry a man of her parents'
choice, for which contumacy she had received many
thrashings.   Of Kitia he knew nothing, except that
she was the pretty and inseparable companion of the
other two.

    .   .   .   .   .

"Ani," said he an hour or so afterwards to the
teacher's daughter, a fat, sullen-faced girl, as he lay
smoking beneath an orange-tree in her father's garden,
"who be the three girls, Kitia, Minea, and Mahekê?"
The sullen features lighted up vindictively.   Ah!
they were a bad, lazy lot.   Mahekê! the shameless
creature that would not marry a good man like
Paturei, who was a deacon.   And why?   Because
she had a dead lover in Pokulā.   She wanted more
beatings.   Kitia, an idle little beast that the white
men favoured because she dressed her head with
flowers and sang heathen Samoan songs, and walked
with bare bosom to the bathing-place, which the
fakafili had forbidden, because it was not modest.
Minea, she who was once so saucy and was now
smitten by God for her sins——

"Oh, shut up, you putty-faced devil!" said the trader, disgustedly, in English.

"Thou art but as a stranger here," the teacher's daughter began again, oilily, "and these are girls whose names have been called aloud in the church by my father for their bad ways. They are three friends—a fourth there is, who is the Devil."

"Ah!" said the white man, mockingly, "then have they a strong friend. Perhaps 'tis he that giveth them so much money to spend in my store."

"What money?" said she, quickly.

The trader, for amusement, magnified the purchases of the Three Friends. The teacher's daughter he knew to be a greedy, malicious creature, and it pleased him to torment her.

Suddenly there came to them from the beach a loud clamour of voices, and with a cry of alarm the fat Ani tore past the astonished trader into the village, calling out something about the Three Friends and the cliffs of Matasuafa.

Before the white man could get to the village to learn the cause of alarm every soul had left it, their brown bodies dashing aside the shrubs and cotton bushes that lay in their way as they hastened with excited cries to the cliffs. Wondering if they had all gone mad, he followed.

.   .   .   .   .

At a point called Matasuafa, where the perpendicular face of the cliffs was highest, the natives—men, women, and children—clustered like bees. Those in front, holding with one hand the branches of the tough scrub that grew on the summit, gazed down at the black ledge of reef that stood abruptly out from the foot of the cliff. There, directly beneath, lay the motionless figures of three girls. Descent at this spot was impossible, and the eyes of the watchers on top moved alternately from the huddled-up forms beneath to those of four or five men who were running along the narrow table of reef a few hundred yards away.

The tide was dead low, yet, as the half-naked men sprang across the pools and air-holes that broke up the crust of the reef, the ocean swell broke savagely against its face and smothered them in misty spray. And now and again a roller heavier than the rest would send a thin sheet of water hissing along the ledge of rock to sway to and fro the long black hair and ensanguined garments of the Three Friends. It came up clear as crystal; it poured back again through the coral gutters and air-holes to the sea tinged with a bloody stain.

.   .   .   .   .

The men dashed on and lifted them up, and then fought their way back through the sweeping seas along the ledge of cruel, black rock, to a place where a narrow path had been cut away in a break of the cliffs.

For some time the trader tried to get near them to see if by any chance they yet lived. Whilst waiting on the cliffs he had learnt the meaning of the mysterious purchase of the morning. After meeting the boy in a lonely sugar-cane patch, the girls had dressed themselves in their best, carefully oiling and combing their long, glossy hair. Then, after making and smoking some cigarettes and sprinkling one another with scent, they bade him come with them a part of the way. They travelled an old, unused path of former days, unknown even to the boy Vetsi, who now began to get frightened, and wept.

Then they stopped, and Mahekê, taking the boy's hand, placed in it the half-dollar she had promised him and bade him go back; but the lame girl, Minea, who seemed moved somewhat, took him to her bosom and kissed and fondled him. Then she pushed him away, and, with the other two supporting her weakly frame, they struck into the undergrowth that quivered to the shock of the breakers dashing against the face of Matasuafa.

.   .   .   .   .

The trader pushed silently through the people and looked. Two, Mahekê and Minea, were dead. Their agony had been brief. The third, the round-faced, laughing-voiced Kitia, who was but budding into womanhood, still lived, but that it was not for long could easily be seen. Both legs and her back were broken.

A woman, with shaking hands and streaming eyes, bent over her and spoke.

The girl's eyes opened, big, soft, black, and tender.

" *Ekê*, where art thou, Mahekê? . . . and thou, my Minea? . . . Shall I fail thee, O my friends . . . my friends? "

The woman laid her lips to the dying mouth.

"My child, my Kitia, 'tis I, thy old mother! "

The bruised and bleeding fingers twitched feebly, and then Ani, the Bitter-Tongued, knelt, and raising the girl's arms, placed the maimed hands against her mother's cheek, and kept them there.

The woman sobbed a question, and in a faint whisper the answer came.

"We had sworn it . . . long, long ago. 'Twas when Mahekê's lover died we planned it. ' I will die ere I become wife to Paturei,' she said. . . . We were friends . . . friends. And Minea said, ' Then shall I die with thee, for I suffer pain always—always.' And then I, I who was strong and well, I jumped too, for we were friends, and I had sworn to them . . . to be with them . . . always . . . for ever. My mother . . . so old art thou . . ."

.   .   .   .   .

The trader, with a sudden mist dimming his eyes and holding his hat in his hand, stood back and turned his face to the sea. Then he walked slowly home to the village.

As he emerged from the narrow path into the open, the chill of the dewy night-breeze struck upon his face.

He stopped a moment on the hill, listening.

'Twas but the muffled boom of the rollers on Matasuafa, sounding in long, solemn symphony the requiem of the Three Friends of Uhomotu.

NIKOA

Nikoa

A WHITE man, thin, brown-skinned, and ragged, was walking along the reef at Henuake, one of the Low Archipelago. In his hand he carried a turtle spear, and every now and then he would examine the deep pools that at intervals broke the hollow crust of the reef. Behind him, carrying a basket, came his native wife.

The tide was very low, and the outer edge of the black wall of reef, covered on the top with patches and clumps of round yellow and pink coral knobs, had dried, and under the fierce sun-rays a sickening odour arose from the countless marine-growths and organisms.

Presently the white man sat down upon a weed-covered boulder on the brink of a pool, and waited for the woman to come up.

.   .   .   .   .

The man's name was Falkiner, and he was about the poorest beachcomber in the group. Not many years before he had been a different man, but he had made money fast in those days, and as fast as he made it he had spent it in drunken orgies at Auckland, Papiete, and Honolulu. Then his luck turned, and from being a man of might and substance and the owner of two pearling-schooners he had sunk to living

on Henuake, planting coconuts for an American firm.
Fifteen months before they had landed him and his
wife and four native labourers, and about twenty
thousand seed-coconuts. Telling him to be careful
of his provisions, and that the schooner would be back
again in six months, the captain had sailed away.

. . . . .

The woman came up, and, taking the basket off
her shoulders, sat down beside him. For a while
neither spoke. The man was tired and savage, and
the woman knew his mood too well to speak until
she was spoken to. Away on either hand stretched
the black waste of reef; in front the oily, glassy ocean,
with here and there a flock of snow-white sea-birds
meandering on the wing or floating on its smooth
surface; and shorewards the long low line of verdure
fringed by the dazzling white beach.

"Show me," said Falkiner, pointing to the basket.

Nikoa opened the basket and showed him a young
turtle of about 20lb. weight.

"That will do us, Nikoa, for a day or two. Perhaps the *kau puaka* will see now that I want nothing
from them."

Now by *kau puaka* (crew of pigs) the white man
meant his native labourers, with whom he had quarrelled. When his provisions ran out—and especially
his liquor—and they all had to live upon native food,
his morose temper soon caused a breach, and it had
gradually widened day by day till at last the white
man and his wife had to seek their own food.

. . . . .

"Harry," said the woman, "why use such bitter
words? These men of Raroia are quick-blooded, and

who is to know of it should thy hot tongue bring death upon us two suddenly in the night?"

"What do you know, what have you heard?" he asked, suspiciously.

"This," she answered, quickly: "but two days ago two of them came to me and asked would I go with them in the boat and seek some other island, for they are wearied of living here and getting naught but foul words from the white man."

The ragged man looked savagely at her for a moment, then snarled: "Well, you sad-faced devil, you can go. I don't want you any more, curse you!"

The woman's eyes flashed fire: "That is the devil in thee that speaks because it calleth for more grog. Now, listen. It will be well for thee to be friendly with these men, for they are four to us two, and they have the boat, and they have money—much money."

"Money," said Falkiner; "where could they get money on Henuake?" and he laughed incredulously.

Then she told him.

. . . . .

Two days before the four natives had been searching for robber-crabs in a dense *puka* scrub, when they had found, lying on the ground, a boat's water-breaker. One of them had taken hold of it to lift it up, and found it to be too heavy. As he placed his hands under each end the bilge gave way, and a great mass of silver coin poured out in a heap. They each set to work and made four strong baskets. Into these they divided the money, and hid it away. Then they consulted.

"Let us tell the white man," said one, "and when he sees all this money he will wait here on Henuake

no longer, but take it and us away with him to
Raroia."

"No," said the others, "let us hide it until the
schooner comes back for us. We can steal it on board
at night-time. Why tell the white man? He will
keep it and perhaps kill us."

But they had told Nikoa, and she had urged them
to let her tell the white man—the money was his, she
argued. Were they not his men? Was he not a
good man to them until all his liquor was gone?—
only then had he become sour and moody. And so
they let it rest with her. And now she told him.

"You're a good girl, Nikoa," said the white man,
pleasantly. "We'll take the boat and go back to
Raroia, and let Henuake take care of itself. Tell the
men we will divide the money evenly—and let us be
friends again."

Nikoa smiled. Loyalty to her husband was always
her first thought, and she thought with delight of her
home at Garumaoa on Raroia—the village of her
childhood, where she was as happy as the day was
long. A year and a half ago Falkiner had bought her
from the chief, and with unquestioning obedience she
had followed him to lonely Henuake. He was occasionally a great brute to her; yet, although she was
sickening to return to her people, she had no thought
of doing so without the white man.

They rose and walked back to the line of palms on
the beach—the woman laughing and talking joyously,
and the man planning black treachery.

In another hour the four brown men had come back
to his house, each carrying his basket-load of silver
dollars. They were emptied on a mat and counted

out in piles of hundreds. There were over four thousand dollars. Falkiner divided it into six shares—one for each of the men, and one for Nikoa.

Then each brown man tied his share up in a piece of cloth and handed it to the white man—to mind till they got back to Raroia.

"Whose money was it before?" they asked him that night, as they sat in his house smoking.

He shook his head. It was mostly in American dollars and half-dollars and Chilian half-dollars. He had heard of some human remains being found in Henuake long years ago, and that a whaleship had been lost there some time about 1850. Perhaps the money had come from her—whaleships in those days often carried as much as five thousand dollars to buy pearl-shell and tortoise-shell.

Then the men went away to their own hut to sleep, and Nikoa, the woman, slept too.

When he was sure she slumbered soundly, Falkiner carefully examined and loaded his Colt's revolver, and placed it in the chest with the dollars.

.   .   .   .   .

At daybreak they pulled out of the quiet lagoon and headed for Raroia. It was calm, and the day became hot, yet the four men pulled unwearingly all day, with but short intervals of rest. At dusk a faint air sprang up, and they hoisted the sail.

"Sleep, strong men, sleep," said the white man, "Nikoa and I will steer by turns till it be dawn."

The four natives lay down. The one who was pulling the bow-oar was a lad named Te Rangi, a cousin of Nikoa. As he coiled his body into the confined space where he lay Nikoa threw him a mat to keep off the chilly night air. Then she slept also till dawn.

.   .   .   .   .

Suddenly the sound of two shots pealed out over the ocean, and, as the woman sprang up terrified, a third. There, under the first flush of the rising sun, she saw three of her countrymen lying either dead or dying, and Falkiner pointing his pistol at the mat-covered figure in the bows.

She seized his arm. "Harry, 'tis Te Rangi, my brother. Let him live?" He shook her off with a savage curse, and fired. The bullet broke the arm of the sleeping lad, who sat up and gazed in terror at the savage face of the white man.

Again the woman caught his hand and begged for the boy's life. He was but a lad, she urged; he was, too, of her own blood—how then could he betray? There was land not far distant. Let him have his life now and he could be landed there.

But Falkiner again thrust her aside, and, this time, sent a bullet through Te Rangi's heart.

.   .   .   .   .

The dead men had been thrown overboard, and Falkiner had changed the boat's course to W. by N. He would get to Samoa, he thought. Once there, he need have no fear. He had spared the woman's life simply because he thought that she would never betray him. As soon as she got over losing Te Rangi she would be all right again and find her tongue.

A few miles ahead of the boat was a cluster of low islands, uninhabited all but one. Falkiner knew them well, and presently he said to the woman—

" Nikoa, we will sleep on Napuka to-night, and in the morning get as many young coconuts as we can for the boat, and perhaps we may find a turtle on the beach. Then we go to Samoa."

She nodded her head. The wild hatred of the man that now filled her heart kept her from speaking.

. . . . .

The current in Napuka Passage was running out fiercely, and the boat could scarcely make headway against it, even with the strong S.E. trade filling her big sail.

" Let us make fast to the edge of the coral till the tide turns," said the white man, and he let the boat's head fall off a little, at the same time standing up to get a better view.

But a sudden whirling eddy brought the boat up against a great knob of coral, and Falkiner lost his balance with the shock and fell over the side.

When he rose to the surface he was a hundred feet away from the boat, which had swung round head-to the current, but was hard and fast on the coral knob.

" Push her off, Nikoa," he called out, " else I am taken out to sea!"

Nikoa stood up and laughed. " Even so, killer of my brother! The heavy baskets of money, for which thou sheddest the blood of four men, keeps the boat firm on the rock. It is a judgment on thee."

Above the roaring, hissing, and swirling of the water her voice reached him, and, still struggling madly to gain the sides of the passage, he was borne out into the blue depths beyond.

Then Nikoa, shielding her eyes from the sun with one hand, saw a splash in the water, and heard a faint cry of agony, and knew that a shark had taken the murderer.

.   .   .   .   .

The boat soon lay high and dry on the coral knob, and Nikoa, lighting a cigarette, sat and smoked awhile. Then she took out the baskets of coin, and cut them open and poured the blood-stained money into the wildly sweeping waters. When the last one was emptied, she lay down and slept till the tide turned.

When she awoke the boat was drifting in quietly to the land, and a canoe full of light-skinned men with strong, wiry beards and moustaches was alongside.

"Who art thou ? " said one.

" Nikoa of Raroia," she answered. "My man fell out of the boat, and was eaten by a shark. What men are ye ? "

"We be of Tetopoto," they replied, pointing to the farthest island ; "had there been men with you we had killed them. But we will not hurt a woman."

.   .   .   .   .

And for years afterwards the children of Napuka and Tetopoto found silver money in the holes and pools of the reef.

THE STRANGE WHITE WOMAN OF MADURŎ

The Strange White Woman of Mādurŏ

A GROUP of four men were seated upon a trader's verandah at Mādurŏ, one of the Marshall Islands. They were smoking and talking about old times. The night was brilliantly moonlight, and the hull and spars of a little white-painted brig that lay anchored in the lagoon about a mile distant from the trader's house stood out as clearly and distinct as if she were but fifty yards away from where they sat. Three of the men present were visitors—Ned Packenham the captain, Harvey the mate, and Denison the super-cargo of the *Indiana*; the fourth was the trader him-self—a grizzled old wanderer of past sixty, with a skin like unto dark leather, and a frame that, old as he was, showed he was still as active and vigorous as when he had first landed on Mādurŏ atoll thirty years before.

It was long past midnight, and the old trader's numerous half-caste family had turned-in to sleep some hours before. The strange, wondrous beauty of the night, and the pleasure of listening to old Charlie Waller's talk of the early days in the Marshalls when every white man lived like a prince, and died in his boots from a bullet or a spear, had tempted the visitors to send their boat back to the ship and accept Charlie's invitation to remain till breakfast next morning. It so happened that the old man had just been talking about a stalwart son of his who had died a few months previously, and Packenham and Denison, to whom the lad had been well known, asked his father where the boy had been buried.

"In there," replied the old man, pointing to a small white-walled enclosure, about a stone's throw from where they were sitting. "There's a good many graves there now. Let me see. There is Dawnay, the skipper of the *Maid of Samoa*, and three of his crew; Petersen, the Dutchman, that got a bullet into him for fooling around too much with a pistol in his hand and challenging natives to fight when he was drunk; two or three of my wife's relatives, who wanted to be buried in my boneyard, because they thought to make me some return for keeping their families after they were dead; my boy Tom; and the white woman."

"White woman!" said the mate of the brig. "Was there a white woman died here?"

"Yes," answered the trader; "but it's so long ago that I've almost forgotten the matter myself. Why, let me see—I came here in '40 or '41. Well, I think it was some time about '48 or '49."

"Who was she?"

Old Waller shrugged his shoulders. "That I can't tell. I only know that she died here, and that I buried her."

"Where did she come from?" asked Denison.

"That I can't tell you either, gentlemen. But I'll tell you all I do know, and a mighty queer yarn it is,

too.   In those days I was the only white man here.
I had come here about six years before from Ebon,
about four hundred miles from here, and, as I had
learnt the language, I got on very well with the natives,
and was doing a big business.   There were not many
whaleships here then, but every ten months or so a
vessel came here from Sydney, and, as I had the sole
run of the whole of this lagoon, I generally filled her up
with coconut oil, and was making money hand over fist.

" The house in which I then lived was, like this one,
built of coral lime, but stood further away towards the
point, in rather a clearer spot than this, for the coconut trees were not growing thickly together around it.
You can see the place from here, and also see that a
house standing in such a position would be visible, not
only from all parts of the inside beaches of the lagoon,
but from the sea as well.   It used to be a regular landing mark for all the canoes sailing over here from
Arhnu (a low-lying coral atoll, densely populated,
twenty miles distant) for, being whitewashed, it stood
out very clearly, even at night-time.

" Well, it was a pretty lonely life in those days, only
seeing a ship once a year ; but I was making money,
as I said, hand over fist, and didn't worry much.   My
wife—not the present one, you know—was a Bonin
Island half-bred Portugee woman, and as she generally
talked to me in English, and had no native ways to
speak of, we used to sit outside in the evenings pretty
often and watch our kids and the village people dancing
and otherwise amusing themselves on the beach.
Rotau, the head chief of this lagoon, was very
chummy with me, and sometimes he and his wives
would come up of an evening and join us.

"One night he told us that a canoe had come from Milli [an island about three days' sail to the leeward of Waller's place], and reported that a ship had passed quite close to their island about a week before. At first I thought it was my vessel coming up from Sydney, but Rotau said it was not a brig, but a three-masted ship with yards on all her masts. Well, at first I thought it was a whaler, but then remembered that it was fully four months too late in the year for a blubber-hunter to be around. Then it occurred to me that it might be some English ship going to China or the East Indies from the colonies; but I wondered why she was beating to the eastward if that were the case.

"Well, after we had sat talking for awhile, my wife called the children in and put them to sleep, and Rotau and I and his wives sat outside a bit longer, smoking. All the rest of the natives had gone away, and the beach was deserted. It was a moonlight night, almost as bright as it is to-night, and the sea was as smooth as a millpond; so smooth, in fact, that there was not even a break upon the reef, and the trade wind having died away, there was not the sound of a leaf stirring in the palm grove, and only just the 'lip-lap, lip-lap' of the water in the lagoon as it swished up the sandy beach.

"We had been sitting like this for about half an hour, when Nera, my wife, just as she was coming out of the door to join us, gave a cry.

"'*Te Kaibuke!* Look at the ship!'

"I jumped up and looked, and there, sure enough, was a big ship just showing round the point and close in—at least, not more than a mile away from the reef.

She showed up so plainly on the surface of the water that I could see that she was under all canvas—except her royals and such.

"For a moment I was a bit scared, remembering that there was not a breath of wind, and yet seeing her moving ; then I remembered the current, and knew that she must have run up to the land from the westward, before dark, perhaps, and that as soon as the breeze had died away the current, which runs about four knots off the weather side of the island, had caught her and was now moving her along. Even by the moonlight I could see that she was a fine-looking ship ; and by her sheer, high bows, white-painted deckhouses, and cut of her sails, I took her to be either a Yankee or British North-American.

"I always kept my whaleboat ready in those days, and, after looking at her for a bit and seeing she was steadily drifting along to the north-east and would be out of sight by the morning, I made up my mind to board her. But just as I had asked Rotau to get one of his women to hunt up a boat's crew, he sang out—

"'Listen ; I hear a boat !'

"In another moment or two I heard it, plain enough—*click, clack ; click, clack*—and at the same time saw that the ship was heading away from the land.

"'That's queer,' I thought. And then Rotau, who, like all natives, had better eyes than most white men, said that she had three boats out towing.

"'Ah,' I thought, 'the captain has got frightened at the current, and, as he can't anchor where he is, he's sending in a boat to try and find a place where he can let go till morning and is towing off the land meanwhile.'

"I knew the ship was right enough, and could not get into any danger, as the current would take her clear of the land in another hour or so; so we all went down to the point to see where the boat was coming.

"As I said, there wasn't even so much as a bit of froth on the reef, and, being high water, no one a stranger to a coral reef would know it was there till he was going over it in a boat and looked over the side. We had just got down to the point when we saw the boat close to. She was being pulled very quickly by four hands, and made a devil of a row coming through the water. The man who was steering was standing up, and I saw that his cap was off, and his face showed white and ghastly in the moonlight.

"As soon as she was within a hundred yards of the beach I hailed them to keep a bit to starboard, as there was a big coral boulder right in front of the spot they were steering for.

"'Aye, aye,' answered the man steering, and he did as I told him. In another minute or two the boat shot up on the beach, and we crowded round them.

"'Stand back, please,' says the officer, speaking in a curious, hurried kind of way, and then I saw that he had a pistol in his left hand, and that the men with him looked white and scared, and seemed to take no notice of us.

"But they didn't give us much time to wonder at their looks. Two of the men jumped out, and then we saw that there was another person in the boat—a woman. She was sitting on the bottom boards, lying against the stern-sheets, and seemed to be either asleep or dead. The officer helping them, they lifted her up

out of the boat and carried her ashore. Then the
officer turns to me, and I saw that though he tried to
speak quietly, he was in a devil of a flurry over something.

"'What's all this?' I said; 'what's the matter?
What have you got this pistol in your hand for, and
what is the matter with this woman?'

"He put the pistol out of sight pretty quick, and
then, speaking so rapidly that I could hardly follow
him, said that the lady was the captain's wife. She
had been taken ill very suddenly, and her husband,
seeing my house so close to, had determined to send
her ashore, and see if anything could be done for her.

"'That's mighty queer,' I said. 'Why didn't he
come with her himself? Look here, I don't believe
all this. How the devil did he know that even though
the house is here that a white man lives in it? And
I want to have a look at the woman's face. She might
be dead for all I know.'

"By this time my wife and one of Rotau's wives
had gone up to the woman, and I saw that although
she wasn't dead she looked very like it, for her eyes
were closed, and she seemed quite unconscious of all
that was going on. She was young—about twenty-
five or so—and was rather pretty.

"'Please take her to your house,' says the officer,
'and as soon as we have towed the ship out of danger
the captain will come ashore and see you.'

"'Hold on,' says I, and I grabbed him by the arm.
'Do you mean to say you're going off in this fashion,
without telling me anything further? Who are you,
anyway? What is the ship's name?'

"He hesitated just a second, and then said, 'The

Inca Prince—Captain Broughton ; but I can't stay to talk now. The captain himself will tell you about it in the morning. As you see, his wife is very ill. You will at least not refuse to help in the matter ? '

" And then, before I could stop him, he jumped back out of my reach into the boat, and the four sailors, two of whom were niggers of some sort, shoved off, and away they went again.

" ' You'd better tell the captain to come ashore at once,' I called out after them ; but although he heard me plainly enough he took no notice of me beyond waving his hand

" Well, we carried the woman up to the house and placed her in a chair, and the moment that my wife took off the woollen wrapper that covered her head and shoulders she cried out that there was blood running down her neck. And it didn't take me long to discover that the woman was dying from a bullet wound in the back of her head.

" We did all that we possibly could for the poor thing, but she never regained consciousness, and towards sunrise she died quietly. There was nothing about her clothing to show who she was, but she wore rings such as would belong to a woman of some position. She appeared to be twenty-six years of age, as I said ; and when she was being prepared for her grave I took particular notice of her personal appearance. That she had been murdered I could not doubt, and perhaps some day, even after all these years, the crime may come to light."

" But what became of the ship ? " asked the mate of the *Indiana*.

" Out of sight by eight o'clock in the morning.

As soon as I saw what was the matter with the woman I knew that we need not expect to see any one from the ship back again. The boats towed her, I suppose, all night, and just before daylight a breeze sprang up, which soon took her away from the land."

"I wonder what the true story of that woman's death was?" said Packenham, thoughtfully, as he looked towards the place where she was buried.

"Heaven only knows," answered the old trader. "Whether it was a mutiny, and her husband was murdered, or whether the officer who came ashore with her was the captain himself and her husband as well, I cannot tell. My own idea is that there was a mutiny, and that she had been shot, perhaps accidentally, in the struggle, and that knowing that she might possibly recover, the mutineers had decided to send her ashore, rather than have to keep her a prisoner on board, and then perhaps kill her to prevent the discovery of their crime. Any way, I have since learnt that there never was a ship named the *Inca Prince.* I've told the story to every shipmaster I've met since that night, and it was written about a good deal in the English and American newspapers. Then the affair was forgotten, and, like many another such thing, the secret may never come out."

.   .   .   .   .

Presently, following the old man, Denison and Packenham went with him in the bright moonlight, and looking over the low white wall of the little cemetery, saw the unknown woman's grave. A faint breath of air swayed the pendulous leaves of the surrounding coco-palms which for a moment rustled softly together, and then drooped into the silence of the night.

THE OBSTINACY OF MRS. TATTON

The Obstinacy of Mrs. Tatton

THE *Indiana* of Sydney, Tom de Wolf's trading brig, lay at anchor off the native town of Niafu, one of the Friendly Group, south from Samoa, when Tatton came on board. He was a short, thick-set, dark-faced man, slow of speech but quick with his hand, and master of the *Lunalilo*, a small trading ketch of a hundred tons or so. Denison had made his acquaintance at Wallis Island about a year previously, and because he found that Tatton hated the intrusion of "the Dutchmen," *i.e.*, the Germans, into the South Seas as much as he did himself, he made friends with him, and they drank and smoked together whenever the two ships happened to meet. And on the same day that the *Indiana* ran into Vavau from Fiji the *Lunalilo* hove in sight from the northward, towed into Niafu Harbour by her boats, for the trade wind had died away at sunset. As Tatton's vessel passed the *Indiana* her skipper, who was standing aft, waved his hand to Denison and called out to him and the captain of the brig to come on board after supper.

An hour later, when their supper was over and Denison and the captain of the brig were about getting ready to go aboard the schooner, the steward came below.

" Here's Captain Tatton, gentlemen."

They opened their cabin doors and shook hands with him. The captain of the *Indiana*, a rough, hard-shell old Connecticut Yankee with a heavy hand and a soft heart, looked at Tatton for a moment, and then asked :—

" What in thunder is the matter with yew, Tatton ? Hev yew got yaller fever or the cholery morbus aboard thet old hooker ef yours ? Any one been and run away with your little missus, or what ? "

Tatton attempted to smile at old Barron's joke, but failed. He lifted the glass of liquor that the steward had poured out for him to his lips, then set it down again on the table with shaking hand.

" No one has run away with poor Luisa, Barron, but "—he turned and stared up at the skylight, and then bent his head upon his hand—" but she's leaving me all the same. The poor girl is dying, Barron. I was bound to the eastward when I left Samoa, but came in here thinking that I might find that Yankee man-of-war, the *Narrangansett*, here. She left Samoa a couple of days after me and passed me the night before last, steaming very fast. Luisa was very, very bad then, and so I burnt the one blue light I had on the schooner, and my crew kept firing their rifles every few minutes ; but she was too far off, I suppose, to see us, or was in too much of a hurry to bother " ; and the sturdy, bronze-faced seaman passed his hand wearily over his face.

In an instant Barron, the grizzled old veteran of thirty years' hardship and adventure in the two Pacifics, reached out his hand to Tatton.

" That's bad news. Is there anything we can do for

you, Tatton? I guess you reckoned on the *Narran-gansett's* doctor? Is your wife very bad? Denison here is a bit of a doctor. Perhaps he can help you. Is she very bad?"

Tatton nodded. "Dying. I can see that. I think she knows it too, poor girl. Still, what can I do? I wonder if the Yankee cruiser has gone on to Tongatabu" (about a hundred miles further south-ward). "If I thought so I would heave up again and try and get there in time."

"Wait till to-morrow, Tatton," said the captain of the brig, "the *Narrangansett* will most likely turn up by then. She's bound to come in here first before going on to Tongatabu—there's coal waiting for her here, I know."

Tatton cheered up a bit at this; then, after drink-ing his grog, asked Denison to go back to the *Lunalilo* with him. "She'd like to see you, I think, Denison," he said, in a hesitating sort of way. "Anyway you knew her and her family, didn't you?"

"I'll come with pleasure"; and Denison, picking up his cap, was following Tatton on deck when old Barron called him back.

"Got any champagne left in the trade room, Denison?"

"About half a dozen."

"Well, look here now, I reckon champagne is jest about the right thing to take. I don't know what's wrong with the gal, but whatever it is yew kin rely that champagne is good fur it. Yew take the lot, and charge it tew me."

When the steward handed Denison five bottles of

champagne, tied up in a basket, the supercargo remembered that only a year or so before, when the *Indiana* and *Lunalilo* were together at Futuna Island, Tatton, Barron, and himself had had an angry dispute over a matter of business, and that Tatton, with blazing eyes, had told the grizzled old skipper of the brig that he was " too blarsted mean to live, like all Down-East Yanks."

.   .   .   .   .

Tatton's ketch lay closer in to the shore than the brig, but the distance between them was short. As the native crew sent the boat over the stilled, starlit water Denison looked at Tatton, who kept silent. He could see that, rude and rough as was the man's nature, he was suffering. Only a few months before their first meeting at Wallis Island, Tatton had married the youngest daughter of an old trader living on one of the Navigators Islands—a delicate-looking, child-like creature, who, were she in civilisation, would hardly have left the nursery. And since then Tatton, the hard-drinking, quarrelsome skipper whose chief argument in any dispute was his fist—and he had many arguments on a variety of subjects—had undergone a wonderful change and acquired an extraordinary renown ; in brief, he became that rare fish in Polynesian seas, a moral trading captain.

.   .   .   .   .

Luisa, born of a Manhikian mother by a white father, was lying on a bed of soft mats spread on the cabin floor. By her side was a native sailor fanning her, for the cabin was close and stuffy. Seated on the transoms a few feet further off was another seaman, a big, sallow-faced native of Manhiki. He was nursing a baby. He looked stolidly at Denison and Tatton for a moment, then bent his face over that of the sleeping child.

"She is asleep," said the man beside her in a whisper. Tatton silently motioned Denison to a seat, and then spoke in a whisper.

" Born just as we passed Beveridge Reef four days ago," and he pointed over to where the big Manhiki man sat solemnly swaying the infant to and fro. " I brought her away from Aitutake because she wanted to get back to Samoa to her mother and her people. So I closed up the station at Aitutake and brought her aboard. Such rotten luck you never saw. Head winds and calms, calms and head winds, for nearly a month ; and then just off Beveridge——"

Here the girl moved and awoke.

"Lu," said Tatton, bending over her, "here is an old friend of your father's."

The girl looked at Denison, then put out her slender hand and said in her mother's tongue, in a voice scarce above a whisper, "Ah, yes, I remember you. Have you forgotten the day when you and my father and brothers went to Apia to the *fa'atau tui* (auction) and Alvord, the big American who rapped on the table with a hammer, gave me a dressed-up doll ? "— and she smiled faintly.

.   .   .   .   .

That was nearly eight years ago. How it all came back to him ! Fat, jolly old Alvord, selling a miscellaneous lot of goods in an Apian resident's house, and the strange, motley crowd that surrounded him ; among them this girl's father, his sons and Denison himself. And he remembered, too, a little girl of about ten coming in at the door, dressed in European style and smiling at him ; and old Ned, her father, bringing her over to him and telling him it was his little girl, "runned down from the Sisters where she was a-schoolin' to see her brothers "; then when the *fa'atau tui* was over how the old dried-up trader, his stalwart sons, the little girl and he, all walked up to the French Mission and gave the runaway back to the good Sisters. And here she was now, a mother, and dying.

The big sailor came over beside her and squatted cross-legged on the mats. Tatton placed his arm around her and raised her up to look at the hideous little bundle of mortality in his arms.

"What an ugly little *aitu* (devil) it is ! " she said to Tatton in Samoan, as the Manihiki man placed it on the mat within touch.

Tatton turned to Denison with something like a smile. "By God, she's pulling herself together again ! If that cruiser would only show up I'd give the ship and cargo." Then he opened the wine and gave her a glass.

Denison stayed another hour or so, and then left them, bearing in his mind the picture of the slight figure of the girl, who had again fallen asleep under the effects of the wine, lying motionless on the couch of mats ; the big man-nurse, and Puniola, the Savage Island sailor, softly waving his fan over the wan features ; and Tatton, with his sun-browned face, resting on his hand, gazing intently down upon the sleeper.

.   .   .   .   .

The morning mists had just begun to shift from the

hills of Niafu when Barron and his supercargo saw the long, black hull of the *Narrangansett* steaming up the harbour. She was one of the famed "ninety-day ships," and made a brave show as she cut aside the calm waters and brought up a couple of hundred yards astern of the *Indiana.* Her anchor had barely touched the ground when they saw Tatton's boat pull alongside, and in another five minutes leave again with another man seated beside Tatton, and pull hard for the *Lunalilo.*

"Waal, now, look at that," said the Grizzled One to Denison, as they sat sipping their coffee on the skylight; "there's a man that, for the past ten years, has been up tew all kinds of red-hot cussedness, plain *and* decorated, nigger-catchin', women-buyin', and sich like Island fixin's ; and, as sure as I ain't one of the saved, but he's jest a turned man, all over that slip of a yaller girl. Land alive ! But he must think a lot of her—to hev the front tew pull the doctor outer of his bunk before coffee in the morning ! "

. . . . .

They had finished their coffee and were watching the movements of those on board the steamer when the *Lunalilo's* boat again left her side and pulled over to the brig, with only two men in her. They bumped up alongside, and one jumped on deck and gave Denison a note from Tatton.

"Come on board as quick as you can. Bring Allan with you."

Allan was the boatswain, a Manaiki half-caste. Wondering what was wrong, Denison called him and got in the boat and went aboard. The moment they gained the deck Tatton met them looking pale and excited. The doctor of the man-of-war was sitting on deck, smoking a cigar.

" How is she ? " he asked Tatton.

" Bad, my lad ; and the doctor says that unless he can attend to her at once she cannot possibly live more than a few days."

" Well," Denison asked wonderingly, " why doesn't he ? "

" Because she won't let him. Says she'd rather die ten times over first. You know what a curious sort of modesty native women have about *some* things. Well, as soon as ever the doctor came on board—of course I'd told him as far as my knowledge went what was wrong—I told her he would soon put her right. She sat up and commenced to cry, and said she wouldn't have him ; and the moment I went on deck to call the doctor down that big Manihiki buck lifted her up and carried her into my cabin, put the youngster in with her, and then locked the door. Now, he's standing guard outside. The fool says he'll kill any one that tries to open it. You see he's a kind of a far-away cousin of the family on the mother's side. That's why I asked you to bring Allan. Perhaps he can talk Rivi over into——"

Allan shook his head. " It's no use, Captain Tatton," he said in English. " If you like I'll go down and scruff Rivi and sling him on deck ; but I'll take his place if your wife wants me to keep out the doctor."

" Curse you for a wooden-headed kanaka ! " said Tatton. " Don't I tell you she's got to die if she won't see the doctor ? "

" Look here, Captain Tatton," said the big half-caste again, "you ought to known enough of native ways by this time to know that no *man* can aid your wife. Take her ashore here to some of the old Tongan women and see what they can do for her. She'd be disgraced for life if you force a doctor on her, and she knows it."

.   .   .   .   .

Poor Tatton was half mad. With Denison he went to the doctor and explained. He was a good-natured man and listened quietly.

"I will wait here another hour—two hours," he said, "if you think she will change her mind. If she won't I think you can't do better than take this man's advice," pointing to Allan, "and let her be attended by some native women. They *may* save her life, but I doubt it. It's a surgical case."

Then he sat down again and went on smoking.

.   .   .   .   .

Allan went down below, and his huge country-man and he talked. Then Allan called to the white men to come down, except the doctor, and the big man opened the door and let them in. Luisa was lying in Tatton's bunk, clasping his hideous little effigy to her bosom.

"Lu," said Tatton, placing her hand on his arm, and speaking in English, "do you understand that if you will not let the American *fò'mai* attend to you that you will die? Is it not so?" turning to Allan and Denison.

The girl's big frightened eyes sought theirs to read the answer, and then slowly closed. She lay quiet a moment or so while the tears welled out and coursed down her cheeks.

"*E pule le Atua*," she said at last. ("It is God's will if I die.")

"Mrs. Tatton," said Denison, "don't you want to see your brothers and sisters again ? Why are you ashamed ? In *papalagi* (the white man's land), when a child is born and a woman is sick to death, it is the custom of all women to have with them a *fo'mai* to save them from death."

She shook her head. "I know. Tatton hath told me that many times. But what woman but a shameless one would suffer such a thing ?"

.   .   .   .   .

The doctor's step sounded overhead. Rivi, the "far-away cousin," with a dangerous look in his eye, shoved past the white men and stood at the head of the bunk. Allan, speaking in Manhikian to him, said, "Have no fear," and he went out again. Poor devil, a perfect slave to Tatton at any other time, he was ready to lay his life down in defence of this ever-so-distant cousin before she should be "made ashamed."

Tatton and Denison went on deck again, defeated. The doctor said he would send some medicine—all he could do. As he stood in the gangway lighting another cigar he said, in answer to Tatton : "Oh, yes ; give her a glass of champagne now and then ; it'll keep her alive a little longer, and do no harm."

Denison went away with the doctor, leaving Allan to help Tatton take his wife ashore to the native women doctors of Niafu village.

.   .   .   .   .

Two days afterwards Luisa died. After the burial Tatton went off to the *Narrangansett*, and the doctor improvised a cunningly contrived feeding bottle with a thick rubber tube for the little Tatton, and gave him a couple of dozen tins of condensed milk " to tucker the kid," as Tatton expressed it, " till he could leave it with its mother's folks."

And just as the shrill whistles of the boatswain's mates piped hands to supper on the war-ship, the *Lunalilo* hove up anchor, and with Tatton at the wheel, payed off before the first puffs of the land-breeze. Seated between the up-ended flaps of the skylight was the big, sallow-faced native sailor with Luisa's legacy in his lap.

DR. LUDWIG SCHWALBE, SOUTH SEA SAVANT

Dr. Ludwig Schwalbe, South Sea Savant

THE *Palestine*, of Sydney, island trading brig, was beating northward along the eastern shore of New Ireland, or as the great island is now called by its German possessors, Neu Mecklenburg, when, going about in a stiff squall, the jib-sheet block carried away and disorganised the internal economy of Thomas Rogers, able seaman, to such an extent that his sorrowing shipmates thought him like to die. Later on, however, Denison, the supercargo—who, by virtue of having amputated a sailor-man's leg in Samoa, was held by the crew of the *Palestine* and the general run of island traders to be a mighty smart doctor —made a careful examination of the damaged seaman, said that only three ribs were broken, and that if Rogers only kept up his normal appetite he would get better.

But that evening it fell a dead calm, and a heavy mountainous swell came in from the eastward, and the *Palestine* "nearly rolled her poor old soul out," as Packenham, the skipper, expressed it. And for three days never a breath of air rippled the hot, steamy

surface of the ocean, and Rogers, A.B., took a bad
turn and couldn't eat.

"We'll have to put him ashore somewhere, Packenham," said the supercargo; "he'll die if we keep
him on board, especially if this calm keeps up."

"Can't put him ashore anywhere about here.
There's no white man living anywhere on the east
coast of New Ireland, and the niggers are a bad lot. If
we were on the west side we could soon run down to
Mioko, on the Duke of York Island, and leave him
there with the missionaries. If we get a breeze we
can get there in a day or so."

But luck was against them, for although a faint
breeze did spring up in the middle watch, it came
from the south-east—dead ahead as far as Duke of
York Island was concerned; and poor Rogers was
getting worse.

Denison was lying propped up against the after-
flap of the skylight smoking his pipe, and looking
at the misty outlines of the mountainous shore that lay
ten miles away on the port hand, when he heard
the captain's cheery voice :

"Come here, Den, as quick as you like." And
then, "Tell Ransom to square away for that camel-
backed island right abeam of us."

"Here we are! Just the very thing," said the
skipper, as soon as Denison entered the cabin, pointing
to the chart spread out on the table. "See? Gerrit
Deny's Island, only twenty miles to leeward. There's
a German doctor living there. I wonder I never
thought of him before. That's our dart. We can
put Rogers ashore there and pick him up when we
come back from the Carolines."

" A German doctor ! What the deuce is he doing on Gerrit Deny's ? No trading ships go there. There's no copra there, no pearl-shell—nothing but a pack of woolly-haired Papuan niggers who are always fighting, and ready to eat a man without salt. We couldn't leave Rogers there ! "

" That's all right, Den, don't you worry," said Packenham, serenely. " I know all about Gerrit Deny's—Nebarra the niggers call it, and I've heard of this Dutch doctor pretty often. He's a bug-hunter —catches insects and things, and wears specs. He'll look after Rogers right enough."

" All right," said Denison, dubiously ; " I suppose he'll stand a better chance there than by staying aboard."

.   .   .   .   .

When daylight came the *Palestine* brought-to under a high, wooded bluff on the lee-side of the island, and dropped her anchor, and the mate got ready to take Rogers ashore in the whaleboat. The island was a wild but picturesque-looking spot, rugged and uneven in its outlines, but clad in a dense mass of verdant forest, stretching from the narrow strip of palm-covered littoral that fringed its snow-white beach, away up to the very summits of its mist-enwrapped mountains, three thousand feet above. Just abreast of the *Palestine* the thickly-clustering grey-thatched huts of a native village showed their saddle-backed gables from out a dense grove of banana trees, and five minutes after the brig's anchor had plunged to its coral bed, a swarm of black-skinned, woolly-haired savages rushed to and fro about the beach launching their canoes, with that silent activity peculiar to some of the Melanesian tribes. Inland, some distance from the grey-thatched houses, a mountain torrent showed here and there a silver line amid the green. Farther away to the northern point, and apart from the village, stood a large house enclosed by a high stockade of coconut logs. This was the white man's dwelling, and soon the people on the brig saw the figure of a man dressed in European clothes issue from the door, walk out to a tall flag-pole that stood in the centre of the great stockade, and bend on a flag to the halliards ; then presently the banner of Germany was run aloft.

"That's him," said Packenham, who was looking through his glasses, "and, hallo, easy with that boat. I think he's coming off to us. I can see some natives hauling his own boat down to the beach. That's bully. We can send Rogers ashore with him straight away and then clear out."

Ten minutes afterward the "bug-hunter," as Packenham called him, came on board, and shook hands with them. He was not at all a professional-looking man. First of all, he wore no boots, and his pants and jumper of coarse dungaree were exceedingly and marvellously ill-fitting and dirty. A battered Panama hat of great age flopped about and almost concealed his red-bearded face, in a disheartened sort of manner, as if trying to apologise for the rest of his apparel ; the thin gold-rimmed spectacles he wore made a curious and protestingly civilised contrast to his bare and dirty feet. His manner, however, was that of a man perfectly at ease with himself, and his clear, steely blue eyes, showed courage and determination.

He listened with much gravity to the tale of the disaster that had befallen the ribs of Rogers, A.B.; but objected in a thick, woolly kind of voice to the task of undertaking to cure him on shore. He had not the time, he said. But he would see what he could do there and then.

Then the captain and the supercargo sought by much hospitality to make him change his mind, and said it would be a hard thing for poor Rogers to die on board, when his life could be so easily saved. And he had a mother and nine young brothers and sisters to keep. (This was a harmless but kindly-meant fiction.)

The cold blue eyes looked at them searchingly for a few moments—" Vell, I vill dry vat I gan do. But if he dies you must nod blame me mit. I vas vonce a dogtor ; but I haf nod bractised vor a long dimes now. I vas ein naduraliz now."

Then whilst Denison got ready a few acceptable gifts from his trade-room, such as a couple of cases of beer, and some tinned meats to put in the boat, the German conversed pleasantly with the skipper. He had been, so he told Packenham, one of the medical staff of the ill-fated *Nouvelle France* expedition, organised by the Marquis de Ray to colonise the island of New Ireland. The disastrous collapse of that venture under the combined influences of too much drunken hilarity and jungle fever, however, and the dispersal of the survivors, decided him to remain in the islands, and follow his entomological and ethnographical pursuits, to which, he added, he was now entirely devoted.

"Does it pay you, doctor?" asked Packenham, with some interest.

He shrugged his shoulders—"Vell, id vill bay me by und by—ven I ged mine moneys from dose zientific zocieties in Germany und oder Gontinental goundries. I haf got me no assistant, und derefore id dakes me a long dimes mine specimens to brebare."

"What is your particular work just now, doctor?" said the captain, filling his guest's glass again.

"At bresend I am studying der habids of der gommon green durdles."

"Green turtle? Oh, indeed."

"Yes; der is mooch zientific droubles mid green durdles. A grade many beobles say dot dose green durdles are like zeals—dot they fights und quarrels mit one anoder in der incubading season—dot is dose male durdles. Und dere is a grade English naturalizd who haf wrote somedings aboud having seen two male durdles fight mit each oder viles der female durdle stood by drembling in her shell mit fear. Und I vant do prove dot dot man is ein dam fool. Der male green durdle never fights vor der bossession of der female—So! Dey haf nod god der amatory insdincks of der zeal, vich leads der male zeals to engage in ploody combats vor de bossession of der female zeal. I haf mineself seen ein female zeal lying down on a rock mit, und vatching der males shoost fighting vor her undil der veakest one dropped dead; und den off she vent mid der besd man. Ach! id is only anoder examples of brude sdrength condending for der bossession of female beaudy."

"Perfectly true, Dr. Schwalbe. I have very often seen the fierce combats of which you speak," said Packenham, and then, being much interested, he said he should like to go ashore and see the doctor's collection ; but the German, with a quick glance at him through his spectacles, said—

"Blease do not drouble. I moosd now ged on shore, so blease put dot zailormans in my boat, und I vill dry and gure him."

A few minutes afterward the "bug-hunter" and student of the moral habits of green turtle had gone ashore, taking Rogers, A.B., with him ; and the *Palestine* was heeling over to the now freshening trade wind as she stretched away northward to the Carolines.

.   .   .   .   .

The German doctor was very kind to Rogers in a quiet, solemn kind of a way. The natives, too, seemed pleased to have another white man among them, and crowded about the German's door when he and his patient (who was carried up from the boat) entered the house. But after a while they were sent away, and Tom Rogers had a chance to study his surroundings and his host, and the interior of the house, which presented a curious appearance.

Instead of boxes of trade goods, such as gin, axes, muskets, powder, and tobacco, taking up most of the space, there were a number of casks of various sizes ranged in a line, and at one end of the room a long table, on which lay surgical instruments, bottles of chemicals, cotton-wool, and other articles. On a shelf above were a number of large bottles, bearing the inscription, "Pyroligneous Acid. Burroughs, Wellcome & Co."

"What the deuce can he want all that bottled smoke for, I wonder?" said Rogers to himself, who knew that many traders in the Solomon Islands used pyroligneous acid for curing pork. "Perhaps," he thought, "he's curing bacon; but what the devil does he do with it? He can't eat it all himself."

At the back of the big room was a smaller sleeping apartment, and when evening came the young seaman was carried there by his host's servants. Then the door was shut, and Rogers heard the clink of bottles and sound of water splashing long into the night.

At one end of the spacious area enclosed within the stockade, and almost adjoining the doctor's dwelling-house, was a long, rambling, hog-backed native house, quite fifty feet in length, and bearing a great resemblance to the big canoe houses which Rogers had seen in the Gilbert Islands. This house, he learned later on, contained some of the most interesting of the doctor's ethnological and ethnographical specimens.

Although, as he had told Packenham, he had no assistant, he had living with him three or four Manilla-men helpers, short built, taciturn fellows, who lived in a house of their own within the stockade, and never associated with the natives of the island. These men, so the *savant* told Rogers, had been sent to him from the East Indies by a brother ethnologist, but their want of intelligence rendered them, he said, quite useless, except in the mere matter of collecting specimens.

For some days Rogers remained in bed, carefully waited upon by his spectacled host, who said he would soon recover.

"Und den," he said, "ven you are quide sdrong again mit, you shall help me in mine business."

Rogers was grateful, and said he would do so

gladly, and as the days went by he became really
anxious to show his gratitude. During conversation
with the German he had learnt that the natives of
Gerrit Deny's were then engaged in a sanguinary
civil war, and that almost every day several men were
killed and decapitated.

So far the seaman had visited neither the doctor's
" vorkshop "—the business-like apartment which ad-
joined the sleeping-rooms—nor the big outhouse, but
in another week or so he had so far recovered that he
was able to leave his bed and walk about. On the
evening of the first day after this he sat down to
supper with his host, who conversed very affably
with him, and told him that though at first he was
very much averse to having another white man on
the island, perhaps it was best after all. It was very
lonely, he said, and he often wanted some one to talk
to when business was dull. And perhaps, he added,
Rogers would be glad of a little money which he
would give him for his assistance.

Amongst other things Rogers learnt that his host
had been exceedingly exasperated by a native teacher
from New Britain landing on the island some twelve
months previously. The man himself, he said, was
nothing but an ignorant savage, and his wife, who
was a native of Gerrit Deny's Island, no better.
The white missionaries at New Britain had, it
appeared, eagerly seized the opportunity of sending to
the island a teacher whose wife could converse with
the people in her own tongue.

" But," said Rogers, " I should think you would be
rather glad of at least having two people on the island
who call themselves Christians. I know that the

20

missionaries have done a lot of good on New Britain. I lived there and know it."

The doctor assented to that ; but said there was no use in sending a teacher to Gerrit Deny's ; then he added—

" Und dis fellow vas alvays inderfering mit mine business."

This interference Rogers subsequently learned was that the native teacher had been telling the islanders that they should not sell the doctor such simple objects of interest as skulls. But as he had not yet made one single convert, no one took any heed of him, and, indeed, his wife, whose conversion from heathenism was by no means solid, had at once reverted to the customs of her people as soon as she returned to them, and casting aside the straw hat, blue blouse, and red petticoat of Christianity, promptly bartered them to an admiring relative for a stick of the doctor's tobacco, a liking for which was her ruling passion, and which could only be gratified by selling vegetables, fruit, or specimens to the white man.

One morning as Rogers was strolling about the grassy sward inside the stockade he heard some one call out " Good morning " to him, and looking up he saw a native, partly clad in European costume, smiling and beckoning to him from the other side. Walking over, Rogers was at once proffered a brown hand, which the owner thrust through a chink in the coconut posts.

" Good morning," said Rogers. " Who are you ? "

" Me missionary. What for you no come see me my house ? What for you stop here with German man ? He bad man ; yes, very bad man."

"Why?" asked Rogers, with a good-natured laugh.

"Oh, yes," the native repeated with emphatic earnestness, " he no good. You come my house some day, then I tell you——" and then catching sight of the doctor coming over to Rogers he took to his heels and disappeared in the surrounding coconut grove.

The doctor seemed annoyed when Rogers told him who had been talking to him, and again said that the teacher was a meddlesome fellow, and then, with a sly twinkle of fun in his eyes, added—

"Look over dere, mein friend, dot lady standing mit her back against der coconut tree is der vife of der kanaka glergyman on Gerrit Deny's Island. She haf come to zell me yams and preadfruits for tobacco. Ach! she is a grade gustomer of mine, is dot voman."

Rogers looked with some interest at the lady—a huge, half-nude, woolly-headed creature, with lips reddened by chewing betel-nut and a curved piece of human bone thrust through the cartilage of her wide, flat nose.

Taking no notice of the strange white man, she addressed herself volubly to the doctor, who seemed to understand her perfectly, and then giving her a stick of tobacco for the vegetables that lay at her feet, he told her to go, and then with Rogers went inside to take a cup of coffee.

Directly in front of the doctor's house, but on the opposite side of the bay, was a small village, and as the two men sat smoking after drinking their coffee, Rogers noticed a canoe crossing and pointed it out to his host, who at once got his glasses and took a long look at the approaching craft. Then he turned to his companion with a pleased expression, and said that the

" glergyman's vife," as he persistently called the horror
he had shown Rogers, had not lied to him after all.
She had, he said, told him that a party of her relatives,
living across the bay, were that day bringing him over
a "specimen," for which he had previously treated
with them but failed to obtain, owing to the outbreak
of hostilities and the diverse claims of various members
of the family who owned the specimen in question.

Half an hour later the canoe drew up on the beach,
and whilst two of the crew carried the "specimen,"
which, if not heavy, was bulky, up to the doctor's
house, the remainder sat in the canoe, took whiffs
from the huge bamboo pipe, which was common
property, and stared at the new white man standing
beside Dr. Schwalbe.

Presently the doctor left Rogers to meet the natives
who carried the burden, which in a few minutes more
was carefully brought into the house, and the seaman
watched the process of untying the bundle with
interest—then he drew back in horror as a grinning
mummy was revealed with its knees drawn nearly up
to its chin and kept in position there by a thin piece
of coir cinnet.

Schwalbe bent down and examined the thing with
keen interest, and then, apparently satisfied with his
inspection, began to bargain with the specimen's
father, who sat close beside it. He was a pleasant-
looking old fellow, with a merry twinkle in his eye,
but was determined to sell his family relic at a good
figure.

A price, however, was soon agreed upon, and with
a smiling face the vendor took his departure, and the
doctor, lifting his prize carefully in his arms, took it

over to his Golgotha—the big house at the other end of the stockade.

That afternoon the *savant* was fairly brimming over with good spirits. A cheerful, child-like simplicity underlay his outwardly grave bearing, and Rogers now began to take a liking to him. In the evening he played dominoes with his guest, and spoke hopefully of returning to Europe with his collection, instead of sending it on in advance. Smoking a long, highly-ornamented pipe the while, he gave Rogers many interesting particulars of his experiences on the island. His collection of skulls, he thought, was about the best ever secured in Oceania, but he deplored the fact of his having had to reject two out of every four offered to him, the crude and inartistic manner in which they had been damaged by heavy iron-wood clubs when their original owners were in the flesh seriously depreciating their value, if not rendering them utterly useless as specimens.

Long before breakfast on the following morning the spectacled scientist was bustling about the house, and as soon as Rogers appeared he greeted him briskly, and asked him to come with him to his Golgotha—a party of his " gustomers " were awaiting him.

As they drew near the big house Rogers saw that the party consisted of but two persons—a man and a woman. Arranged in a row before them were five skulls. Though quite black-skinned and woolly-haired, like most Papuan-blooded people, both man and woman seemed a quiet, gentle-voiced pair, and were, the doctor said, a betrothed couple. They smiled pleasantly at him as he examined their wares, and sat patiently awaiting him to make an offer.

The man, whose mop of fuzzy hair could never be approached by the Paderewski heads of this world, let his eyes wander alternately from the doctor to the object of his affections sitting beside him. To him the price he obtained meant much, for the father of his *fiancée* was a hard-hearted old fellow, who insisted upon one hundred sticks of tobacco over and above the usual dowry of ten hogs. The woman, too, watched the scientist with timid, anxious eyes. Two of the skulls belonged to defunct female members of her family; of the other three, two had belonged to men who had fallen to her lover's spear a year before, and the third was that of a despised nephew.

At last the scientist made a bargain for the two biggest of the relics for eighty sticks of tobacco and two butcher knives; and with joy irradiating their dusky faces the lovers followed him to his house and received payment. And Rogers, as he watched them walk smiling away, carrying the rejected relics with him, saw the woman give the man a sly hug as they went through the gate—the happy day for her was not far off now.

A few evenings later Rogers, who was tired of idleness, asked his host to give him something to do. They were sitting playing dominoes at the time.

"Very well," he answered, "but you haf berhaps nodiced," and he looked at the young man through his gold-rimmed spectacles, "dot I alvays keeps der door of mine vork-room glosed. Dot vas pecause I did not vant you to zee me at mine business undil you vas sdrong. Und dere is nod a goot smell from dose gemmicals. But to-morrow you shall zee me at my vork, und if you vill help me I vill be glad mit. Bud you moost nod dell any beobles vat my businees is. So ? "

Rogers promised he would not.

At breakfast next morning he was disturbed by loud, triumphant shouts outside. It was not the first time that he had heard similar outcries, and he now asked his friend, who was placidly drinking his coffee, what was the cause.

" Dot is some gustomer," he replied, briefly ; " ven ve haf finished preakfast you shall zee, und den you und me vill do some vork at mine business."

But before the meal was over, the clamour became so great that Rogers followed his host to the door, which the latter threw open, revealing a number of natives who were gathered outside.

Some two or three of these now entered, and the sailor saw that one of them carried a gore-stained basket of coconut leaf. This his German friend opened, and took out a freshly-severed human head !

Grasping it by the reddish-brown woolly hair, the investigator of turtles' morality took it to the door to obtain a better light, and examined the thing carefully. His scrutiny seemed to be satisfactory, for, placing it in a large enamelled dish on the long table, he opened a trade-box and gave the vendor some tobacco, powder, musket-balls, and fish-hooks.

" What in God's name are you going to do with it ? " asked Rogers, in horror-stricken tones.

The German looked at him in placid surprise without answering ; then he abruptly told the natives to go away.

" Come back to our preakfast," he said, motioning to Rogers to go first ; " ven ve haf finished den I vill

show you vat I do mit dis thing—dot is pard of my
business here in Gerrit Deny's Island."

And then, to the young man's horror and disgust,
he learned that the man he had looked upon as a mere
skull collector, also bought and cured human heads.
That was one of the departments of his business.

"Vy," he said quietly, "vot harm is there? Dese
black beobles do kill each oder and eat de podies of
dose who are slain. I buy der heads—dot is if der
skulls are not broken mit bullets or clubs. Und I
vork very hart to make dose heads look nice and goot,
und I sell dem to the museums in France und Russia,
und Englandt und Germany. I dell you, my friendt,
it is a goot business. Ach! you may spit on der
groundt as mooch as you like, my friendt, but I dell
you dot is so. Und I dell you some more—it vas at
von dime a grade business in New Zealandt, und a
goot many of your English officer beobles make blenty
of money buying dose schmoked Maori heads und
selling dem to der Gontinental scientists. But by and
by der British Governments put it down, and now der
business in Maori heads is finished."

"I'd hang every one connected——" began Rogers,
when the blue-eyed German stopped him.

"So! but der heads are *dead!* Und dey are vorth
money. Blenty of beoble vant to study such dings as
dese. Und dese heads from Gerrit Deny's Island are
prim full of inderest to *savants,* for they presend a
remarkable illusdradion of the arporeal descend of man.
Und I don'd care a tam apout durdles—dot vos a lie I
dold to your captain; durdles haf no inderesd vor me.
Now, better you trink your coffee und come und see
my gollection, before some more gustomers gome in."

Feeling as if he had eaten too much breakfast, Rogers followed his host back to the big room ; and then lifting off the head of one of the casks, the German showed him eight or ten of the nightmares in a pickle of alum and saltpetre.

"Dot is der first brocess," he explained, briefly.

In the next cask—the second process—were others, and more in the third. These latter were all ready to be put into the "smoke-box," a contrivance so designed that after being thoroughly dried by the smoke of a wood fire they were ready for a final bath in pyroligneous acid. That was the last process.

"Come und zee mein schmoke-box."

Rogers followed him to the corner of the stockade where the smoke-box was erected. A withered old Manilla man, with a face like an anthropoid ape, was attending to the fire, and moved away to let him look inside. One look was enough—a dozen or so of the horrors hung suspended from the cross-beams, and seemed to grin at him through the faint blue smoke, their nostrils distended with pieces of stick and eyelids sewn together over the cotton-wool-stuffed sockets.

.   .   .   .   .

When the *Palestine* arrived six weeks later, Rogers bade his host a hurried but fervent goodbye, and said he'd like to see him give up such a beastly business.

"Ach ! I cannot help mineselfs. I musd stay here mit my gollection for some dimes yet. But I am quide satisfied—my gollection is a goot one. My friendt, if you could at somedime see dose heads in Europe you vill see that Ludwig Schwalbe gan preserve heads more better den dose Maoris did. Ven dey are exhibited in a glass case mit, dey vill look mosd beautiful."

A year or so afterwards Denison read in a colonial paper that the distinguished German naturalist, Dr. Ludwig Schwalbe, had left the Bismarck Islands for Singapore in a small schooner, on May 2nd, 18—. About ten days later she was found floating, bottom upward, off the Admiralty Group, near New Guinea. "The unfortunate gentleman had with him an interesting and valuable ethnographical collection, the labour of ten years."

THE TREASURE OF DON BRUNO

The Treasure of Don Bruno

MANY hundreds of tales have been written about the discovery of buried treasure, and the wise people of to-day laugh and shake their heads when some boy, pondering over an exciting treasure story in which doubloons, and pieces of eight, and pirates, and buccaneers inflame his imagination, asks some one " if any part of it at all is true." Yet, although ninety-nine out of a hundred of such tales may be, and probably are, the purest fiction, treasure *has* been found, not only in the haunts of the old-time pirates of the Caribbean Sea and the Spanish Main, but in both the North and South Pacific Oceans ; and the story of the finding of the treasure of Bruno do Bustamente on an island in the North Pacific is true—true in every detail as here narrated, save that the name of one of those who found it has been changed. He was an Englishman, and less than thirty years ago was well known in the Southern Colonies as the chief officer of a steamer trading between Sydney, Hobart, and Melbourne. At that time he was a young man of twenty-six.

. . . . .

In those days there was a line of mail steamers running between Sydney and Panama. They were rivalled in size and speed only by the Peninsula and Oriental Company's steamers, and were named the *Rakaia, Mataura, Ruahine,* and *Kaikoura.* To be appointed to one of these liners was considered a distinction, and therefore young Forrest—for so I will call him—naturally felt elated when he was offered the berth of first officer on one of the new liners. He therefore was not long in making up his mind; and bidding goodbye to the captain and officers of the *City of Hobart,* he went on board the mail steamer, and immediately tackled the duties of his new position.

.   .   .   .   .

Two months had elapsed, and the steamer was in Panama Harbour coaling for the return trip to Sydney, when Forrest was sent for by the agent on some business that required his presence at the office. A number of passengers for the Sydney steamer had just arrived by train from Aspinall, or Colon, as the Americans call it, on the Atlantic side of the isthmus, and the agent's offices were thronged.

Forrest was anxious to return as quickly as possible, and, sending in his name by a clerk, waited for five minutes or so with a fair amount of patience. After taking in his name to the agent, the clerk had returned and said that Mr. Macpherson would see Mr. Forrest presently. At the end of ten minutes Forrest, pacing angrily to and fro on the pavement outside, strode in again, and in sharp tones asked the clerk to tell Mr. Macpherson that he could not possibly remain another five minutes.

The clerk disappeared into the inner office, and Mr. Macpherson himself came out.

Now this Macpherson was a man to whom Forrest had an intense dislike. He had been sent out from England to take charge of the Panama office, and during the passage over from Sydney his offensive and haughty manner to his fellow-passengers and the ship's officers had caused him to be heartily detested. He was a measly-looking, insignificant little creature, with very weak eyes, but a hideously strong Scotch dialect. And yet his wife—who had come over with him in the *Rakaia*—was the prettiest and sweetest little Scotswoman imaginable.

The moment Forrest saw him he endeavoured to get through the crowd of people in the front office, who, seeing by his uniform he was an officer of the *Rakaia*, made way for him.

. . . . .

"What is it, Mr. Macpherson?" said Forrest, shortly.

"I'll no' hae ye addreesin' me in such a disrespectfu' way, young man. An' I'll no hae ye stormin' and fumin' and sendin' in messages for me to come oot tae ye when ye ken I've varra important beesnis ta attend to."

Forrest was not a bad-tempered man, but the audible titter that ran round the office angered him almost beyond endurance. Gulping down his wrath, he said—

"You sent for me—on an important matter, you said. We have, as you know, only twelve hours to finish coaling in. Tell me what it is. I have no time to waste here."

"Hoo daur ye talk to me like that," and the little man's watery eyes shone green with rage. "Weel,

it's just this. Ma wife tells me that there is a watter-
colour peecture belonging ta *me* hanging up in your
cabin. Ye'll just understand I'll hae no nonsense
aboot it, and sae I sent for ye ta tell ye so mysel';
ye'll please send it ta me directly."

"You infernal little sweep!"

The passengers fell back hastily on either side, and
Mr. Macpherson tried to get back into his office, but
he was too late—Forrest had got him by the collar.
His temper had quite mastered him now, and his face
was black with passion.

"You d——d miserable little beast! So you only
sent for me to insult me? Well, you've done it.
And now I'm going to take it out of you. Will any
one lend me a cane?"

There was a quick response of "Si, señor," and a
short, nuggety-looking man, who looked like a
Spaniard, handed Forrest a light Malacca cane.

Quick as lightning Forrest pulled the little agent
over his knees, and then for a minute or so he be-
laboured him savagely. Then he stood him up on his
trembling legs again, and, dragging him through the
crowded front office to the street door, he gave him a
kick and sent him flying head first out on to the
pavement.

"By Jove, sir!" said a big fat man to Forrest, as he
stood glaring contemptuously at the prostrate figure,
"you'd better get aboard again. Served the cheeky
little beast rightly, *I say*. Gad, he won't be able to
sit down for a month; but I think he's stunned.
Hallo, here's a couple of *aguazils*. Look sharp, sir,
and get away."

Muttering his thanks, Forrest proceeded on his way

to the railway wharf, where a launch awaited to take him over to Flamenco, where the *Rakaia* was coaling.

Just as he had reached the wharf he heard hurried footsteps behind him, and turning, he saw four police-men, who at once arrested him, and in half an hour he was in prison—the result of hanging pretty little Mrs. Macpherson's gift, the "watter-colour peecture," in his cabin instead of stowing it away in his chest, as she had desired him. At dinner-time his captain came, and Forrest learned he was in for more serious trouble than he had apprehended. The little agent, so the captain said, was stated to be dying from a cracked skull, and Forrest would have to stay in prison till he was tried on a charge of attempted murder.

Two days afterwards the *Rakaia* was gone, and Forrest lay in prison cursing his luck, hoping that it wasn't true about the fractured skull, and wondering, if it were, if he should propose to the widow after he came out of prison.

On the third day his gaolers told him that a gentle-man wanted to see him. He had had plenty of visitors, principally Englishmen, from the Consul down to merchant's clerks. They all tried to cheer him up, but said that little Macpherson, who was still very bad, meant to press the charge of attempted murder, and that the Consul could do nothing for him. However, he was glad to have another visitor.

The moment he entered Forrest recognised him. He was the little, square-built Spanish gentleman who had lent him the cane.

"Good-day, señor," he said, extending his hand ; and then, in a low voice, he added in English, " What

21

is this fellow's name?" pointing to the gaoler who stood in the corridor.

"Manuel."

Calling him over to him, the Spaniard put in his hand a ten-dollar gold piece, and said—

"Friend Manuel, I want to have half an hour's talk with my friend here. I am interested in him. Every time I come here I will beg of you to accept a ten-dollar piece from me."

Señor Manuel discreetly withdrew, and the Spaniard, taking a little stool, placed it in front of Forrest, who sat on a bench, and commenced to talk to him in English.

.   .   .   .   .

"Señor Forrest," he said, "I desire to assist you, and in two days, if you will accept my assistance, you will be a free man. In the State of Colombia a little money goes a long way with those in power. Do you understand?"

The Englishman was about to thank him, when he stopped him with a smile.

"Be patient, please, and listen, and I will tell you why I desire to see you free. First of all, though, answer me one question. Will you, when free, enter into my service for one year, at a salary to be named by you?"

"What is the nature of the employment?"

"I wish you to take the command of a vessel."

"Ah!" and Forrest instantly jumped to the conclusion that his visitor was connected with some revolutionary project. "I am not a naval officer; I am in the merchant's service."

"Precisely; I know that. But the service upon

which you will be employed is one that, while you—
and I—may be exposed to a certain amount of danger
and run risks, does not need the training of a naval
officer, and it is a perfectly honourable and legitimate
adventure. Does that satisfy you ? "

" Perfectly."

" I was informed, Mr. Forrest, that you are a skilful
navigator."

He was silent for a while, and the Englishman took
a good look at him. Not a sailor, thought Forrest,
looking at his small, well-kept hands. Perhaps he was
a soldier. He certainly had the bearing of one. Presently he looked up and caught the young seaman's
eye. He smiled pleasantly, and stroked his pointed
beard and iron-grey moustache.

" You are wondering who I am. I should have
been more courteous. My name is Pedro do Bustamente. Until six months ago I was a captain of
infantry in the Spanish army in garrison at Malaga.
My father then died—in Cuenca. At his death certain property and documents came into my possession.
I read the documents, and, placing faith in what I
read, I sold the property, threw up my ¦commission,
took passage to Colon, and, had it not been for my
witnessing your beating of the little man, would now
be on my way to San Francisco or some American
seaport, where I could buy a small vessel for the purpose I have in view. But, señor, I like your face. I
believe you to be an honourable man, and that a good
Fate designed our meeting. Goodbye for the present ; in less than forty-eight hours you will be out of
Panama."

" Well, that's queer ! " muttered Forrest, as he

watched the obsequious Manuel bow his visitor out.
"What the deuce does he want me for? Any way,
I'll go—that is if I don't get stabbed or garotted here.
I wonder if that poor little beggar is really dying?"

.   .   .   .   .

But although Mr. Macpherson was a long way off
dying, both the English and American Consuls knew
that Forrest was in for a long imprisonment, and so
did Captain Pedro do Bustamente. And Bustamente
also knew that by judicious expenditure he could be
quickly got out. So he lost no time.

At midnight as Forrest lay asleep, Manuel came to
his cell, awoke him, and handed him a note. It read—
"Put on the cloak and follow Manuel."

The gaoler handed him a heavy woollen poncho,
and motioned him to follow. In another minute they
were out of the prison and walking quietly down the
street. For half an hour they continued on in the same
direction, till they came to where a man was waiting,
holding three mules. It was Bustamente. Without
a word they mounted and jogged quietly along,
following the coast-line northwards. At daylight
they drew up beside a small roadside *fonda*, and, to
Forrest's surprise, Bustamente said, "Let us halt and
get some breakfast; these people here are expecting
us. There is no fear of any pursuit—that is, if money
has any virtue." As they ate, Bustamente told Forrest
that he had learnt English in England, having been
for many years on the suite of the Spanish Minister in
London.

All that day they rode northwards, and at nightfall
entered a little seaport town on the shore of Parita
Bay. Here Manuel left them, and Bustamente and

Forrest in another ten hours were on board an American steamer bound to San Francisco. Bustamente had arranged with the captain of the steamer to call for them on her way down the coast.

.　　.　　.　　.　　.

As the clumsy old side-wheeler *Nebraska* steamed along the coast of Costa Rica, the Spaniard and Forrest sat in their deck cabin, and Bustamente put his hand in his bosom and pulled out a bundle of papers.

"Now, my friend, I can talk. I think you will find my story interesting."

And it was interesting. Briefly told, it was this : In 1850 his father, Bruno do Bustamente, a Spaniard by birth, was the richest merchant at Mazatlan, on the coast of Mexico, and traded largely with the East. The Governor of the province of Durango, whose hostility he had incurred, had him imprisoned on a trumped-up charge, and from that day he was the prey of the Mexican authorities, who sought to subject him to a continuous process of extortion and blackmail. His wife was a Mexican lady of San Blas. By her he had two children, a son and daughter. The son, Pedro, he had sent to Spain to enter the army. Upon regaining his freedom and paying a fine of 5,000 dollars to the Governor of Durango, he determined to leave Mexico and return to Spain. About this time his wife died. Quickly but cautiously, he realised upon his various estates, and sold his vessels as well—all but one, a brig of 120 tons, named the *Bueno Esperanza*. The captain of this vessel was an American named Devine, a man in whom he had the most implicit confidence. At that

time there was but little gold coin in use in that part
of Mexico, and he had in many cases to take payment
for the properties he had sold in silver Mexican dollars.
Of these he received something like ninety thousand,
and about twenty-five thousand dollars in gold coin.
The money was secured in bags made of green hide,
and conveyed from time to time on board the *Bueno
Esperanza*. Fearing every moment that he would be
detained, and his money seized by the Mexican
authorities, he gave out that he was despatching the
brig on one of her usual voyages to San Blas, and that
his daughter, Engracia, was going there also to visit
her mother's relatives. Accompanied by her nurse,
the little girl went on board, and Don Bruno had the
satisfaction of seeing the brig get safely away without
suspicion arising as to the treasure she carried. But
instead of San Blas, the *Bueno Esperanza* was bound
to Manilla, in the Philippine Islands, where Devine
was to await the arrival of his master.

A month later, Don Bruno, having disposed of the
remainder of the property, followed them in an
American trading schooner he had chartered for the
purpose, and after a quick passage arrived safely at
Manilla, and, to his dismay and grief, learned that
nothing had been seen of the *Bueno Esperanza*,
which should have reached Manilla a month before
him.

Month after month passed by, and then the distracted merchant, broken in health and fortune,
returned to end his days in his native town of Cuenca.
His death was very sudden, and his son Pedro learnt
from the old housekeeper that it occurred on the same
day on which he had received a letter, bearing a

foreign postmark. Upon reading this letter he became terribly agitated. Telling his housekeeper that he desired to write to his son in Malaga, she left him, and upon returning a quarter of an hour afterwards she found him with his head upon the table, quite dead. Under his cold hand was a sheet of paper, on which were scrawled a few words to his son. Death had smitten him too quickly to write more, and beside it lay the letter bearing the foreign postmark.

These were given to Captain Bustamente as soon as he reached the house a few days later.

.   .   .   .   .

" Here are my father's last words," said the Spaniard, and taking up a paper he read—

"The money will be there. Seek for it. I command you in the name of the Holy Virgin to give Christian burial to the bones of your sister. I pray——"

The remaining two or three lines were undecipherable.

"And now," continued Bustamente, "read this— the letter he received an hour before his death. It is in English, and is dated just one year and two months ago. The enclosure is in Spanish."

"Ship 'Sadie Wilmot,'
"*New Bedford, U.S.A.*,
"*6th March,* 1861.

"Mr. Bruno do Bustamente,
"*Cuenca, Spain.*

"Dear Sir,—The ship *Sadie Wilmot*, of which I am master, while cruising for sperm whales between Mindanao (Philippine Islands) and the Pelews, on the 14th August, 1860, picked up a ship's boat containing the dead bodies of five persons, who had evidently died from thirst and starvation. In a tin box found in the boat was the enclosed letter to you, and the sum of one thousand dollars in Mexican gold coin. If you can establish a claim to this I am prepared to forward same, less charges. My second mate, who is a native of the Azores, read the letter addressed to you. I believe that the island mentioned is uninhabited. I was too far to the westward when the boat was found to go back and see if any of the crew had remained there. Please reply to A. Wilmot, New Bedford.

" Yours truly,
" Amos Wilmot."

Forrest handed him back the letter, and then Bustamente slowly unfolded a single sheet of paper, written upon in pencil. On the top of the sheet was written in English—

"In case of my death I ask that this may be sent to Don Bruno do Bustamente, Cuenca, Spain, or to his son Pedro, at Malaga."

Then in Spanish—

' Wrecked on an uninhabited island in lat. 7° 29′ N. long. 160° 42′ E. Six of the crew drowned, also owner's child, Engracia Bustamente, and her nurse. The body of the former was buried at a spot above high-water mark, about 300 yards from a large round knob of rock, covered with vines on the eastern point, and bearing E. by N. from the grave. No provisions were saved except some jerked beef, packed in hide bags. Were four months on the island. Left there July 3rd, in open boat, to try and reach Manilla.

" Devine."

With flashing eyes the Spaniard sprang to his feet and placed his hands on Forrest's shoulders.

" Ah, that brave man, that Devine! Cannot you understand ? These words of his were written so that my father, if ever they came to his hand, would know that the treasure had been saved and hidden. ' The jerked beef in hide bags.' The money was in hide bags! And I think that instead of my poor sister being buried on the spot he speaks of, there we will find it."

He walked up and down the cabin quickly, and then resumed.

"And then, see how careful he has been to avoid telling the name of the brigantine, where she was from and where bound to. He knew that my father would return to Spain after he had given up all hope of the *Beuno Esperanza*; that in Cuenca, his birth-place, he would spend the rest of his days; he feared to say more. My good friend, I am certain that un-less my father spoke of those bags of bullock-hide to people in Manilla, not a living soul but you and I know that the brig carried a hundred and fifteen thousand dollars in gold and silver. And we will go to this island and get them."

Their course of action was soon decided upon. By the sale of the little property he had inherited from old Don Bruno his son had realised nearly a thousand pounds. Out of this he had paid nearly two hundred pounds, the greater part of which had gone to effect Forrest's escape, and with something like seven hundred pounds ($3,500) he and Forrest landed in San Francisco.

A week afterward they had chartered a small fore-and-aft vessel of ·fifty tons, the *Marion Price*, for five hundred dollars a month, provisioned her for six months, and with three Hawaiian natives for a crew, sailed out of the Golden Gate for the island.

On the twenty-seventh day out the little *Marion Price* passed the first of the Caroline Group, a chain of low, sandy atolls, covered densely with coconuts. That night Forrest hove-to, for if the position of the island they sought was given correctly in Devine's account of the wreck they were not more than forty miles to the eastward of it.

At daylight Forrest stood away to the westward, and sent one of the Hawaiians up aloft; and whilst he and Bustamente were at breakfast they heard the cry of "Land, ho!"

The breeze was steady and of good heart, and at eleven o'clock the *Price* was within a mile, and the two white men were scanning the strange island with interest.

.   .   .   .   .

It was, for its smallness—being barely two miles in circumference—of considerable height. On three sides gray coral cliffs rose steep-to from the surf that lashed and foamed unceasingly at their base; for only on the lee-side was the island protected by a fringing reef. In some places the summits of the wall of cliff sunk to perhaps fifty or sixty feet, in others it rose to nearly two hundred or more, but preserved the same grim and savage monotony of appearance throughout. Right to the very verge the broken, jagged pinnacles of coral were concealed by a dense, impenetrable growth of short, stunted scrub and masses of vine and creepers. Here and there these creepers had grown over the face of the cliff itself and hung down over the boiling surf below like monstrous carpets of green and yellow, in other places they clambered up and wrapt around sharp pinnacles of rock, so that from the deck of the *Marion Price* these pinnacles looked like densely-verdured and neatly-trimmed pine-trees.

"Small hope for a man did a ship strike here," said Forrest, with an involuntary shudder, looking at the wild seeth of the breakers as they dashed in quick succession against the beetling heights, and fell back in frothy, streaming clouds and whirling flakes of foam. "Ah, we're opening up the south point now, and there's a long reef running out there. Get aloft, one of you fellows, and see if there is a break in it anywhere."

As the schooner stood out again they got a better view of the island, and could see that although on the weather side it was clad in short, impenetrable scrub, it sloped gradually to the westward, and presently the man aloft called out that he could see the tops of coconut trees showing up over the other vegetation, and then : "There is smooth water, sir ; I see beach and passage, too."

Rounding the point of the long stretch of reef, Forrest hauled up and ran close in again, and then his arm was seized by the Spaniard.

"Look !" and he pointed to the shore.

.   .   .   .   .

On the eastern point of the island, which they had now opened well out, there stood out in bold relief from the points and knobs of vine-covered rock, a huge, round boulder, flattened at the apex, but perfected in the symmetry of its outlines by a closely-fitting mantle of vivid green.

The two men grasped each other's hands in silence. It was the rock spoken of by Devine.

Another half-hour and Forrest had let go his anchor in five fathoms, on a bottom of white sand, and taking one native, he and his friend lowered the boat and pulled ashore.

.   .   .   .   .

The *Bueno Esperanza* had evidently struck on the long, fringing reef before mentioned, as the first objects they saw were some spars, a lower-mast and a broken topsail yard, the ends of which were protruding from a heaped-up pile of loose coral slabs that the action of the surf had backed up above high-water mark. Further along they could see a part of her decking and other wreckage.

The Spaniard leading, they clambered over the bank of stones and sand, and directly in front of them they saw a grove of coconuts, beneath which were the ruins of a deck-house and a quantity of planking, barrels, ironwork and other material saved from the brigantine. There for two years the wreckage had lain undisturbed, blistering and cracking under the rays of a tropical sun, ever since the hapless men that had tenanted the deck-house had left its shelter to die of the horrors of thirst in a small open boat.

.   .   .   .   .

Fifty feet or so from the rotting, tumbledown deck-house was that which they sought, the grave of the little Spanish child; a rude, square structure of coral slab, over which the kindly creepers had crept and bound lovingly together.

Pedro do Bustamente, baring his head, knelt for a moment and prayed for the soul of the little sister he had never seen since they had played together in the days of his childhood.

Then, by a motion of his hand, he directed the Hawaiian sailor to cut away the binding creepers from the stones.

In a few minutes this was done, and the three men rapidly removed the small slabs of loose coral, and then the sandy nature of the soil rendered the rest of their task easy.

The coffin of the little girl had been constructed very solidly, and as a protection from decay had been covered with copper taken from the wreck.

After carefully lifting it out and placing it aside, Forrest, at the Spaniard's request, made an examination of the bottom of the grave. He was soon satisfied that it had contained nothing else but that which they had taken from it.

To his surprise Pedro showed no disappointment, and asked him in quiet tones if he would help him to carry the coffin to the boat.

This was done, and they returned to the schooner. Placing the coffin on the cabin table and covering it with a flag, the two men came on deck again.

" My friend," said the Spaniard, " now that that duty is done, let us get the treasure."

" Where shall we look for it ? "

" There," said Bustamente, pointing to the great round green mass outlined clearly before them, " three hundred yards east by north from the grave ! "

Taking with them the three Hawaiians, who were provided with long, heavy knives to cut through the scrub, they returned to the shore.

It took them some time to clear a way, but at last they stood at the foot of the great round boulder. A thorough examination revealed nothing in the way of any cave or hollow anywhere about the foot or sides.

With great difficulty the two white men, by clinging to the vines, succeeded in gaining the top, and immediately discovered that the flattened summit of the rock was in reality a large depression in the centre, over which the luxuriant creepers had grown and formed a thick network.

Standing in the centre they found that, although the bed of vines sank under their feet, there was still a hollow space between them and the bottom. Then the Hawaiians were called up and set to work slashing the vines all round the edge of the miniature crater with their knives.

Then the five men, hauling on the heavy mass, dragged it to the edge and tumbled it over the side, and Bustamente, with an excited face, jumped down into the hollow, and sank up to his knees in the accumulation of dead leaves and *débris* from the vines.

In a moment he plunged his hands amongst this and groped about. Then he looked up.

" It is here ! "

Forrest and a native sprang down after him.

The moment Forrest's feet touched the bottom Pedro's calmness gave way, and in his wild excitement he threw his arms around his comrade and embraced him. Releasing him, he turned to the native sailor—

" Clear away these dead leaves."

There was barely standing room for them to work in ; and as they had neither bags nor baskets, the sailors took off their shirts and threw them down to Pedro and Forrest, who quickly filled them with *débris* and then passed it up to the men above, and as they worked they could feel under their feet the rotted hide bags giving way and bursting under their weight ; and as the last shirtful of rubbish was collected the native sailor dragged up a piece of hide bagging, clinging to the inside of which were some Mexican sun dollars, stained and discoloured.

And then, tearing away the uppermost side of the rotting bags of hide, there lay at their feet the lost treasure of Bruno do Bustamente, just as his faithful captain had placed it in the hollow rock two years before. So rotten and decayed were the topmost layer of bags, that the contents, under the pressure of their feet, had spread out and formed a thick and even surface of silver coins, which hid from view the bags beneath.

For an hour the two white men and one native sailor worked collecting the loose Mexican dollars together ; and then, whilst two of the sailors were sent back to the schooner for some canvas needles, palms and twine, Forrest, clambering to the top again, was passed up handful after handful of money, which he poured out on the rock beside him.

As soon as the sailors returned, the five men set to work at the canvas, cutting it up and sewing it into rough bags, into which the loose coin was placed and sewn up. Then they descended again.

The rest of the bags, with careful handling, were taken safely out, and then they came to eight smaller packages, which proved to be wooden boxes covered with hide. Taking a hatchet, Bustamente knocked the outside covering off one, and then prized open the lid. It contained gold.

Securing it firmly again, the eight boxes were lifted out and placed on the rock beside the bags.

Then, satisfying themselves that all the treasure was secured, they had a hurried meal, and each man picking up a box or bag, they all made their way in single file back to the beach, and returned again and again till the last load had been brought down and put in the boat.

It was dark before their work was finished, and then the two white men went below to the cabin again. Around them lay the bags and boxes of gold and silver, and the light from the lamp fell upon the flag-covered coffin of the little Spanish girl.

" Poor little one," murmured Pedro do Bustamente, placing his hand tenderly on the flag, "thou shalt rest beside our father in Spain."

.   .   .   .

That night they opened the boxes of gold and counted the money. Each box contained three thousand dollars, and in one, a little larger than the rest, they found a paper written by Devine, which gave a detailed account of the wreck of the *Bueno Esperanza*, and concluded by saying that he had opened the largest of the boxes, which contained £4,000 and had taken from it a thousand dollars, for it was his intention to leave the island and endeavour to reach Manilla, where he expected to find Don Bruno awaiting him. They could then charter a vessel and return to the island for the treasure.

As Forrest surmised, the *Bueno Esperanza* had run ashore at night on the long horn of reef stretching out from the south point. The sea was fairly smooth at the time, but the ship ground heavily on the coral ; and seeing no hope of floating her, Devine and his crew proceeded to save all they could. The treasure was safely landed at daylight, and then the sea rose, and the ship commenced to break up. In returning to the shore both boats were capsized by a huge sea, and six men drowned from the mate's boat, and the Mexican nurse and the little Engracia, who were in the captain's boat, were, although rescued from drowning, so badly injured by the coral, that they died from exhaustion the next day. The nurse was buried on the beach, and the little girl, who lingered longest, in the grove of palms.

.   .   .   .   .

After reading this sorrowful record the two men proceeded to open and count the bags of silver. In all it amounted to ninety-three thousand Mexican and Spanish dollars.

The next morning Bustamente called the three Hawaiians aft, and told them that on the arrival of the schooner at Manilla he would give them five hundred dollars each over and above their wages ; but he asked them to swear secrecy.

Kahola, a huge broad-shouldered native from the island of Oahu, looked intently into the Spaniard's face, and then, bidding his fellow-countrymen stand back, he said, gravely—

" What I swear, those two men he swear too. If you please, sir, you wait till I get something."

He walked for'ard and disappeared below, returning in a minute or two with a book, whose size was only surpassed by its dirty appearance.

Standing before Bustamente, the Hawaiian saluted, beckoned to the two others to stand beside him, and held out the book to the Spaniard.

" All right, sir, now. You go ahead and swear me and this two man here on book."

Taking the volume from him, the white man opened it. It was in a language utterly unknown to him. He called to Forrest, who was steering, and asked him what it was.

22

Forrest shook his head. "What book is that, Kahola?"

The seaman looked at him in mild surprise.

"That Bible in my country language, sir."

Forrest grasped the situation at once, and rapidly explained the man's wishes to Bustamente.

The Spaniard nodded gravely, and took off his cap; the Hawaiians already held their battered old *fala* hats under their arms, which were crossed over their broad and naked chests. With their dark eyes fixed upon his face, they waited. He raised the book.

"Will you, Kahola, and you, Liho, and you, Bob, swear to me, Pedro do Bustamente, to speak to no man about the money on board this ship till you return to your own country, or till such time as I and Captain Forrest shall fix upon?"

Kahola conversed rapidly with his countrymen for a brief space. Then, with gravely respectful demeanour, but intense earnestness, he said—

"I think, sir, all us man here swear. But, sir, if you please, me and my countrymen like you swear something too, first."

"What would you have me swear, Kahola?" said Bustamente.

"Me and my countrymen like you swear, sir, on this good book, that this money belong to you. Suppose you no swear, me and this two man here no swear. We 'fraid you steal money."

The Spaniard raised the book to his lips. "On this book, which is the Word of God, and by the body of my dead sister, who lies in her coffin beneath us, I swear to you Kahola, and you, Liho, and you, Bob, that the money we have taken is mine. It was once my father's. He is dead ; but before he died he told me where to seek for it."

" Good," said Kahola, and he reached out his brawny hand for the book, and then added, in Hawaiian, " What is the father's shall be the son's, for that is the law of God and the law of man."

So in his simple, earnest manner the big native sailor swore the oath—

" I, Kahola, will no tell no man one word about the money. Suppose I tell something, I hope God kill me dead, and give me dam bad luck."

Liho and Bob repeated the same words, and then with smiling faces they shook hands with Bustamente and Forrest, and turned to again to their duty.

At noon the island had sunk to a purple speck on the horizon, and Pedro and Forrest, with joy bubbling in their hearts, were sitting on the deck talking.

. . . . .

" My dear comrade," said Pedro, placing his hand affectionately on Forrest's shoulder, " you must—you *shall* do as I wish. Both you and I are alone in the world. Let us be comrades always. See now, it was so intended by God for us to meet, and therefore fifty thousand dollars of the money is thine ; that will leave me sixty-four thousand."

Forrest began to remonstrate, but Pedro placed his hand on his mouth. " But that I had found such a true man, I may have never succeeded in finding it."

And this is the story of the finding of the lost treasure of Don Bruno do Bustamente.